The Energy Merchant

The Energy Merchant

by Rufus Jarman

Published in 1977 by Richards Rosen Press, Inc.
29 East 21st Street, New York, N.Y. 10010

First Edition

Manufactured in the United States of America

Richards Rosen Press, Inc.
New York, N.Y. 10010

Robert E. Thomas Founder and Chairman of the Board

Acknowledgments

As author of *The Energy Merchant,* I wish to thank all executives, staff members and employees of MAPCO, Inc. with whom I worked for their generous help and readily-given cooperation in supplying me with material for the book. I have written books and magazine articles for 30 years about business concerns, but I cannot recall any group of employees whose intelligent enthusiasm about their work and their company equalled that of the people of MAPCO.

I would like to thank especially the following, upon whose time and patience it was necessary for me to make unusually large demands: First, the following women: Helen Jones, Helen Malone, Becky Staines and Peggy Carroll. Also, the following MAPCO executives: Robert J. Swain, David A. Roach, Gilbert V. Rohleder, J. Lee Wright, Bruce C. Wilson, Dean Cosgrove and Grover C. Denison.

The following Pipeliners gave me of their time and assisted me above and beyond the call of duty: Harvey Henderson, Billy Hunter, Bob Hunter, Isadore Zaleski and Bud De Masters. I would also like to express my appreciation for their efforts to Gene Grounds, Superintendent of the Fractionating Plant at Conway, Kansas, and Don Holliman, Manager of the Production Division's Northern office at Billings, Montana.

I am particularly grateful to Roger Shelley, Joseph P. Tully and Charlotte Lowe of Ruder & Finn, Inc., of New York City and Patricia Coleman for their help, advice and encouragement.

—Rufus Jarman,
Weston, Conn.
April, 1976,

Contents

The Impossible Dream 1

The most important message contained in the story of MAPCO, Inc., a young and remarkably successful developer and merchandiser of energy, headquartered in Tulsa, Oklahoma, is this: In these regulated times, when business is enslaved by the Computer, restricted by Government and regimented by "Accepted Practices," the pioneering spirit that built the great business empires of the past is not yet dead, and it is still possible to create a flourishing industrial enterprise out of energy and dreams.

Those old-fashioned business virtues of hard work, long hours, dedication to a purpose, expertise, know-how and aggressive, intelligent management, however, are still very much required. But when a concentration of these factors combines with dominating desire and an unshakable purpose to attain a goal, an enterprise apparently grows and prospers over and beyond the understandable results of the physical and mental efforts of its force of workers. They seem to set in motion forces that we generally call "luck"—for want of a better explanation—which appear to arrange for seemingly unrelated personalities, developments and chains of events to fit into the fabric of the enterprise and help it to attain the goals which have been formed in the minds of the people who conceived and founded it.

Over the centuries, the above phenomena have been observed and commented upon by sundry philosophers and even business men regarded by their peers as unusually "lucky" to wit: "Shallow men believe in luck . . . strong men believe in cause and effect." (Ralph Waldo Emerson, in *Conduct of Life,* 1860.) "Diligence is the mother of good luck." (Benjamin Franklin in *Poor Richard's Almanac,* 1736.) "It always seems that the harder I work, the luckier I get." (William K. Warren, founder of the Warren Petroleum Company of Tulsa, Oklahoma, 1975.)

"The most remarkable thing about MAPCO is that it ever got formed and financed in the first place," according to George F. Bennett, President of the State Street Investment Corporation of Boston, a former Treasurer of Harvard College and a board member of some of the country's best-known corporations, including MAPCO's during its first few years. "MAPCO was based on nothing more than dreams," he says. "The definition of 'creation' is making something out of nothing. And that is how MAPCO was built. God moves in mysterious ways His wonders to perform."

The corporate name "MAPCO" is formed by the initials of "Mid-America Pipeline Company." This was the first name of the enterprise, which originated as the world's first long-distance pipeline devoted to carrying liquefied petroleum gases—propane, butane, ethane and natural gasoline. The pipeline commenced operations in late 1960, so that 1976 represents the fifteenth anniversary of the company's first full year of business. It began with a great deal of debt and very little equity, and in those years was often characterized as "The Scrappy Little Pipeline." The company's name was changed to "MAPCO" eight years after it started because its management had added to its list of activities operations other than pipelining. These include the production of oil, liquefied petroleum gases and natural gas; the merchandising of natural gas liquids; the manufacture and merchandising of liquid plant foods; the nation's first anhydrous ammonia pipeline, carrying this liquid fertilizer to the wheat and corn belts; and, finally, a strong commitment to coal production, in response to the nation's energy shortages, beginning in the early 1970's.

These widening activities, along with an increase of several hundred percent in its LP Gas Pipeline throughput, have brought MAPCO's sales and operating revenues from a little under $7,000,-000 during its first full year of operation to nearly $350,000,000 annually 15 years later. Net income rose from a loss of about $2,500,-000 in 1961 to net earnings of more than $49,000,000 in 1975. Dividend payments increased from around $185,000 in 1965, the first year they were paid, to about $13,000,000 in 1975. And the value of MAPCO's securities, adjusted for splits, had increased in value from $2 per common share in 1960 to around $45 by the middle of 1975. The value of MAPCO's common shares had continued to rise steadily, despite the stock market doldrums of the early and middle 1970's.

In 1975, MAPCO was listed for the first time among *Fortune* magazine's Top 500 Companies. This was a remarkable accomplishment, indeed, considering that a mere 15 years earlier, MAPCO consisted of little else than some 2,300 miles of steel pipe in the ground, served by 60 pumping stations and seven unloading terminals along the way, a control room in Tulsa and a large amount of determination and debt.

On the basis of gross sales for 1975, MAPCO was ranked *449th* among the *Fortune* 500. Its rating was considerably higher, however, in the areas of performance and profits:

MAPCO's *net* income, for instance, was *174th* from the top in 1975.

MAPCO ranked *seventh* from the top in net income as a percentage of sales.

2

During the decade, 1965–1975, MAPCO ranked *fourth* from the top in average return to investors.

MAPCO ranked *ninth* in net income as a percentage of stockholder's equity.

During the decade, 1965–1975, MAPCO ranked *17th* in growth rate per share earnings.

Investment bankers, securities analysts and other financial authorities place MAPCO in the top portion of the top 1 percent of major American industrial corporations on the basis of steadily increasing gross revenues, earnings for its stockholders and performance generally. They attribute these things mainly to excellent management and an exceptional ability by MAPCO to anticipate America's energy needs and to move aggressively and effectively to help fulfill them, even before such shortages became apparent.

In 1960, MAPCO began operations in two or three offices borrowed from the Williams Brothers Company in Tulsa. It occupied several floors of Skelly's Oil Center Building for 15 years. Then, in 1976, the company moved into its own 10-story building, formerly the Shell Building, in downtown Tulsa, overlooking a park and a scenic vista of the Arkansas River. It easily accommodates MAPCO's over 200 home-office employees with plenty of expansion room.

The individual most responsible for building MAPCO from an idea into a highly successful reality and who has continued as its top decision-maker and leader ever since is Robert E. Thomas —a man of strong opinions, overwhelming determination and persistence, great powers of concentration and a remarkable capacity for hard work. Mr. Thomas' career has progressed from accountant to financier and finally to industrialist. He is widely admired in the financial community as a man who moves boldly into areas where more conservative executives fear to tread—but whose judgments, to date, have almost always been right.

Although he'd had no experience in that field, Bob Thomas seized on the idea of building the world's first liquefied petroleum gas pipeline at a time when, as it turned out, such a project was badly needed. As a result, the Mid-America Pipeline has been extremely successful. His motivation was to try to improve the situation of a financially distraught railroad he then headed—the Missouri-Kansas-Texas—and, in so doing, to pick up his own career, which, because of the railroad's almost impossible problems, was sitting on dead center at the time. The M-K-T Railway, which originally was to control and operate the pipeline, was so weak fiscally, however, that it could provide only extremely limited financing. So it was largely Robert E. Thomas, with the help of several financial and legal advisers, who built the 2,184-mile-long pipeline, through his own persistence, his reputation as a financier and the force of his personality. Mid-America was, in fact—and will probably remain—the only major pipeline to be financed and built without any contracts from suppliers or customers and in the face of opposition by major oil companies. This feat has caused some observers, who know details of how it was conceived, financed, constructed and put into operation, to call the Mid-America Pipeline "The Impossible Dream."

Having gotten the Mid-America Pipeline into the ground and operating, Mr. Thomas used it as the nucleus around which to build other related industrial operations. Some observers see these accomplishments as even more remarkable than the achievement of building the pipeline under adverse conditions. "To my thinking," says Edward A. Merkle, President of the Madison Fund of New York City and a former associate and rival of Mr. Thomas, "Bob's most remarkable achievement in the handling of the company has been his ability to reach out and get Mid-America into other profitable areas. For instance, the coal business prospects for the future are now very bright—but Bob had the guts to get into coal when these prospects were not so bright. Most people in his position would not have done it. And he now has the backing from financial people to get whatever money he needs. If you haven't got money, guts won't do you much good. But Bob has a lot of respect in financial circles now."

Horace C. Bailey, Vice President in Charge of Petroleum and Related Matters at Kidder, Peabody and Company, Inc., of New York City, makes this comment: "Everybody [in the financial community] used to talk about the extraordinary success that [the late] Gardiner Simons had with the Tennessee Gas Transmission Company and how he had built it into a national industrial institution after its start in 1946. I would say that what Bob Thomas has done with Mid-America and MAPCO rivals what Simons did. Bob's achievements have been exceptional."

David Leslie, a New York Public Relations executive who has worked closely with Robert E. Thomas in years past, has these observations: "Many Bob Thomas observers are always talking about how 'lucky' he is. I don't think Bob Thomas' accomplishments have anything to do with 'luck.' I believe there are things beyond our comprehension that the human mind is capable of—powers we are not conscious of. Some people call this the 'Power of Positive Thinking.' I believe that such a thing truly exists, and I think Bob Thomas transmits it because he believes so strongly in what he is doing. I think he believes it to the extent that it kind of radiates from him and creates an environment that *makes* things happen. That is why, in my opinion, so many seemingly unrelated people and situations have come together from out of left field to join in the creation and success of the Mid-America Pipeline Company, later MAPCO."

Vincent Butler, Project Manager in building the Mid-America Pipeline and who now heads his own engineering firm

4

in Tulsa, says: "Bob Thomas is my kind of executive. He is the sort of person who will give you a decision and, having made it, he will stand behind you as you try to carry it out. In today's world, that kind of person is at a premium. He retains those old-fashioned ideas that a truly successful business is based upon hard work and integrity. And in today's business world, when so many enterprises seem to be based upon gimmickry, it is refreshing to see from MAPCO's success that those old-fashioned principles still work."

"The thing about Mr. Thomas—busy as he is—is that you can go in there and get a hearing on anything within reason," says G. Dean Cosgrove, MAPCO's Treasurer, who joined the firm in 1960 at the time it began operating. "Mr. Thomas is very decisive, however. He will tell you 'Yes' or 'No,' and if he says 'No,' you might as well forget it and go on to something else. As far as we in management are concerned, it is the old story: Change what you can change and don't worry about the things you can't. That is the way this company is operated and it is an important reason why we have been so successful. We can move more quickly. We can move in a day's time, where it might take a much larger corporation that does not have the Thomas Open Door Policy six months or a year—and by then, the opportunity is often gone."

"Bob Thomas is no dictator," an associate has pointed out. "He believes deeply in the capitalistic system and that a company's Board of Directors is an extremely important part of the capitalistic system. Some presidents of companies go to their boards with fear, some with power in their hands to bend the board to their beliefs. Bob regards his Board of Directors as a group of specialists, available to help with guidance and counseling."

MAPCO has always had a strong Board of Directors, and its members agree that they work harder at the MAPCO Board meetings than at those of most other companies on whose boards some of them serve. "I always try to make it to the MAPCO Board meetings because here, we Board members are deeply involved in making decisions," says Albert B. Alkek, who has ranching and oil and gas production interests and is Board Chairman of a couple of Texas banks. "The managements of some companies have everything all cut and dried ahead of time and expect the Board members to act as mere rubber stamps. I fought with Bob Thomas on some of his projects—but it turns out that he is almost always right. He is a man of remarkable vision and he has got a hell of a good company—great leadership, loyal employees. Bob takes care of his people. He doesn't take all the cream and give them the water. He is fair with everybody. He made it on his own and he remembers."

MAPCO's two remaining Board members in 1975 who have served since the company was formed are William N. Deramus III, Chairman of the Board of Kansas City Southern Industries, Inc., of Kansas City, Missouri; and John Hawkinson, President of Supervised Investors Services, Inc., of Chicago. "Bob Thomas is a very aggressive, very strong, very tenacious individual, as most entrepreneurs are," Mr. Hawkinson says. "Another of Mr. Thomas' characteristics is that sometimes he doesn't proceed with caution and prudence that a typical corporate executive probably would. This has never been negative as far as the company's progress is concerned because he has always had quite a good Board of Directors who have taken a much greater interest and have been much more closely involved with this corporation than is usually the case with board members. Based on our collective experiences, our counsel and votes, we board members have helped to prevent the senior executive staff from making serious mistakes. I might add that as a member of the financial community, my association with MAPCO and the degree of success it has achieved have reflected favorably on me. I know that this is the case also with several other Board members."

The youngest member of the MAPCO Board is Philip C. Lauinger, Jr., President of the Petroleum Publishing Company of Tulsa, which publishes *The Oil and Gas Journal* and other periodicals. He has observed: "Bob Thomas has a strong personality, but he also has the wisdom to listen to the fellows on the Board, especially those who have done their homework and developed a studied opinion. He is quite sensitive to the feelings of people he respects. The MAPCO Board is certainly not a rubber-stamp group. Our meetings are filled with a great deal of informal give and take, often in earthy language comparable to the Watergate tapes. And yet the Board is a cohesive group; there is a real fraternity among its members."

In 1975, Robert E. Thomas was a young sixty-one years old —a big, well-built, vigorous man, standing six feet two and weighing about 195 pounds. His decisiveness is reflected in his posture, walk and general demeanor, which are commanding, and in his facial expression, which is usually pleasantly serious. But he does laugh frequently and enjoys a couple of drinks before dinner. Bob Thomas is a good-looking man with a high forehead, level, light blue eyes, a prominent nose, firm mouth and chin and thinning, graying, light-colored hair, parted on the left side. He has a strong, at times rather rasping, voice and a definitely impressive presence, at all times—whether he is talking to one person, or presiding at the annual meeting, or speaking to the Rotary Club somewhere or being interviewed on television.

His manner is sometimes rather distant and almost always formal. His confidential secretary, Mrs. Helen Jones, reports that Mr. Thomas has never called her anything but "Mrs. Jones" since she began working for him when he opened his Mid-America Pipeline office in Tulsa back in 1960. Only once in all that time has she seen him in his office when he was not wearing his suit jacket, and the time she did see him in his shirtsleeves—the air conditioning was not working on a sweltering summer day—so startled her that Mrs. Jones hasn't quite gotten over it yet.

Mr. Thomas has become a sort of legendary figure, especially in the minds of MAPCO employees who work out in the field away from Tulsa. Although they seldom—if ever—see him, many of these employees say they believe Bob Thomas is probably the wisest businessman in the U.S., and whatever he decides must be correct, in view of the company's growth and success and the feeling of fulfillment that they personally experience in working for MAPCO under his direction.

Tom Patterson, a Vice President in MAPCO's Coal Division, puts it this way: "Bob Thomas is a good gentleman. You know, he puts me in mind of the way a company President *ought* to be. I think most people sometimes picture a company President in their mind and how he ought to look and act. I worked for a lot of coal companies and some big ones, and met the Presidents, but not one was like Mr. Thomas. I mean, he is *really the President of MAPCO* period! He has a lot of class. He has been in our home and is just as common as anyone you would want to see . . . but . . . at the same time he is . . . oh . . . I don't know . . . somehow different . . . I think he is remarkable. He has built a fine organization, and I'm just damn happy to be part of it. That's all . . . I feel about him just like everybody else who works for MAPCO. Bob Thomas is our spiritual leader . . ."

For a man who has in his bearing the grand sweep of a tycoon, Robert E. Thomas was born in modest circumstances in Cuyahoga Falls, Ohio, a suburb of Akron, on July 28, 1914—the day, he sometimes points out, that Austria declared war on Serbia, thus precipitating World War I. Robert was the eldest of the three children of Talbott Earl and Jane Eggleston Thomas. The middle initial in Bob's name stands for his mother's maiden name. His sister, Marilyn, is married to Dr. Benjamin Holder, of Midland, Michigan; his younger brother, Talbott Earl Jr., lives in Costa Mesa, California, and works for the Firestone Tire and Rubber Company.

"Our family wasn't poor, but we weren't well-to-do, either. Average, I guess," Bob Thomas reports. "My father was never out of work or anything of that sort. He held his job as an accountant at Firestone in Akron throughout the 1930's Depression." At first, young Bob wanted to be an architect and spent one summer working in an architect's office and another summer in the drafting room at Firestone, while getting architecture out of his system. After finishing high school, he worked for two years in a small stationery wholesale house in Akron, getting money to go to college, while learning accounting at home from his father. Besides keeping books for the Akron Stationery Company, he drove a truck, made deliveries, worked at the warehouse and learned quite a bit about running a small business. "I didn't make much money," he reports, "but it was good experience and I was never out of a job during that period between high school and college, even though we were in the midst of the Big Depression. I've had the feeling ever since that if a person really wants to work, he can find a job. The problem with so many people is: 'This is beneath my dignity,' or the pay isn't enough.'"

In September, 1933, Robert Thomas enrolled in the distinguished Wharton School of Finance and Economics of the University of Pennsylvania, majoring in accounting. Because of his father's instruction and his own experience at the stationery company, he knew more about accounting as a college freshman than some of his instructors and breezed through his courses, often finishing three-hour examinations in 45 minutes. The ease with which he got through his freshman courses caused Bob to take on extremely heavy academic loads during the next two years and he was able to finish the four-year course in three.

"I was fighting for money all the time," he says. "My father couldn't send me much, if any. I was borrowing my tuition from the University and by finishing in three years, I owed the University four hundred dollars less than I would have otherwise.

"I lived free of charge with my uncle, Raymond Eggleston, my mother's brother, and his wife in a suburb of Philadelphia. Uncle Raymond was in the road contracting business and, during my senior year at Wharton, I kept all the books for his two companies, working at night and on weekends, sleeping only three or four hours a night. My uncle paid me for this work. He was very good to me and I was quite close to him. He owned a yacht, a 38-foot power boat, the *Mira*, named for his wife. He kept his boat in Chesapeake Bay and I spent considerable time aboard her during the summer months. This is when I got my love for yachting. I looked up the *Mira* recently at the New York Yacht Club in *Lloyd's Yachting Register* for 1932. That really brought back memories."

Yachting has remained Bob Thomas' main—and practically only—diversion. Every few weeks, he abandons his frantic schedule of working in Tulsa and flying about the country to attend business meetings and make speeches on energy so that he and his wife, Barbara, can take off for Fort Lauderdale, Florida, where he keeps his boat. Bob serves as Captain of the 55-foot custom-built power cruiser, *Seabird,* and Mrs. Thomas is First Mate. They manage to get in some sailing between Bob's frequent long-distance telephone calls to various business associates and contacts about the nation and the world. Yachting is his great love and relaxation. "When I begin to feel the roll of the sea under my feet," he likes to say, "my cares roll away."

During his years in college, Bob had no difficulties with his instructors about his academic status, but now and then he *did* have disagreements on matters of political philosophy with some of the professors, whom young Thomas regarded as "Pinks." "I have always been a rugged individualist and a strong conservative," he says. "When I was in college, I didn't go through any period of liberal leanings, like a lot of college students. My attitudes have remained pretty much the same all through life. I have a strong belief in the individual—a strong belief in noninterference by Government—a strong belief in paddling your own canoe and not running to the Government every time you have a problem, which so many businessmen do. No businessman wants the Government interfering with his affairs when times are good, but too many of them run to Washington the minute things turn bad. I think a lot of this inflation we have is due to the expansion of the Government and expansion of governmental regulations. All this costs money and there is only one person who pays that bill—the customer, the consumer, the taxpayer.

"When it comes to the oil business," he said in 1975, "Congress has taken away the statutory depletion allowance from the major oil companies. Congress professes to have kept this allowance for small independent oilmen to continue encouraging them to make further explorations for new oil, but actually, Congress threw a hooker into that, technically speaking, and took the depletion allowance away from most of them, too. This will certainly have a deflating effect on efforts to find new oil and solve our energy crisis. Nobody realized that the bill had taken away the independents' incentive until the legislation was already passed. Congressmen didn't even have a copy of the bill to read when they voted on it. One of them voted with his fingers on his nose. To me, that is completely irresponsible."

Robert Thomas makes frequent speeches along such lines to groups throughout the United States these days. But at the time he finished college, in 1936, he never pictured himself as a public speaker, as he was strictly interested in his business career. Back before he started to college, Bob was much impressed when an engineer who lived down the street from his parents told him that, in order to succeed in life, a person must have definite goals. So young Thomas set for himself the following: He resolved that he would be making $12,000 a year by the time he was thirty years old. He would be making $50,000 a year at age forty and would retire when he reached fifty. He reached his $12,000-a-year goal at age twenty-six, back when a dollar was worth about four times what it is now. He passed the $50,000-a-year goal before he was forty, but gave up the idea of early retirement when he became involved with the building of MAPCO. Although the going salary rate in 1936 for hiring college graduates was $125 a month, Bob Thomas, who was twenty-two when he graduated, decided he was worth $200 a month as a starter. He got it from Keystone Custodian Funds, a mutual fund headquartered in Philadelphia. In fact, with salary and bonus, he made $3,000 his first year as assistant to the general manager, helping to select investments for Keystone's portfolio. His $3,000 first-year income exceeded Bob's goal by $50 a month.

Keystone's General Manager, a man named Theodore Rehn, was a Wharton School graduate and a friend of one of Bob's professors, Canby Balderson, who recommended young Thomas for the job. Bob could never understand why because he regularly slept through Professor Balderson's eight A.M. class, weary after his three- or four-hour night's sleep. Bob also got an offer from General Motors, but their starting figure was only $125 a month. "Maybe they got up to $150; I don't remember," he says. "Anyway, I turned them down. I was also interviewed by Armstrong Cork and they met my price. But their letter containing the $200-a-month offer got delayed in the mail for six weeks and I didn't receive it until after I had started work with Keystone. If the letter hadn't been delayed, I probably would have started to work for Armstrong and, who knows, I might be President of Armstrong Cork today. Whether or not Providence arranged the delay of that letter from Armstrong is hard to say. But whether I had gone with Armstrong or had swallowed my pride and joined General Motors, I probably would not have been making $12,000 a year when I was only three years out of college, which I did at Keystone. It was quite a small company when I went there, and one thing that attracted me was the belief that it was going to grow quite rapidly, which it did. Keystone had only about $3,500,000 worth of assets when I went there. Today the company has close to $2,000,000,000 worth of assets."

Bob saw no military service during World War II. He was wearing special glasses to correct an eye problem at the time, and the Army turned him down because there was no way of providing these special lenses in the field. At the war's end, Keystone had a large portfolio of railroad securities, and the railroads throughout the country soon began to have problems. Bob was placed in charge of Keystone's railroad holdings "to sort of clean up the debris," he says. "And I did." He became known as a railroad financial expert during this period, and his experience with railroads was to have an important influence upon his subsequent career. Throughout the war, railroads had enjoyed immense business, but when the hostilities ended, their traffic went down and payroll costs went up. Equipment and trackage had been allowed to run down during the war, and now the roads were faced with replacing and repairing them at ever increasing costs. Many roads were having trouble making ends meet because of their heavy indebtedness. This made recapitalization advisable—rearranging the debt structure so that the road's obligations would be spread out over a longer period of time.

Keystone was the largest bondholder of the Lehigh Valley

Railroad, a rather weak company struggling under a stifling debt structure, which young Thomas overhauled. He took the lead in preparing a new plan of recapitalization and testified at hearings before the Interstate Commerce Commission. The recapitalization was quite successful—for a time at least. Bob also arranged for refinancing the Boston and Maine Railroad, which had been handicapped by a big preferred dividend arrears. Most of his railroad work was done after the Keystone Fund moved its headquarters from Philadelphia to Boston in 1938.

Bob Thomas lived in Boston from 1938 to 1953 and during this time, in 1949, married his present wife, the former Barbara Darcey. They have one daughter, Barbara Ann, who is married to Brian H. Kennedy. At this writing he was employed in sales for a heating and air-conditioning company in Atlanta, Georgia, where Barbara Ann worked in the computer department of a bank. Mr. Thomas has one son by his former marriage, Robert E. Thomas, Jr., who was living in Oceanside, California in 1976, operating a sales agency for catamaran sailboats.

Bob Thomas left Keystone in 1953, after 17 years, and became a Vice President of the Pennroad Corporation in New York City. The Pennroad Corporation had been organized by the Pennsylvania Railroad as a railroad holding company, and at one time owned controlling interests in quite a number of railroads. When Bob Thomas joined the firm, the Pennroad Corporation was converting over some of its railroad holdings and becoming a closed-end investment company, whose stock is traded on the Exchange, as contrasted with a mutual fund, whose shares are not traded. Pennroad's name was subsequently changed to the Madison Fund. Bob took its offer when assured that the job would be worth "something like $50,000 plus a year." The Pennroad management wanted to enlist the Thomas railroad expertise for improving the financial status of the railroads in which it still had investments.

After Bob Thomas had been with Pennroad for two years, the opportunity arose, in 1955, for Pennroad, along with the State Street Investment Corporation of Boston, to acquire controlling interest in the Missouri-Kansas-Texas Railway, one of the Midwest's largest and most troubled railroads. The management of the two purchasers—Pennroad and State Street, decided to buy control of the M-K-T (Katy) Railway jointly, with the understanding that Bob Thomas would devote a great deal of his time to bringing the ailing Katy out of its financial difficulties.

And this marked the great turning point in the career of Robert E. Thomas—away from the investment business and into railroading. Eventually this would result in the materialization of "The Impossible Dream" of the Mid-America Pipeline Company.

The Katy Railroad: 2
Color and Confusion

The spark that was to become MAPCO, Inc., sprang from an apparently unrelated assortment of people, events and circumstances that came together along the devious and seemingly senseless path that Fate sometime chooses to follow when fabricating its more spectacular creations. And of all these components, one of the more extraordinary was an individual by the name of Edward N. Claughton.

Mr. Claughton died in 1955, before MAPCO was even dreamed of, and he probably never heard in all of his life of Robert E. Thomas. Nevertheless, E. N. Claughton had a large responsibility in laying the foundation of what was to become—five years after his death—the Mid-America Pipeline Company, now a division of MAPCO, Inc. The catalyst who brought the work of Mr. Claughton into the orbit of Robert E. Thomas is Salim L. ("Cy") Lewis, a legendary personality on Wall Street for nearly 40 years, and Senior Partner in the prominent investment banking house of Bear, Stearns and Company.

"I had this man for a client who was an unbelievable character, and who became very much attached to me," Mr. Lewis recalled during a dinner at a private club in New York City one night in the summer of 1975. "He would only do business with me when buying securities. He used to ask my opinions all the time but couldn't care less what I told him. He was going to do what he wanted to anyway. His name was Edward Napoleon Claughton, and he was a man with a great history.

"He was born in Columbus, Georgia, in 1895, educated in public schools at Macon and Atlanta, Georgia, and studied architecture in night classes at Georgia Tech. After working for the Ford Motor Company as an employee and a dealer and operating in real estate in Georgia and Alabama, he became connected with a bank in Atlanta that went busted during the 1920's. He was thrown into jail and after coming out, became an abject drunkard for a period. Finally he moved to Miami, Florida, where he managed somehow or other to rehabilitate himself, and from then on I don't believe he ever had another drink. Ed Claughton was a very imaginative man and he knew a lot about real estate. He became closely associated with Ed Ball, head of the duPont Foundation at Jacksonville, and he gave Ball some marvelous ideas in real estate, from which the duPont Foundation made a lot of money. Ball did this in a manner that allowed Claughton to make some money, too, and thus he began his financial comeback in Florida real estate."

Mr. Claughton had moved to Miami in 1936, and from almost the first, until his death there 19 years later, he was a firebrand in local real estate, business and political circles. He always claimed that he arrived in Miami with "just enough money to buy a ham sandwich." First, he sold radios, next he built a theater and leased it to a chain, then another. Before his death, the Claughton Company owned half a dozen motion picture houses in the Greater Miami area. Mr. Claughton acquired 20.7-acre Burlingame Island in the mouth of the Miami River with the idea of making it into a housing development. He helped develop Edison Center and the Allapattah business districts and duPont Plaza on Biscayne Bay in Downtown Miami, where the duPont Plaza Hotel now stands. The controversial Mr. Claughton figured in various court suits and threatened suits, both as plaintiff and defendant, involving a list of litigants that included stockholders of the Missouri-Kansas-Texas Railway Company, six leading motion-picture producers—whom Claughton sued for $9,450,000, claiming they had conspired to keep his theaters from obtaining first-run films—the Internal Revenue Service and, especially, the City Fathers of Miami. Only a month before his death, he achieved national publicity by breaking up the Republican Lincoln Day Dinner in his Urmey Hotel in Downtown Miami because Negroes attended. This action was termed "disgraceful" by the Mayor of Miami, who "apologized to the rest of the nation" for the behavior of citizen Claughton.

But the most important of Mr. Claughton's many operations, as far as our story here is concerned, was his penchant for buying railroad securities. First, he acquired substantial holdings in the Florida East Coast Railroad and then fought the city's attempts to remove its antiquated station and tracks from Downtown Miami. Later, he accumulated considerable holdings in the Chicago and Eastern and the Chicago and Great Western Railroads that he tried unsuccessfully to merge with the Missouri-Kansas-Texas (Katy) Railroad, in which he had also become a major stockholder.

"Somehow or other Claughton got involved with me, or I got involved with Claughton—I can't remember which," Cy Lewis recalls. "I think our connection emanated from our Chicago office but I can't remember for sure. Claughton was very much interested in those three railroads. He would buy stock in them when he felt like it and he would tell me to deliver it to various banks.

As far as I could see, he used practically every damned bank in the country. Sometimes it was slow pay—but he never defaulted; it was always paid.

"Finally, E. N. Claughton got sick. I didn't realize how serious it was until, on my way home from Cuba, I came through Miami and stopped by to see him at his home. Then I realized he had terminal cancer. I went on from there to Scotland to play golf, and while over there, I got a cable from some lawyers in Miami who reported that Ed had died and they wanted me to come there and help them out. When I got back to Miami a week later the lawyers told me they discovered that Mr. Claughton just happened to own something over 525,000 common shares of the Katy Railroad. The entire capitalization of the Katy was not very much over 800,000 shares of common stock. In other words, Mr. Claughton had more than 60 percent—controlling interest—in this Midwestern railroad, which he had never reported to anybody. This was strictly against all the rules, but he always felt the rules were for somebody else, not him.

"So, the lawyers, Mrs. Claughton and I got together to see what we could do about these shares, which seemed to be lodged in practically every bank in the country. And on a very tight margin. They asked me if I thought I could sell the railroad to somebody and I said I thought I could," reminisces Mr. Lewis, long considered one of the greatest salesmen on Wall Street. "And I did sell that block of stock—to the Pennroad Corporation of New York City and the State Street Investment Corporation of Boston. And that is how it all came about. Instead of taking cash for my services in that transaction, I accepted my commission in stock. Which I might add was a hell of a mistake.

"At the time, M-K-T stock was being traded at 13½ to 13¾," Mr. Lewis went on. "I sold the entire block for 13⅜ and I felt—and I think almost anybody in the securities business would agree—that I made quite an achievement, since the stock was held on a very, very slim margin of maybe a couple of points. The buyers were satisfied. The lawyers for the Claughtons were relieved because the estate wasn't going to be killed. But the very next day after publication of the announcement that these two very powerful corporations had bought control of the Katy, its stock rallied —hell, it exploded!—up eight or ten points to 23. Whereupon, Claughton's widow sued my firm and me because we had not gotten a higher price. We won the case and pretty soon Katy's stock dropped down to about three or four, which is about where it belonged—and it stayed there."

The two corporations had bought control of the railroad with the understanding that Robert E. Thomas, who had become known as an expert in refinancing ailing railroads, would have overall control of the Katy's management as Chairman of the Executive Committee. "I had been interested in the Katy Railroad for quite some time before this deal came up and knew what was going on there pretty well," Bob Thomas says. "I felt that operational conditions of the road could be changed considerably for the better. When Cy approached us on this deal, I went to see Bill Morton, a Vice President of the State Street Investment Corporation and also a Director of the Seaboard Railroad. He and I had been friends for a long time. I told him some of my ideas for reforming the Katy, based on studies of their employee force and things of that sort. The Katy had about 9,300 people on the payroll and we believed that was too large. There were lots of other things we felt could be remedied. Bill was quite interested. And so State Street agreed to go in, provided the Pennroad Corporation would free my time so I could run the show. Pennroad was agreeable. And on that basis we bought the deal."

At the time the new management took over, the Katy Railroad was 85 years old—some 3,500 miles of track running from St. Louis to Kansas City in the North through the principal cities and towns of Kansas, Oklahoma and Texas, going down to Wichita Falls in the north and San Antonio, Houston and Galveston to the south. Much of the railroad's past was an exciting, colorful and picturesque history. Ahead lay financial chaos, the like of which the Eastern financiers never anticipated. Or else they never would have acquired the old railroad. Although moneymen are seldom moved by such intangibles, perhaps Robert E. Thomas and his associates were influenced to a degree by the romance of the Katy's history in their decision to acquire that railroad property.

"The early chapters of the railroad's life," the St. Louis *Post-Dispatch* commented editorially in 1945 on the occasion of the Katy's 75th birthday, "were filled with frontier chaos, bandits and Indians, longhorn cattle, dust and mud, squalor and sudden riches, fire and flood, gun-toting train and engine men, armed as a requisite of continued existence. Superhuman labors by pioneer workers and gambles by financial brokers all have a place in the history of the Katy Railroad. It was begun less than five years after the Civil War, and the men who built it were largely veterans of the Northern and Southern Armies who were accustomed to hardships of life in the open. The Katy was the first railroad to enter Texas from the north. Its coming meant swift, dependable transportation for hundreds of thousands of settlers seeking homes in a virgin empire. It brought markets for cotton, cattle and other products weeks nearer than the old trail days with their grueling overland cattle drives and their cumbersome wagon trains. Within half a decade after the advent of the Katy, such picturesque transportation, as well as the horse-drawn passenger stagecoach, had become memories."

The road's owners were young men just emerging into the world of finance—August Belmont; J. Pierpont Morgan (the elder) ; Levi P. Morton, later a Vice President of the United States; John D. Rockefeller, a little-known Cleveland, Ohio, oilman at the time; Levi Parsons, and George Denison. The railroad traces its beginnings to May 23, 1870, when the young financiers decided to build the line to take advantage of the Government's offer of free land for development of western railroads to provide transportation between Army posts and help in the development of the West. It turned out, though, that instead of receiving a bonus of 3,600,000 free acres, the financiers got only a 200-foot-wide right-of-way through Kansas and the Indian territory (now Oklahoma) to Preston, Texas.

The Cherokee Indians gave their consent only reluctantly for the railroad to pass through their land in what is now Oklahoma. Indian leaders conducted a campaign of harassment with claims of damages against the railroad for land, livestock, orchards and timber. Cherokee priests and medicine men also gave the railroad a bad name by attributing all the tribe's bad luck to the "devil's iron rails." One time when a severe drought was gripping the area, the Indian rainmakers explained at the council fires that their efforts had not been successful in bringing rain because the clouds could not get across the Katy Railroad tracks.

Although the Indians offered no physical opposition, the railroad in its early days had to cope with much violence from Western "badmen." These toughs were generally known as "Terminuses," because they hung around the end of the railroad looking to make a dishonest dollar by causing trouble. They sometimes opened switches to send a train into the ditch, and committed robbery and worse crimes. Their behavior finally became unbearable in 1872 during the visit of Secretary of the Interior Jacob D. Cox to a new railroad terminus in Indian territory called Eufaula. The "badmen" got fired up after laying their hands on a big shipment of illegal whiskey and, during the Secretary's inspection of a collection of dives and brothels, several tough characters spoke boldly to him, blustering that they had as good a right as anybody to stay in the Creek Nation. Meanwhile, a man killed the night before "for a mere caprice" lay in a tent the Secretary was invited to enter. When Secretary Cox attempted to speak to the unruly crowd, somebody fired a pistol and a bullet passed close to his head. The Washington dignitary retreated inside his private car and a railroad official telegraphed Washington about what was happening. This brought to Eufaula the Tenth Cavalry, which quieted down the toughs and ran them out of the area.

During the era of Jesse James, Katy trains were occasionally victimized by robbers as they wound their way through the lonely valleys and hills of Missouri and Kansas and the wilds of Indian territory. The last Katy train robbery—in fact, the last train robbery to occur in Oklahoma—came on the night of August 23, 1923, when a robber band headed by the notorious Al Spencer stopped

Katy passenger train No. 234 near Okesa, Oklahoma, by building a big fire in the middle of the tracks. The robbers rifled the mails of $21,000 worth of negotiable bonds and took to the hills. J. K. Ellis, of Fort Worth, Texas, Katy's Superintendent of Special Services, organized a manhunt composed of federal, state and local law enforcement officers. Al Spencer, leader of the band, was killed in a hail of bullets when he sought to shoot his way out of an ambush near Coffeyville, Kansas, where he was attempting to dispose of some of the stolen bonds. All other members of the gang were sentenced to 25 years in prison. Two were later killed during an attempted break from Leavenworth Penitentiary. A third, Frank Nash, escaped from there, but died later in the infamous massacre at the Kansas City Union Station during the 1930's when a band of gunmen headed by Pretty Boy Floyd, while attempting to rescue Nash as he was being taken back to prison after recapture, killed several officers and shot Nash by mistake.

When robbers and toughs were not preying on the railroad, it sometimes seemed that the Katy was trying to destroy itself. One time, in 1896, the Katy's general passenger agent, William George Crush, got a great promotional idea for staging a deliberate train wreck for the entertainment of thousands of spectators. He plastered the territory with great circus-style billboards proclaiming the unparalleled spectacle of two great trains meeting head-on at top speed. On September 15, M-K-T excursion trains hauled 40,000 spectators to the temporary tent city of Crush, Texas, between Waco and Hillsboro. The crowds dined from lunch baskets filled with fried chicken and boiled ham while others patronized a restaurant under a circus tent that Crush had provided, along with five Katy tank cars filled with drinking water.

Two hundred specially recruited deputy sheriffs herded and pushed the crowd back to what was considered a safe distance from a sign reading "Point of Collision." Then two ancient locomotives, one painted red, one green, and each pulling six cars loaded with crossties and adorned with colorful posters advertising a fair at Dallas and a circus at Waco, chugged slowly toward each other. They touched cow catchers in a ceremonial salute, then backed up a mile or so and stood panting. Crush waved his sun helmet; the two train crews opened the throttles, leaped to safety and the doomed engines lunged toward each other whistling and shrieking. Dozens of signal torpedoes placed along the track exploded as the trains passed over them, adding fire and color to the spectacle. At the climax, the two great engines crashed together, reared up on their hind ends like fighting lions and then each fell over sideways.

But railroad officials had not anticipated the tragic anticlimax. The boilers of both locomotives exploded, and immense clouds of wood and metal rained down upon the landscape and spectators. Miraculously, only two people were killed and a relatively few injured. The remainder of the crowd took time to give aid to the victims, while picking up the pieces to carry home as souvenirs.

By the time Robert E. Thomas took over control of the railroad in 1955, all these colorful carryings-on were past history. But rising costs, neglected maintenance and changing trends in transportation away from railroads were now giving the Katy more grief than all the combined past efforts of hostile Indian medicine men, robbers, outlaws and the perils of the frontier. The Katy had weathered the financial depression of the 1930's without going into bankruptcy, but just barely. The road had enjoyed a booming business during World War II, but shortly after war's end signs of strain began to appear. The railroad had not been able to reduce its $100,000,000 debt. Profits continued to go down, expenses up; proxy fights broke out between groups of stock-holders; efforts were made to recapitalize the company's debt, and management began requesting permission from Federal and regulatory bodies of the states to abandon certain areas of track and discontinue nonprofitable trains. On September 25, 1952, even the sixty-two-year-old "Katy Special," one of the road's prestigious trains, puffed into Union Station at St. Louis for its last time. The decline of the Katy Railroad had definitely set in.

When Bob Thomas took over, he found conditions in the M-K-T organization so much worse than he had expected that in a few months he went to his close friend, William N. Deramus, Sr., President of the Kansas City Southern Railroad, and requested permission to ask his son, young Bill, to join Thomas in his efforts to straighten out the Katy. Young Bill, at the time, was President of the Chicago and Great Western Railroad, in which the Kansas City Southern owned a substantial interest. Bill Jr. was building a reputation as a comer in railroad circles for streamlining operations and diversifying the income-producing activities of the Chicago & Great Western. The elder Deramus gave his permission, and in 1956, William N. Deramus III became the President of the Missouri-Kansas-Texas Railway Company to work with Bob Thomas, Executive Committee Chairman.

Young Bill was forty-one years old at the time, the youngest president of a major railroad in the country. His family had wanted him to be a lawyer, and sent him to Harvard Law School. But, after graduation in 1939, Bill renounced the law and went to work in St. Louis as transportation apprentice for the Wabash Railroad. After the U.S. entry in World War II, young Deramus went with an Army Transportation Unit, sponsored by the Wabash, and for two years ran a ramshackle, meter-gauge railroad carrying supplies and reinforcements through the jungles of Burma and India. He left the military with the rank of Major and joined the Kansas City Southern. In two years, he was Assistant to the General Manager. Then he went with the Chicago and

Great Western as Assistant in charge of operations, and when the president of that road died, young Bill succeeded him.

William N. Deramus III is tough and taciturn and believes in working a seven-day week. He immediately began cutting and slashing away at the Katy's top-heavy expenses and cutting down the payroll at a rate of about 100 people a week. The new president ran into difficulties when he attempted to reduce the Katy staff from about 1,300 to approximately 700 people at Parsons, Kansas, a main division point for many years. Deramus announced that the accounting office there was being abolished and the remaining 45 accounting employees would be moved to the company's division point at Denison, Texas.

But, on March 18, 1957, a temporary court injunction, obtained by the State of Kansas, prevented him from shipping a baggage car loaded with accounting records and equipment from Parsons to Denison. Great cries of anger arose from several quarters against the Katy management for its wholesale dismissals. Said George Harrison, President of the Brotherhood of Railway Clerks: "Deramus is engaged in a slaughter of jobs. . . . He is violating our contract."

The greatest outburst of indignation, however, broke loose a week later on a Monday morning when, according to the St. Louis *Post-Dispatch,* "about one-hundred and fifteen Accounting Department employees of the Katy reported for work today [in the St. Louis Office] but found their offices locked, dark and a sign directing job seekers to report Wednesday at Denison, Texas. . . . The employees, angry and stunned, milled about the fifteenth-floor corridor of the Railway Exchange Building. Security officers armed and wearing western-style hats, stood beside the door and objected when a *Post-Dispatch* Reporter and Photographer wanted to make a copy of the text of a sign that stated:

"This office has been transferred to Denison, Texas, March 23rd and employees who desire to transfer will report to Denison starting duty at eight A.M., Wednesday, March 27, 1957. Pullman cars for use of all employees will be attached to the head end of the Texas Special, leaving St. Louis at 5:40 Tuesday, March 26th. You will be permitted to stay in these cars at Denison for a period of one week and you will be allowed four dollars a day for meals for the period you occupy the Pullman cars. You will be paid your wages for March 25th and 26th and those who do not desire to transfer and who are entitled to vacations will be paid for their vacation. The railroad will reimburse those employees who move their household effects to Denison."

The *Post-Dispatch* had reported the previous day, in its Sunday morning edition, that the Missouri-Kansas-Texas Railway Company had begun moving truckloads of records from its headquarters in the Railroad Exchange Building in the dark hours of Saturday night and Sunday morning without making any public explanation of the move. The paper said that the parking space beside the building was reserved for a number of large trucks, and a guard refused to allow a reporter from the newspaper to go to the Katy floor. Later on, the newspaper disclosed that it had learned that the original plan was to move the trucks loaded with records pick-a-back on freight trains but management had decided to send the trucks "by a secret route through East St. Louis and Illinois to avoid possible reprisals from employees and the union."

The press, unions and even the St. Louis Chamber of Commerce were aghast at what they considered high-handed treatment of employees by management. Two days later the Chamber of Commerce of Metropolitan St. Louis expelled the Katy Railroad from its membership "for violating responsible business practices in its treatment of employees." It was the first such action the Chamber had taken against a large corporation member for at least 45 years.

Senator Warren G. Magnuson, Democrat of the State of Washington and Chairman of the Interstate Commerce Committee, issued an order for an immediate investigation of the M-K-T's action. "It looks pretty high-handed to me," he commented.

The St. Louis *Globe Democrat,* a morning newspaper, denounced Robert E. Thomas in an editorial as "the master criminal mind from New York," and called President William N. Deramus III "a murderer of jobs, a heartless bully."

The St. Louis *Post-Dispatch* said editorially: "It is a long time since 1880 when William H. Vanderbilt, the ruthless financier and railroad mogul, commented upon a cut in services with the classic remark, 'the public be damned.' " That newspaper's Pulitzer Prize-winning cartoonist, the late Daniel Fitzpatrick, drew cartoons about the Katy situation during the next few days. One picture was a truck with "Texas or Bust" painted on the side. A small locomotive, a couple of account books and a forlorn-looking woman were sitting on the tailgate. The cartoon was titled, "Katy Jones Got Another Poppa." Another Fitzpatrick cartoon showed a train trailing away into the night. A big, gross-looking gangster-type wearing a silk hat and smoking a big cigar, was pictured leaning out of the rear platform from which waved a banner saying, "The Employees Be Damned." The train was labeled M-K-T RR and the title of the cartoon was: "The Old Slogan Revised."

A week after the Katy's retreat to Texas in weekend darkness, 24 gloomy employees who had gone to Denison and worked there for a few days returned to St. Louis to report on conditions to other Katy employees. They said that morale was extremely low among the expatriates—that nobody knew if they were going to keep their jobs long—and that Denison was a dull town.

The outcries of indignation became so intense that, for the first time in his life, William N. Deramus III consented to an interview. He told a writer for the *Post-Dispatch:* "We didn't have

20

time to stop and explain every move." He explained that employees were not given notice because the Katy could not afford to have its retrenchment program delayed by court proceedings, such as happened at Parsons, Kansas. "We are trying to save a railroad with emergency measures and the sooner these measures take effect, the sooner we will turn the corner and stop losing money," he added.

A special article from New York City in the *Post-Dispatch* quoted Robert E. Thomas as saying that the previous owners of the M-K-T had allowed its properties to deteriorate to the extent that drastic measures were needed to save the railroad. "The Katy was dying and an emergency operation had to be performed," he said. "We went into the deal believing that under the right conditions and with the solution of the railroad's financial problems, the Katy could become a strong and prosperous part of the Southwestern Transportation System."

Despite the angry outcries and the all-time low in public relations, the new Katy management continued to cut, slash and consolidate, laying off employees and abandoning sections of track and little-used railroad stations. On May 1, 1958, the M-K-T's last passenger train across Missouri, the once renowned "Katy Flyer," rolled into Union Station at St. Louis, two hours and forty minutes late, on its death run. Aboard were only two through passengers from Parsons, Kansas. The "Katy Flyer," which began running in 1899, was once a household word throughout the Southwest for speed and class, but these qualities were now long forgotten. Dropping the "Flyer" and its sister train meant a saving of $120,000 a year.

The railroad's economy measures continued to draw flack: U.S. Representative Morgan M. Moulder, Democrat of Camdenton, Missouri, in opposing discontinuance of service on the Franklin-Moberly Branch, called Deramus "a road wrecker" and charged that the Katy was being mismanaged.

A poultry raiser of Windsor, Missouri, said at another hearing that the proposed abandonment of service west of Nevada, Missouri, to the Kansas line would have a debilitating effect on the economy of Henry County, "The Baby Chick Capital of the World."

One citizen, in a letter to the editor, annoyed because the line had brought back into service some ancient chair cars on the run from Parsons, Kansas, to Kansas City, suggested that Bill Deramus peddle liniment to passengers to soothe their sore backs.

Despite the Thomas-Deramus emergency service, the Katy's condition did not improve significantly. Every time management saved a few hundred thousand dollars by abandoning a stretch of track, closing a station or retiring another train, it had to spend even more money trying to keep in passable condition the property still left in operation. Beyond that, railroad salaries continued to rise throughout the nation. During Bill Deramus' first year as president, although he reduced by more than 1,000 the number of M-K-T employees, the payroll was larger at the end of the year than it had been the year previous.

Meanwhile, efforts to recapitalize the railroad were handicapped by dissension between owners of common stock—mainly State Street and Pennroad Corporation—and holders of 667,005 shares of $100 dollar-par value, 7 percent preferred stock. These had been in default for years in the amount by now of about $110,000,000. Finally, on a third try, Eastern management hammered through a plan that wiped out all of the debt on the preferred shares and the preferred shares themselves, by substituting for each share one $100 dollar 5½ percent debenture along with a non-interest-bearing $100 certificate against earnings, plus one share of common stock.

William N. Deramus III resigned as President of the Katy in November, 1961, to take over Presidency of the Kansas City Southern, following his father's retirement. In 1975, he still held that position and also retained his post as one of the original Directors of the Mid-America Pipeline, now MAPCO, which, as we shall see, grew out of the troubles of the Katy. In 1976, Bill Deramus looked back over his administration of the Katy and summed it up as follows: "I agreed to take over the presidency of the Katy because Bob Thomas was a close friend of my father and me and he needed badly somebody of proven ability to try to run the line. The Katy had too much mileage but not enough revenue and its previous management had not spent the money it should have during the lush war years to bring up its physical facilities. What were we able to do? Not nearly enough. We spent a lot of money on maintenance and way. We should have spent more but we did not have the cash. We did manage to improve the financial situation of the road—somewhat. Still its condition was not too great when I left—and still isn't."

Long before Mr. Deramus left Katy, however—in fact only a few months after he had joined that railroad as president—he and Robert E. Thomas had caught a glimpse of what they hoped might be a light at the end of the tunnel. The first small glimmer was reported in the St. Louis press on October 24, 1957, in the following short item: "The Katy Railroad, in cooperation with the New York Central, has signed a contract with Williams Brothers Company of Tulsa, Oklahoma, a consulting engineering firm, to explore the feasibility of installing a liquefied petroleum gas pipeline along the railroad's right-of-way, it was announced today. A spokesman said the possibility of the pipeline becoming a reality is at this point necessarily vague . . ."

This dispatch resulted from a luncheon-meeting in New York City attended by Robert E. Thomas and the late Colonel T. C. Davis, Chairman of the Board of the bankrupt Missouri-

Pacific Railroad. Colonel Davis told Mr. Thomas that the Missouri-Pacific and New York Central Railroads had been discussing with Williams Brothers of Tulsa the idea of building a pipeline, to carry mainly propane, along the railroads' rights-of-way from the Texas oil fields into New York State. He added that he had been unable to get the Missouri-Pacific to go along. Colonel Davis told Bob Thomas that the Katy was welcome to take the Missouri-Pacific's place in the plan if Mr. Thomas thought it had merit and could get his Board to back him.

Mr. Thomas knew little about pipelines but he saw in the idea a hope to save not only the Katy, but his own career as well. Edward A. Merkle, who had recently become President of the Pennroad Corporation in New York—now called the Madison Fund—did not favor Thomas' spending practically all his time and effort trying to salvage the Katy. And so, President Merkle had asked Vice President Thomas to leave the Madison Fund.

Bob Thomas seized on the pipeline idea and would not let go until it resulted, three years later, in the Mid-America Pipeline, which followed a somewhat different route than originally proposed. Since it had been founded with Katy money, Katy owned about 18 percent of the new pipeline. Mr. Thomas retired from the Katy Railroad in 1964 to give his full time to the booming business of the Mid-America Pipeline Company that was to develop into MAPCO, Inc., the highly prosperous, well-rounded energy company and a sensation of Wall Street for the past half a dozen years.

The Katy evokes rather painful memories in Bob Thomas these days when he looks back on his years of trying to revitalize that railroad. "We took over the railroad with high hopes and great plans," he said in the summer of 1975. "The Katy just turned out to be a much bigger job than any of us had anticipated. I would consider getting into that deal one of the big mistakes of my life. I got to the point where I was sorry I had ever heard of the Katy.

"But at the same time—from the standpoint of my own personal career—if I had not made that mistake, I would not be running MAPCO today. A stockbroker friend of mine in New York City, who was once on the Katy Board, said to me one day that he thought I was the luckiest guy he had ever seen. 'If you fell into a sewer,' he told me, 'you would come out wearing a full dress suit.'"

KATY JONES GOT ANOTHER PAPA

Daniel Fitzpatrick, Pulitzer Prize-winning cartoonist of The *St. Louis Post-Dispatch*, attacked with his charcoal pencil the Katy management's abrupt and unannounced "midnight move" of its accounting office and staff from St. Louis to Denison, Texas.

(Reprinted with permission of The *St. Louis Post-Dispatch*.)

AN OLD SLOGAN REVISED

Fitzpatrick created a new version of William H. Vanderbilt's notorious pronouncement, "The Public Be Damned," to express local outrage at the Katy's "secret midnight" shift of employees to a "dull town" in Texas. Meanwhile, the rival St. Louis daily, *The Globe-Democrat*, was editorially branding Robert E. Thomas "the master criminal mind from New York."

(Reprinted with permission of The *St. Louis Post-Dispatch.*)

A crack Katy passenger train highballs down the line, through the lonely reaches of Missouri, Kansas, Indian Territory (now Oklahoma) and Texas during the early 1870's. In those pioneering times, the railroad was beset by many colorful vicissitudes, including train bandits, border ruffians and the hostile incantations of disgruntled Cherokee medicine men. But none of these proved as disastrous to the Katy's prestige and financial situation as did the railroad economics of the 1950's.

You lose some; you win some. In St. Louis, the Chamber of Commerce had ousted the Katy Railroad from its membership "for violating responsible business practices in treatment of employees." But in Texas, where the Katy had moved its accounting office and staff, Governor Price Daniel presented Awards of Merit to Katy Executive Committee Chairman Robert E. Thomas (far right) and to Katy President William N. Deramus, III (next to Mr. Thomas.)

The Anatomy of an Idea   3

When asked how he got the notion of building the world's first liquefied petroleum gas pipeline, Bob Thomas always replies that he was "handed the idea on a silver platter" by the late Colonel T. C. Davis, then Chairman of the Board of the bankrupt Missouri-Pacific Railroad. Actually, Colonel Davis was only the "waiter" who served up the idea. The "chef" who had prepared and arranged the contents of that "silver platter" was a young lawyer from the East named Hugh Robinson, who originated and developed a concept that finally resulted in the Mid-America Pipeline System, while struggling to keep his job with the Williams Brothers Company in Tulsa, Oklahoma.

Hugh Robinson, who was in his early thirties when he got the idea of building an LP Gas pipeline, is a native of Washington, D.C., son of a U.S. Army Colonel and a graduate of Princeton College and Harvard Law School. He served in the U.S. Artillery during World War II, and left the service when the war was over with the rank of Captain. For a short while he was associated with a law firm in New York City but left because, as he says, "I wanted to get into some sort of 'intellectual outdoor life.' I picked pipelining, which had always fascinated me. Don't ask me why— it just did. So, in 1953, I managed to get a job with Williams Brothers, one of the best-known names in pipelining."

Williams Brothers sent young Robinson out to work with its pipeline-laying crews, for a year in Canada, then two years in Alaska. During the latter stint, Robinson says he heard for the first time about liquefied petroleum gas. "That Alaska project was for the U.S. Air Force and it was enjoyable work," Hugh Robinson reminisces. "One of the nice things about outdoor life, whether it is soldiering, pipelining or whatnot, is the interest older men often take in showing youngsters the ropes—how an oldtimer will tuck a youngster under his arm, as it were, and guide him and look after him and tell him what a damn fool he is now and then and how he can do the job better. I had a welder friend like that, a West Texan, and one day I said to him: 'Joe, what is this LP Gas that I keep hearing about?'

"Joe shifted his cud of tobacco from one jaw to the other and he said, 'Well, now that's liquefied petroleum gas.' I said, 'That's interesting, Joe, but what is liquefied petroleum gas?' 'Well, now, son, that is mainly butane and propane.' I asked, 'What in hell are butane and propane?' And then he said, 'Well, god-dammit if you were to strip the moisture out of a wet fart, butane and propane is what you would get.'

"And so, that is about all I knew on the subject of propane and butane in 1955. But Joe's earthy definition had made a strong and lasting impact on my mind—and that may have been partly responsible for my becoming interested in LP Gas in a practical way a couple of years later. Early in 1956 I had been shifted from field work to the Williams Brothers central offices in Tulsa, where they had me doing feasibility studies with the idea of developing new pipeline projects."

Williams Brothers was an old and honored name in pipe-lining, but the current management was fairly new, consisting of the younger generation of the family and several associates, headed by John Williams. They had taken over six years earlier from the two Williams Brothers, who had founded the business. The younger generation's new management was low on capital but high in energy, ambition and know-how. They were anxious to enlarge the Williams Brothers Engineering Department by going out and determining areas where pipelines were needed, then finding the operational management with the capital to pay Williams Brothers to do a turnkey job. They visualized creating the entire project, surveying the route, obtaining rights-of-way, laying the pipe, installing the pumping and other operational equipment and, in short, turning over a complete system to an operator in condition to go to work immediately.

"A day or two after I started to work," Hugh Robinson recalls, "John Williams and Vincent Butler, head of the company's Engineering Department, met with me and told me to start by drawing a map of all the pipelines and all the refineries in the United States to familiarize myself with the situation. Then I was to look for pipelines of various types that needed to be built. My budget was quite limited, amounting to a secretary and what support the Drafting Section and the Engineering Department could give me. It soon became apparent to me that undertaking a natural gas pipeline was out of the question. For that you needed a lot more money than I had in my budget. Natural gas is controlled by the Federal Power Commission and a natural gas pipeline amounts to a monopoly situation. To build one you've got to get from the Federal Power Commission a Certificate of Public Convenience and Necessity to serve a certain area. This is possible, if you're lucky and if you have a million dollars or so to spend on studies and reports and entertaining the proper people —and we didn't have that kind of money.

"Pipelines carrying liquids—mainly crude oil—were not controlled by the Federal Power Commission but by the Interstate Commerce Commission. They did not represent a monopoly situation, did not require Certificates of Public Convenience and Necessity and, therefore, it was much easier to build a liquid-carrying pipeline. That seemed the only field open to us at the time. So I began examining prospects for building crude oil and products lines. Along about March, 1956, I began thinking about LP gas and playing around with the figures on its consumption. On the basis of sales of these products over the past five or ten years, I extrapolated what the consumption was likely to be in the future. I distinctly remember one evening while working late at the office at the end of a long nice spring day when I really wanted to get out, but these figures were getting exciting. Suddenly I said to myself, 'Well, by 1959, the consumption will be big enough that there is going to be room for a pipeline system carrying nothing but liquefied petroleum gas.' "

Robinson prepared a memorandum showing the history of LP Gas, what it was, its rate of growth, and he proposed the building of a pipeline from the producing areas of the Southwest to follow the rights-of-way of railroads all the way to a major freight yard near Albany, New York. His reasons for such a proposal were:

1. The densely populated East—and the New York sector in particular—represented potentially immense consuming areas for LP Gas and were ripe for further development.

2. At the time it seemed a sound idea for a pipeline to follow the rights-of-way already owned by railroads. This meant that if the railroads operated the pipeline there would be no expense of acquiring more land. Robinson figured this idea should interest railroad managements, in trouble financially because of competing forms of transportation.

3. Since practically all of the liquid-carrying pipelines were owned by major oil companies, Hugh Robinson believed that if he could get one or two large railroads to back his proposed pipeline, these railroads would have enough muscle to keep the oil companies from getting into the act and fouling up his project. The reasoning was that, since railroads had little or no pipelining experience, their managements would almost certainly depend on Williams Brothers to build the pipeline, which would not necessarily have been the case if one or more of the major oil companies became involved.

"Here is what is likely to happen," Hugh Robinson says, "when somebody in my position working for a company like Williams Brothers proposes a new long-distance pipeline to some major oil company: You call somebody on your level in the oil company and invite him to lunch. You feed him a couple of martinis on the expense account and the nicest lunch on the menu and you say, 'Have you fellas ever thought about building a pipeline from A to B?' The answer will be, 'Yes, no, or maybe—why?' And you say, 'Well, I just happen to have a study here and it looks pretty good.' Now here you have a study from one of the leading pipelining engineering firms, and the oil company man is a damn fool if he doesn't take it back to his superiors. So you give him the study and sit on the edge of your chair waiting for results. A couple of months later the oil company guy calls you on the phone and he says either, 'We don't think we will do it,' or 'Yeh, it looks pretty good—as a matter of fact we're going to take it to the board next month.' And you ask what day it will be and you mark that on the calendar and when that day arrives, you telephone the guy at the oil company and he says, 'Well, what do you know—the board approved it—isn't that great! And if your company is the low bidder, you'll get the job.'

"Now, a wide-ranging, international company like Williams Brothers often has trouble being low bidder on a domestic pipeline because they have got to maintain a fairly large staff all the time and a great mass of equipment. They often have to bid on a job against an outfit whose headquarters are mainly in the general manager's hat, and he hires workers and leases the equipment only when he gets a job. And so, when somebody like myself working for a big company like Williams takes his great idea to a major oil company, some other engineering outfit often ends up with the job. I didn't want this to happen to my LP Gas pipeline concept. I decided to try to spark the interest of some forward-looking head of a railroad, with a right-of-way along the course of our proposed pipeline."

Hugh Robinson took his idea to Colonel Davis in New York City. His Missouri-Pacific Railroad went down into the oil- and gas-producing country. Colonel Davis was also a great friend of the late Robert Young, head of the Allegheny Corporation, which then controlled the New York Central Railroad. Robinson envisioned the proposed pipeline following the Missouri-Pacific right-of-way to St. Louis, then the Central to its end.

Both Colonel Davis and the New York Central management showed keen interest in the idea, but Colonel Davis was not able to develop a similar interest in the Missouri-Pacific headquarters in St. Louis. The Missouri-Pacific was in receivership at the time and a fight for control was going on between the common stockholders, represented principally by Colonel Davis, and the bondholders who really dominated the railroad and who opposed Colonel Davis. Beyond that, the Traffic Department was very much opposed because of the potential loss of valuable tank-car shipments. Management of the New York Central on the other hand, according to Hugh Robinson, was anxious to get going—they wanted to make studies of the project, but without the Missouri-Pacific Railroad to bring the LP Gas up to them at St. Louis from the oil fields, the Central was stymied. And so Robinson spent the latter part of 1956 and early 1957 waiting and hoping for some development that would allow the two railroads to proceed with the line. That didn't happen.

"Finally, Colonel Davis telephoned me in Tulsa one day and said that the Missouri-Pacific Board was not going to approve the pipeline idea," he relates. "He then asked if I would have any objection if he discussed the proposed project for a liquefied petroleum gas pipeline with Robert Thomas, Chairman, and his associate, Bill Deramus, President, of the Missouri-Kansas-Texas Railway Company. I didn't know either Mr. Thomas or Mr. Deramus, but I certainly had no objection. My project was sitting idle on dead center and the Katy Railroad was just one more opportunity.

"The next thing I knew, three or four days later, I got a telephone call—I can't remember whether it was from Colonel Davis or Bob Thomas—asking that we meet with them in the offices of the Kansas City Southern Railway in Kansas City, Missouri. I then told John Williams for the first time about this new development involving the Katy Railroad. Both he and Vincent Butler recognized the possibilities. So the three of us and old Mr. Miller Williams, one of the founders of the original company, went up to Kansas City and met with the Katy Railroad officials. We gave them details of our studies and direction of our thinking thus far. They told us they would be in touch with us later. A couple of days after we got back to Tulsa a call came from Mr. Thomas, who said he had discussed the idea over long-distance telephone with William K. Warren, of Warren Petroleum Company, who was also a director of the Katy Railroad. Mr. Warren had told him, Bob reported, 'This is a marvelous idea—come on down here and let's talk about it,' or words to that effect."

The pipeline promoters considered Mr. Warren's support vital, since Warren Petroleum was one of the three leading producers of liquefied petroleum gas, the other two being Phillips Petroleum Company and the Skelly Oil Company. Bob Thomas and his associates badly needed a throughput agreement from Warren, but they never got one. "Bill Warren's early enthusiasm soon cooled on the subject," Robinson reports. "I believe he had begun to think of the LP Gas pipeline as something that Warren Petroleum ought to do. It finally became impossible for us to get the time of day from Warren Petroleum. The Warren people were never openly hostile; there was just a total wall of silence insofar as us getting any of the reports, surveys and such that they had which would have been very useful to us.

"We now began to run into real opposition on all sides, mainly from the giants of the petroleum industry," Hugh Robinson remembers. "The big companies were polite enough. They would listen courteously to us but wouldn't give us any commitment. Shell would not; Mobil would not. I remember making a trip to Humble Oil, Exxon's subsidiary. They listened carefully and were quite polite; they gave us all the time we wanted. The interview opened and closed and that was the end of it. This was the very first time anyone outside of the oil patch had really beaten the big boys to the punch. I think they resented the possibility of us messing up their established marketing arrangements. They didn't want to see the rules of the game changed. We were making a new game of it in which smaller, independent marketers could compete with them by using a common carrier pipeline that was not controlled by major oil companies."

The new pipeline project got opposition rather than support from Phillips Petroleum Company. According to Hugh Robinson, Phillips was batching through its own pipeline thousands of gallons of propane to the Chicago Transit Authority to fuel all of that city's buses, a highly profitable operation. Phillips also owned an interest in the Great Lakes Pipeline, and Robinson believed it was partially, at least, Phillips' influence that caused the management of Great Lakes Pipeline to refuse to deal with Bob Thomas, John Williams and Vincent Butler when they approached Great Lakes with the idea of tying the proposed propane pipeline into the Great Lakes system for distribution throughout the upper Middle West.

The Thomas group made this move after it had become apparent early in 1959 that any hope of building a pipeline into the East was dead. There wasn't as much demand in the thickly populated megalopolis areas for LP Gas as in the farming areas of the Midwest. And the idea of using the railroads' rights-of-way for pipelines turned out to be impractical. A high-pressure pipeline built that near any railroad was potentially dangerous every time there was a derailment. Besides, as Bob Thomas says, "Railroads wiggle around too much." It would be cheaper to buy the land and go straight across country with the pipeline.

"It came as quite a shock to Bob, John and Vince when they learned from its management that Great Lakes wanted no part of their project," Hugh Robinson says. "I think they began to realize for the first time the extent of the opposition we were getting from most of the major oil companies. I knew about it because I had been living with that project day by day.

"I knew our project was definitely in trouble—and so was my future. I considered myself middle-aged at the time and had no other immediate jobs in prospect. It looked like I would be laid off during the course of that year. John Williams was running into static from various oil companies who kept saying in effect, 'Hey, we give you a lot of business. What the hell are you doing down there competing with us?' In fact, John almost abandoned the project at one point. Some of the companies had begun to protest so vigorously that finally John told me just to drop the whole thing.

"But I didn't drop it. I didn't tell him one way or the other, but I just kept on trying to line up support for that pipeline. I could not afford to drop the project. If I did, I was out of a job. Fortunately, John's moment of weakness happened just before we got our big breakthrough. When that came, John quickly reversed himself and we went ahead. That was the only time I had to go beyond the scope of his instructions."

The "big breakthrough" came from the Skelly Oil Company. When he realized that the idea of going East with the pipeline was dead, Hugh Robinson decided the only possibility left was to go North through the rich wheat and corn belts and into Minnesota and Wisconsin. And the only way to accomplish this was to get a throughput agreement from at least one of the big three producers of liquefied petroleum gas.

"Both Warren and Phillips were out," he says. "That left only the Skelly Oil Company. Without at least one major supplier, we were dead. It had become obvious to me by this time that Skelly was our key. If we could get the backing of that one major supporter, that would allow us to gather some strength and the smaller suppliers would probably join the bandwagon. So I telephoned a young fellow I knew with Skelly's LPG Department named Wesley Baker and invited him to have lunch with me at the Mayo Hotel, which in those days put on a very good buffet. At lunch that day I told Wesley we would be willing to lay out our proposed pipeline pretty much at Skelly's convenience, providing Skelly would sign a throughput letter of intent. I pointed out that Skelly, which didn't have a long-distance pipeline, would continue to be outmaneuvered as long as Phillips had its line and carried some LP Gas in it, and that Warren was getting strong support since being taken over by Gulf. Skelly needed something to keep up its competitive position and I said, 'Wes, what would Skelly want in the way of a pipeline?'

"He said that Skelly might be interested if we built a pipeline starting down near the Skelly plant in southeastern New Mexico in the Hobbs area, then went north through Skellytown to accommodate the big Skelly installation there. Then he said, 'We would like for it to go near Conway, Kansas, so we could get some salt cavern storage there, and we have big markets up in the Iowa and Minnesota areas. We ought to have a branch up there.' And then he said, 'How about coming over here in the direction of St. Louis and see if we could pick up some good markets in Missouri and go on up through Illinois and Wisconsin?' I said, 'That all looks pretty good to me.'

"So, right there in the old Mayo Hotel dining room, I drew for him on a linen napkin the map of the proposed LP Gas Pipeline, almost identical to what it later became in reality, an irregular Y going into Minnesota to the west and Wisconsin to the east, terminating at Pine Bend, Minnesota, and at Janesville, Wisconsin. I left the napkin there at the hotel dining room without realizing its historical significance, so I guess it went to the laundry and our penciled map got washed out. I wish, though, I had brought that napkin away with me. I'd sure like to have it today."

A few days later during a luncheon at the Tulsa Club, Robinson showed Bob Thomas and John Williams a redrawn version of the map he'd done originally on that hotel napkin, and told them, "I think we're going to get Skelly support to go north along this lop-sided Y route." Then he says, "I kept emphasizing that we *had to have Skelly*. Without Skelly, we were dead. I said I had drawn this route pretty much for the convenience of Skelly, but it would be satisfactory for a number of other shippers. Bob and John said to me, 'All right, follow that up.' They always gave me the most wonderful support.

"During the course of that summer, Skelly showed more and more interest and we kept constantly pointing out to them that this pipeline was their only hope of keeping anywhere on near even terms with their major competition. By late summer 1959, it began to appear that we were about to crack through the opposition. One weekend Bob and I went up to Kansas City and met with Don Miller, the Marketing Vice President at Skelly. When we explained the line, Don was enthusiastic about it. Bob had the flu that weekend. I never saw anyone sicker who was still trying to work. He had a temperature of 103 but kept on the phone, calling New York, Minneapolis and places trying to line up some of the marketing companies. I had the feeling that this was a sort of make or break weekend for the project.

"Even when he was sick, Bob kept going full steam all the time. When we met with the Skelly people he put on a magnificent show of acting, although I knew he didn't have his financing all in a row. Until he did, he couldn't make firm commitments to potential suppliers. But Bob played a beautiful hand, never promising flat out that there would be a pipeline; he would just say this was subject to a lot of negotiations and developments and, in his opinion, yes, there would be a line. He had a very fine, convincing, affirmative approach to the potential shippers. Conversely, when his potential underwriters were wobbling, Bob would reassure them with a positive approach. I have tremendous admiration for the way he conducted that campaign."

By the early fall of 1959 it had become obvious that the President of Skelly now favored the pipeline. But at that point, J. Paul Getty, who owned 60 percent of Skelly, fired the President. For a short while it appeared that the main support for the pipeline was gone. But then luck smiled on the project. Getty promoted Don Miller from Marketing Vice President to President of

Skelly—and Miller was even stronger for the pipeline than his predecessor had been. And so, on November 20, 1959, Don H. Miller signed on behalf of the Skelly Oil Company a letter to the Midcontinent Eastern Pipeline Corporation (the original name of the Mid-America Pipeline Company) stating that it was Skelly's intention to use the proposed LP Gas pipeline if it was constructed. This was the big breakthrough.

"I got that letter from Skelly on a fine, gorgeous Autumn afternoon," Hugh Robinson likes to recall. "They handed it to me at their offices, and I was walking along the street away from the Skelly Building about five o'clock. I remember, a fellow I knew who worked for the Tuloma Oil Company spotted me about a block away and seemed to sense the elation I was feeling. He shouted at me, 'Well, you surely look happy—what have you got there?' I remember waving the letter—the original letter—in his direction and yelling back, 'Here's a sixty-million-dollar letter that I just got.'

"I was shouting partly because of the elation of success and partly for reasons of propaganda. I realized that this letter meant that we probably were going to win and I wanted the word to get around. Tuloma was Standard Oil of Indiana's LP Gas Division. Their people had shown interest in our pipeline and I knew there was no quicker way for the word to circulate in the industry that we were about to get there than to give somebody in the industry something he could report of a positive nature. By the end of that week everyone knew that Skelly had signed, and they realized that this signing was pretty damned important.

"After that, our pitch to the various potential supplying companies was something like this: 'If you sign a throughput agreement, we will build a spur to your plant at *our* expense. We will put your plant into the initial design of the line. If you do not give us a throughput agreement, you're going to be in the position of *having* to use the line once it is in operation. But if you wait until then, you can damned well build your own spur over to us at *your* expense. And that began to chip away at quite a number of them.

"A few weeks later, at Christmas time, Bob brought representatives of the Prudential Insurance Company of America and the underwriters and some New York bankers out to Tulsa to listen to the potential suppliers express their attitudes about the pipeline, which by then were quite enthusiastic. This meeting was highly successful. The money people from the East were obviously convinced as to the feasibility of our project. After that, things just sort of fell in place as far as I was concerned. They had a lot of paperwork and stuff to do in New York, I know, but by the Spring of 1960, the crews had started to work laying the pipeline. I would like to emphasize, though, that without Bob's personality this project would never have gone anywhere. John Wil-

36

liams was not prepared to do it on his own. He had not yet reached that point of independence. Bob kept the ball bouncing between the industry and the financial support until he finally got his pipeline in the ground."

After leaving Williams Brothers, Hugh Robinson worked for Mid-America Pipeline for a while, and he is still retained by MAPCO as a consultant. He lives a quiet life these days with his family in a small town in northern Connecticut near the Massachusetts border, where he is associated with a country law firm. But Hugh Robinson often looks back nostalgically to the tumultuous days when he was trying to save his job by converting the dream of the world's first LP Gas Pipeline into reality.

"That was the most exciting, satisfying and happiest period of my entire life," he says these days.

What is LP Gas, Anyway?   4

The general consensus among Robert E. Thomas watchers is that the man is not only smart, determined and persistent—he is also shot full of plain ole luck. Edward A. Merkle, President of the Madison Fund of New York City and the one-time associate and rival of Mr. Thomas within that company, describes the present MAPCO President and Chairman as follows:

"Bob is ambitious and he is smart," Mr. Merkle said in the Spring of 1975. "And he has got guts. It is very important to have guts, you know. Very few people do. And Bob is lucky, too. You have *got* to have some luck. Hell's bells! I don't care how smart you are, if you're not lucky—*forget it.*"

Most people probably regard a "lucky" individual as merely the fortunate recipient of favors from fickle chance. Others hold that there is no such thing as chance or coincidence and that a person who seems to be "lucky" is really receiving inner guidance, although the recipient is generally unaware of this. Whatever the case—although his knowledge of both pipelines and hydrocarbons was almost nil at the time—Bob Thomas grabbed onto the idea of building an LP Gas pipeline the first time it was suggested to him.

For 20 years Robert E. Thomas had been regarded in financial circles as a "railroad expert"; he was enthusiastic about railroad securities as potentially good investments. But then he took over management of the Missouri-Kansas-Texas Railway Company, and that eventually disillusioned him about the future of railroad investments generally—and even the ability of railroads to survive physically. During an interview with the Tulsa *World* in November, 1961, Mr. Thomas, who was then Chairman of the Executive Committee of the M-K-T and President of the Mid-America Pipeline Company, said that he had become convinced that "railroads may die . . . unless they diversify and get into businesses other than running trains. That's the reason Katy Railroad is in pipelining. Katy owns about 20 percent of Mid-America, which is the first step to diversify our (Katy's) business activities." He blamed the railroads' plight on truck and barge competition, the high wage cost situation in railroads and competition from "private carriage," in which many large firms move their own products, rather than rely on common carriers.

At the time of this interview, the Mid-America Pipeline had been operating about a year, and Bob Thomas had become an authority on both pipelining and hydrocarbons. But four years earlier when he was given "on a silver platter" the idea of the Katy Railroad's helping to build and operate an LP Gas pipeline, "about all I knew about pipelines," he now says, "was that they were underground and they generally made money." He had heard vaguely that there was such a thing as LP Gas, and that about covered his knowledge on the subject.

When the Mid-America Pipeline began operating, in 1960, the LP Gas business had already become an industry of respectable size. It was then forty-eight years old and, especially during the sixteen years prior to 1960, had grown rapidly—from total sales of 76,000,000 gallons in 1946 to 10,000,000,000 gallons in 1960—an increase of some 800 percent. Since 1922, the daily consumption had multiplied 44,843 times. By 1960, however, it had become obvious to experts that if the business was to continue to enjoy substantial growth, improved methods of transporting the product were essential. In short, it was now high time for somebody to build a major pipeline devoted exclusively to carrying LP Gas. As it turned out, Mid-America became the first to build such a pipeline—the first in the world and forerunner and inspiration of other LP Gas pipelines that were to follow. The fact that Robert E. Thomas, who knew practically nothing about the national LP Gas situation, jumped at the idea *at the crucial time he did* and continued to persist, against formidable odds, until he got the pipeline built is a striking example of "Thomas Luck" or, as some might say, inspiration or inner guidance.

The reason that no major LP Gas pipelines had been built up to this time was that liquefied petroleum gases were largely a stepchild of the oil industry—a by-product that the big oil companies seemed to regard more as a problem than an economic opportunity. As a result, the derivations, properties and potentials of LP Gas had remained pretty much of a mystery to most Americans. As most people know, hydrocarbons were formed over millions of years by decaying plant and animal life trapped in the earth. Some of this residue comes from the earth in liquid form, which is refined into several classes of combustible products for fuel, including heating oils and gasoline. During the process of fermentation and formation of crude oil, the decaying plant and animal life gave off various gases—something like sewer gas—that are highly combustible. The most abundant and familiar of these is methane, the dry "natural gas" that is piped direct to consumers through tributary lines leading off major pipelines from the oil and gas fields.

But "natural gas" does not emerge from the earth in a condition suitable for immediate transportation via pipeline. It is somewhat like fog, heavily laden with moisture, caused by the so-called wet gas that emerges along with the methane. The wet gases include propane, butane, ethane, natural gasoline and other lesser gases. Natural gas is derived from two sources. It is harvested from regular gas wells, drilled specifically to obtain natural gas. It also comes out of the earth as a by-product of crude oil from oil wells. For many years most natural gas came from oil wells and most of that was wasted. Oil producers simply burned, or flared, the bulk of it to get the stuff out of the way because there were not nearly enough pipelines to handle this valuable gas commercially.

During and shortly after World War II came a great wave of long-distance pipeline construction to take natural gas from the oil and gas fields to the great urban centers, especially in the East. This put to commercial use almost all of the methane being produced in this country. But a great deal of the LP Gas that emerged from the ground with the methane, and which was separated from it, continued to be flared, or wasted. It was necessary to separate this wet gas from the "dry" methane in order to transport methane effectively to market via pipelines. Otherwise, the wet gas would condense in the line and block the transmission process.

One reason that pipelines intended to handle LP Gas exclusively were so late in coming was that these products are more difficult to transport, because LP Gases must be kept in liquid form until they are actually burned. This meant that a pipeline handling such products had to be built strong enough to endure high pressures at all times. Propane, for example, boils, or vaporizes, when the temperature gets warmer than 44 degrees below zero, at normal atmospheric pressure. In order to keep propane in liquid form while it is in the pipeline or in storage, this wet gas must be kept under pressure of at least 200 pounds per square inch, thus raising its boiling point above outside normal temperatures. That is why, when a propane pipeline breaks, it freezes the surrounding ground. The escaping propane absorbs the nearby heat so rapidly that it freezes everything in the vicinity, by producing, in effect, a "heat vacuum." It is this principle that makes a spray from an aerosol can cold to the touch.

Liquefied petroleum gas is more potent than the more familiar methane, better known to consumers simply as "natural gas." A cubic foot of propane—the most popular, adaptable and abundant of LP Gas products—gives off 2,316 units of heat (BTU's) when burned, as compared with about 1,000 units produced by a like amount of methane. It takes a smaller amount of propane to do the same heating or fueling job than straight natural gas.

LP Gas products are called hydrocarbons because they are

made up of carbon and hydrogen. The chemical formula of propane is C_3H_8, which means that a molecule of propane contains three atoms of carbon hooked together with eight atoms of hydrogen. This is why propane is often called "C-3."

About 70 percent of all LP Gas comes from wells mixed with natural gas, and about 30 percent emerges from the ground mixed with crude oil. The liquefied petroleum gases are separated from crude at refineries that produce gasoline and other products; they are removed from natural gas at "fractionating plants," then confined under sufficient pressure to keep them in a liquid state until time to burn them. As the LP Gas escapes through a burner, it vaporizes in normal atmospheric pressure. Thus, it reverts to a gas, and that is what burns to produce heat or power.

To get a clearer perspective of the LP Gas picture at the time Mid-America Pipeline began operating and to better appreciate how this Mid-America pipeline fit into the needs of the industry, it is a good idea to look back briefly at the history of natural gas in general and especially at the development of the wet gas or "bottled gas," and the LP Gas industry. We are indebted for this information to the National LP Gas Association, of Chicago.

A thousand years or so before Christ, herdsmen on Mount Parnassus, in Greece, observed a strange vapor escaping from the ground. After smelling it, they became light-headed, giddy and talked in a strange and wild manner. A temple was built at this spot, and in the centuries that followed priests would breathe the fumes, causing them to speak in strange tongues. Thus originated the famous Oracle of Delphi, which the Greeks consulted for centuries to get advice and predictions for the future. This is one of the early recorded instances of a natural gas discovery.

About the same time, on the other side of the world, the Chinese had discovered a gas escaping from a soft-coal bed near Peking, which was highly combustible. They piped it through hollow bamboo tubes to their salt works and used the gas as fuel to boil precious salt from brine. The same gas was also piped into Peking and served to light and heat the temples and palaces there.

In Persia, 500 or 600 years before Christ, priests of Zoroaster erected temples near Baku on the shores of the Caspian Sea, where faithful followers flocked in, awed by the "sacred fires" that burned there continually. One of these temples stood as late as 1880. After it was torn down, a pipe was found that conducted natural gas from a nearby well to the temple altar.

The first natural gas reported in the United States was discovered in 1775 by Jesuit priests exploring the valley of the Ohio River. At about the same time, George Washington discovered what he called a "burning spring" in the Kanawha River Valley in western Virginia. The place has since been dedicated as a national park.

The first practical use made of natural gas in the United States was at Fredonia, New York, in 1821, after two small boys discovered gas bubbling up through a pond. Their father piped it to the inn that he operated in the village, where it fueled thirty burners. Four years later, when General Lafayette stopped at the inn, he found it brightly lighted with natural gas and some of the food for the banquet in his honor was cooked with natural gas. The National LP Gas Association said in 1961 that natural gas from the same source was still burning in that old village inn.

In 1830, salt makers along the Muskingum River in Ohio were using natural gas to boil down brine, as the Chinese had done nearly 3,000 years earlier.

Meanwhile, in England, William Murdock, an employee of James Watt, inventor of the steam engine, had discovered how to make artificial illuminating gas. He burned coal, wood and other materials, trapped the gases and piped them through 70 feet of tubing to light his house at Redruth, in Cornwall. Four years later an Italian fireworks manufacturing concern used coal gas to illuminate an amphitheatre in Philadelphia, Pennsylvania.

The American House, in Boston, became the first hotel in the United States to be lighted with coal gas. This was in 1835, nine years before any hotel had a private bath. Coal gas was used in many cities in America for 150 years until finally the increased use of natural gas following World War II drove it off the market.

In 1859, Colonel Edwin L. Drake brought in the nation's first oil well at Titusville, Pennsylvania. Nearby Oil City became the nation's first oil boom town. It was lighted by manufactured coal gas, while natural gas from the oil wells nearby was being flared away and wasted in the hills day and night.

In 1865, the Fredonia (New York) Light and Waterworks Company became the first concern in the United States to sell natural gas. Seven years later the first "long-distance" pipeline—25 miles—was laid from a well at West Bloomfield, New York, to Rochester. The pipe was made of hollowed-out logs, called "pump-logs."

The first "bottled gas" used in the United States was called "Pintsch Gas" and was imported from Europe in 1880. It was not liquefied, but compressed, made by cracking oil, and consisted of a mixture of methane and heavier hydrocarbon gases. It was known as "bottled petroleum gas" and its uses included lighting railroad cars. Liquefied "bottled gas" was developed by Herman Blau, of Augsburg, Germany, in 1903–1904. It was a mixture of permanent gases, liquid gas and light fractions of gasoline. This expensive product cost 10 cents a pound to manufacture.

The founder of the LP Gas Industry is generally conceded to be Walter O. Snelling, Doctor of Chemistry with degrees from Harvard, Yale and George Washington universities, who developed an underwater detonator for explosives for the U.S. Geological

Survey. After perfecting this device, which was credited with saving over $500,000 during excavations for the Panama Canal, Snelling and others of his staff moved to Pittsburgh with a Government operation that later became the U.S. Bureau of Mines. It was here that he began experimenting with the so-called "mine damp" gas that caused numerous disastrous explosions in coal mines.

One day in 1910, a Pittsburgh man who owned an automobile walked into Dr. Snelling's office and complained that the gasoline he purchased was evaporating at a rapid and expensive rate. He suggested that the Government look into why these substances disappeared into the air. Dr. Snelling thought this was a good idea, went out and bought some gasoline which he brought back in a laboratory container. He quickly learned why the gases were escaping. They were too light to be contained in a regular bottle and were continually blowing the stopper out of the mouth of the laboratory container. The chemist checked the composition of the escaping gases and realized that the gasoline contained butane, propane and other hydrocarbons.

Since no facilities existed to separate the various fractions of this fuel, Dr. Snelling, who had mechanical as well as chemical skills, built a distilling apparatus with coils from an old hot-water heater and some pieces of laboratory equipment. With this he was able to separate, or fractionate, the "wild gasoline" into liquid and gaseous components. His work became the basis of one of the two major patented inventions that contributed largely to the early development of LP Gas. Perhaps the term "bottled gas" originated in this country at that time because the only container Dr. Snelling had capable of holding these materials was a seltzer "squirt bottle" covered with a wire mesh. Later on he obtained a sealed container, made in Germany, that allowed him to transport the new fuel for demonstration purposes such as lighting gas lamps, fueling hotplates, cooking, and heating metal.

The other early major patent in the development of LP Gas was obtained by Frank T. Patterson, an employee of the Bessemer Engine Company. He succeeded in condensing liquid from natural gas by packing tons of ice around gas mains. Later, he used a heat-exchange type of refrigerating device to obtain this result.

On November 11, 1911, Dr. Snelling, Frank Patterson and three others incorporated the first LP Gas company under the laws of West Virginia, known as the American Gas Oil Company. Assets of the company included the Snelling and Patterson patents, Dr. Snelling's little shop in Pittsburgh, his LP Gas demonstration apparatus and a lot of faith. It took the new company six months to find its first customer, a farmer named John W. Gahring, of near Waterford, Pennsylvania. The system was shipped May 8, 1912, and it took the A. F. Young Hardware and Plumbing Company of Union City, Pennsylvania, 28 hours to get it installed and working. A. F. Young charged for this installation work $11.20— 40 cents an hour. On May 17, 1912, the system went to work lighting the lamps and cooking the meals in the farmhouse of the Gahring family. *The LP Gas Industry dates its beginning from that day.*

The Gahring home and gas installations are gone now. But, according to the LP Gas Association, just down the road is the home of E. E. Wheeler, where the second installation was made. At last report, this house was still standing; the same family lived there, and on the back porch is the first steel cabinet that replaced a wooden box which had been used to shelter the tanks and equipment of the early LP Gas system. Other early customers in Pennsylvania included the St. Paul Lutheran Church at Penryn, the home of Henry S. Bombach at East Petersburg, and the home of Dr. George W. Gerwig, for many years Secretary of the Pittsburgh School System.

During the 1920's the big oil companies took over leadership in the LP Gas field. Phillips Petroleum Company, the leading producer of natural gasoline, turned its expensive research facilities on problems of LP Gas. In 1927, Phillips designed and obtained approval for the first special railroad tank cars to haul LP Gas. Phillips got railway classifications and realistic rates for shipping the product; it set up bulk plants to receive tank-car shipments and arranged for tank-truck delivery to customers. The first railroad tank car of LP Gas (butane) was shipped May 31, 1927.

In July of that year, Shell Oil Company introduced Shellane, a mixture of propane and propylene, which was handled mainly through company-owned depots. Skelly Oil Company entered the LP Gas field with Skelgas the same year. Skelly was among the first to recover LP Gas experimentally from cracking stills used in gasoline production. The Pure Oil Company also worked successfully at this technique. It was also in 1927 that the Tappan Company developed an insulated gas range to utilize LP Gas more economically. And down in Georgia, the Atlanta Gaslight Company held the first-known "old stove roundup" to promote replacement of old appliances with new LP Gas-burning ranges.

In 1928, gas meters were adopted to measure the customer's use of LP Gas. Union Carbide built the first cylinder-filling plant in New York City, and the Servel Company, in June of that year, introduced the first LP Gas refrigerator. Pyrofax advertising in *The Saturday Evening Post*, and Rockgas radio advertising in California did much to publicize and popularize LP Gas. And Germany's Graf Zeppelin used LP Gas as fuel during its epic-making world voyage.

By 1931, a total of 123 cities in the United States were served by butane-air mixtures through underground mains. The

44

U.S. Navy's dirigible *Akron* was equipped with LP Gas for cooking and water-heating on ranges made by Tappan. The National Electric Light Association warned its members against the rising competition from LP Gas, which it called "the best fuel obtainable for cooking, water-heating and refrigeration." And yet, it was pointed out, more than 13,000,000 families living beyond gas mains still used coal, wood, gasoline and kerosene for cooking and water-heating.

The Phillips Petroleum Company, in 1937, introduced ranges, refrigerators and water heaters bearing its trademark, Philgas. The Ford Motor Company installed a butane standby system at its River Rouge plant. The Union Pacific Railroad powered a streamlined train, "The City of Salina," with LP Gas. The Carnation Company at Los Angeles converted a 1936 Ford truck to run on butane. The performance was so superior that the company converted its entire fleet of 210 vehicles to run on that product. And the following year the first Russian LP Gas service station opened in Moscow.

In 1940, Servel, Inc., produced an LP Gas all-year air conditioner for summer cooling and winter heating in one unit. The U.S. Army and Air Force adopted LP Gas-powered field kitchens, where portability was required. About 1,200 railroad tank cars carrying butane and propane were in service by now, and a rash of discriminatory ordinances, prompted by the electrical industry, broke out across the country. The U.S. Department of Agriculture published its first leaflet on "Liquefied Gases in the Household." The number of LP Gas customers passed the million mark for the first time, but the Japanese attack on Pearl Harbor, December 7, 1941, disrupted the industry's plans for expansion for the next few years.

Despite the war, however, use by utility companies of LP Gas increased 138 percent during those years. A high proportion of defense plant housing was equipped with LP Gas utilities, after the War Production Board announced that electric ranges failed three times as frequently as gas ranges. Meanwhile, the Phillips Petroleum Company warned that butane was on the way out of the domestic market because of its usefulness as a chemical raw material. The company advised the industry to make all of its new storage tanks suitable for propane.

During the immediate postwar years, in agriculture, flame control of weeds, using propane, and propane-fueled crop dryers became popular. Rainmaking methods, using LP Gas to vaporize silver iodide for seeding the clouds, came into use. The Chicago Transit Authority ordered 500 new LP Gas-powered buses. The process for storing LP Gas underground in salt caverns was perfected and by 1952, 26 producing companies had completed 77 underground storage facilities with an aggregate capacity of 246,-

204,000 gallons. Meanwhile, LP Gas consumption continued to increase, and by 1951 there were about 8,000,000 customers and 4,500 bulk plants that marketed 4,227,275,000 gallons.

Four years later, in 1956, the total national consumption of LP Gas had risen to 6,635,763,000 gallons. A survey showed that 40 percent of production was being consumed on farms, 40 percent in small towns and 20 percent in the suburbs. It was forecast that the future would see the ratio change to 50 percent on farms, 35 percent in small towns and 15 percent in suburbs. A five-page report in the *Electric Light and Power Magazine* reported impressive inroads by LP Gas into the electric market. A headline read, "How're Ya Gonna Keep Them KW Down on the Farm After They've Seen LP?" The magazine commented editorially that liquefied petroleum gas is "the greatest threat we have today . . . to the future growth of Kilowatt sales in rural areas."

And this was approximately the situation in the liquefied petroleum gas industry when Robert E. Thomas first became enthused with the idea of building the world's first pipeline solely to transport the product. Actually, according to authorities in that field, the industry's growth from the middle 1950's on would probably have been extremely slow because of a lack of adequate transportation had not that first LP Gas Pipeline been introduced at this point by Mr. Thomas, the Katy Railroad and his and its associates.

Although Bob Thomas knew almost nothing about the background of LP Gas and very little about pipelining when he latched onto the idea, his "luck"—or perhaps his inner guidance —told him that the time was right for just such a pipeline. And the results have proven he was correct.

Christmas Week at the Mayo

5

The business career of Robert E. Thomas, which had flourished and grown and shown great promise for 20 years, dipped to its all-time low in 1959. A friend has described his situation this way:

"Bob had gotten himself into this deal of running the Katy Railroad—and that wasn't going well at all. He and the new President at the Pennroad Corporation had reached the parting of the ways. That left Bob's future tied to the Katy, which was a shaky support, indeed. In trying to cut the railroad's expenses, he had gotten some of the most unfavorable publicity in Katy territory since the passing of Jesse James. Bob did not know then how he was going to put the Katy on a paying basis—and he didn't know what the hell he was going to do with his own career. He badly needed a viable idea. And, as it turned out, Colonel T. C. Davis had given him one two years before."

"I guess that pretty well describes my situation at the time," Robert Thomas admits these days, "but I wasn't depressed about it. I knew I had a hell of a struggle ahead, but I don't get depressed easily and I don't discourage easily either. I guess that basically I am a scrapper. If I believe in something, I will keep fighting.

"Bradley Gaylord, who was President of the Pennroad Corporation at the time, had brought me into that organization. After Bradley retired, Ed (Edward A.) Merkle succeeded him as president, and Ed and I never really got along. I disagreed with some of his philosophies and he disagreed with some of mine. I didn't approve of the way he looked at things; I felt he was quite short-sighted. In my opinion, he was basically a trader and I had a longer picture in mind."

Mr. Merkle's viewpoint was: "My main trouble with Bob was that he spent more time looking over Katy's figures than he did thinking up ideas for us to make some money at Pennroad. I didn't like railroads at the time and never did especially favor Pennroad getting in on the Katy deal. Bob and I are different. He wants to build and operate something, but I only want to buy and sell stock."

"The idea of building a pipeline of any kind had never entered my mind," Robert Thomas says, "until that day in September, 1957, when I had lunch in New York City with Colonel Davis. I was just looking for business. He handed me the pipeline idea on a silver platter. Colonel Davis told me that the railroad he represented, the bankrupt Missouri-Pacific, and the New York Central had been talking with the Williams Brothers Company of Tulsa about the possibility of building this liquefied petroleum gas pipeline from Texas into New York State. He said, 'We are not going to do anything with it on the Missouri-Pacific, and if you want to try this pipeline idea with the Katy, you are welcome to it.' I said, 'Thank you very much.' I didn't decide at that moment to plunge into building such a pipeline, but I did *immediately* start to work on the idea.

"Within half an hour after getting back to my office, I had telephoned Al Perlman, President of the New York Central, and made an appointment to meet with him the next morning and discuss the pipeline. The Central was very pleased to have the Katy step into the Missouri-Pacific's shoes on this deal—and it looked like we were off and running. I then made two long-distance calls to Tulsa. One was to John Williams, who was quite intrigued that the Katy management was interested in the pipeline. The other call was to Bill Warren, who was Chairman of the Warren Petroleum Company and also a Director of the Katy Railroad. Bill sounded enthusiastic and said he thought we ought to go ahead and investigate the possibilities of the pipeline immediately.

"When we began to put this idea together, it became obvious that this LP gas pipeline was going to require considerable time and money—a *lot* of my time. The Katy Board of Directors ended up by capitalizing a portion of my time and my expenses for travel and everything else and for engineering fees we were going to incur in getting into this thing. In all, I think the Katy Railroad spent something like $480,000, in return for which the Katy got about 18 percent of the initial stock of the Mid-America Pipeline Company."

Salim L. "Cy" Lewis was a member of the M-K-T Railroad Board of Directors. His investment banking firm, Bear, Stearns and Company of New York, was in on the financing of the proposed LP Gas pipeline from the first. Two or three months after the Katy Board's decision to proceed with its investigation, Bob Thomas moved to enlist the support of White, Weld and Company, also of New York City, the leading investment house in the field of pipeline finance. Its Senior Partner was Francis Kernan, generally regarded in fiscal circles as the father of pipeline financing. As one authority has said, "Frank Kernan is the man who saw to it that most of the important pipelines in the United States got properly financed and built. The pipeline executives got more publicity, but people who know the industry will tell you that Frank Kernan is the man who really saw to it that the proper things got done. The whole idea of mortgage indentures for pipelines . . . was a product of Frank Kernan's mind."

Mr. Thomas did not know Frank Kernan personally at the time, but the Katy Executive Committee Chairman had met another partner in White, Weld and Company, Curtis Neldner. By 1975, Mr. Neldner had retired but remained as a consultant and member of the Advisory Board of White, Weld. He recalls his first meeting with Robert Thomas this way: "Sometime early in December, 1957, I called on Robert E. Thomas in his office to try to sell the Pennroad Corporation an issue of private placement securities of the Carolina Pipeline Company, a natural gas pipeline. Pennroad turned us down. But, several months later, Mr. Thomas was nice enough to come to see me and tell me that my presentation of the story of Carolina Pipeline had made quite a favorable impression on him. 'I know of your firm's reputation in the pipeline industry and I have come down to talk to you about a pipeline in which *I* am interested,' he told me." Soon the White, Weld Advisory Board decided to join with Bear, Stearns and Company as financial managers of the LP Gas pipeline the Katy Railroad proposed to build. A main reason for this decision, according to Frank Kernan, was that "the proposed pipeline had the Pennroad and State Street Investment and some good, solid people behind it.

"This was the great era of pipeline building," Frank Kernan says. "They had started to go in a big way right after World War II with such as Transcontinental Gas Pipeline, and Tennessee Gas Transmission. . . . I had been connected with the financing of a good many of the larger pipelines and thus had rather wide experience in the field. Therefore, I did not view a new pipeline project with a jaundiced eye, but quite the contrary. Pipelines were interesting things to look into. In this case, the big question was: Could we get a supply of product at one end and an assured market at the other?

"The Transcontinental Pipeline, for instance, was financed in 1948, after having been started three or four years earlier. Its financing was based on a guaranteed supply of gas from the producing areas, while on the other end, companies such as Consolidated Edison and Brooklyn Union in New York City, the Philadelphia Gas Company and the Delaware Power and Light Company were taking its gas on a contract basis, and the Sun Oil Company backed up the line by agreeing to take gas on an off-peak basis. But Mid-America didn't have any of these guaranteed supplies and customers. And that distinguished the Mid-America line from anything that had been built in the way of pipelines up to that time.

"One of the early campaigns that we at White, Weld set ourselves to was quieting down the enthusiasm for using the existing railroad rights-of-way for the pipeline right-of-way on the part of Mr. Thomas and his people. Actually the cost of a right-of-way for a pipeline is a small percentage of the entire expense of the project. The minute we took a look at what the right-of-way for this one was likely to cost, as compared with the ultimate cost of the entire pipeline, the idea of using the railroads' rights-of-way didn't send us the way it had sent the others."

Actually, relatively little material progress was made toward getting the pipeline moving until the Spring of 1959 when the Southern Management Company, a subsidiary of the M-K-T Railway, undertook engineering and economic studies of a pipeline system proposed to run from gasoline plants in New Mexico and west Texas to the upper Middle West to carry butane and natural gasoline to refineries in the McPherson, Kansas area and to take propane on into the upper Middle West. As a result of these studies, a news item appeared in a St. Louis newspaper September 16, 1959, that began: "The Missouri-Kansas-Texas Railway Company has abandoned plans to build a one hundred million-dollar Texas-to-New York pipeline, Chairman R. E. Thomas said today. Instead, he says, the M-K-T plans to build a fifty-five million-dollar LP Gas Pipeline from West Texas to the Upper Midwest. The Texas–New York line would have run along the rights-of-way of the M-K-T and New York Central Railroads. . . ."

George F. Bennett, President and Chief Executive Officer of the State Street Investment Corporation of Boston and for years Treasurer of Harvard College until his resignation in the mid-1970's, was a Director of the Katy Railroad during the time of the formation and early years of operation of the Mid-America Pipeline Company. He was also one of the original directors for five years of Mid-America. Mr. Bennett has given some insights into the difficulties and dissensions within the Katy Railroad itself that complicated and delayed the birth of the world's first liquefied petroleum gas pipeline:

"The pipeline was really organized as a creature of the Katy Railroad under the auspices of the new management [the Pennroad and State Street Investment Corporations]," he explains. "Since the Katy didn't really have much credit—that was one of its chief difficulties—there was a problem of financing the pipeline. It was financed really by the ingenuity of the men connected with the new Katy management, all financially oriented—Mr. Thomas, Mr. Lewis and myself, chiefly, in combination with some expert advice and assistance from underwriting firms in New York, White, Weld and Bear, Stearns. We had our problems getting the pipeline project organized and operating because there was within the Katy a certain amount of friction between two factions in the ownership. One group was the holders of the majority of common stock—ourselves—and the other group owned preferred stock. They had two directors on the board. The two factions had difficulty seeing eye-to-eye in various things, because we owners of the common stock maybe had different objectives than those who owned the preferred. The preferred group had a prior position and wanted to enforce it; we holders of the common stock had control and wanted to capitalize on it. The representatives of the preferred stockholders were not too cooperative in our efforts to form a new venture [the pipeline]. And yet when it became clear that the pipeline was to be formed, there was great desire by the owners of the preferred stock to be represented on the board of the pipeline. In the early stages I think that one of the services I performed was to insist that the Mid-America Pipeline Company Board be constituted only of the people representing the common stock of the Katy Railroad. We'd had too much friction and difficulty reaching decisions between the two different factions in the railroad, and I was completely unwilling to see that perpetuated in the pipeline.

"And so the original Board of the Mid-America Pipeline Company was constituted only of people representing the common stock of the Katy Railroad. William N. Deramus III, then President of the Katy, became Chairman of the Pipeline. Mr. Thomas, Chairman of the Katy's Executive Committee, was named President of the Pipeline. I became Chairman of the Executive Committee of the Pipeline. Mr. John Worcester, of Boston, Senior Partner of the firm Sullivan and Worcester, which was counsel to the State Street Investment Corporation, joined the Board. And I believe John Hawkinson, of Chicago, was an early Director. It was a relatively small Board and because we all had the same objective —that was to make the pipeline successful—there was no dissension on the Board of the pipeline as there had been on the Board of the railroad.

"If we had failed to get outside financing, the Katy would have lost the approximately $500,000 it had put into the planning of the pipeline—and the Katy could ill afford to lose anything. But we felt that the railroad stood a much better chance of gaining a lot than in losing its investment. Initially, we had hoped that the Katy's ownership of the pipeline would be as much as 30 percent, but it became necessary to make more stock available to the lenders and that meant less for the entrepreneurial efforts of the Katy, which wound up with about 18 percent of the common stock."

In the Autumn of 1959, after it had been decided to build the proposed pipeline into the upper Midwest instead of going East, things began to roll. The prestigious Stone and Webster Service Corporation was employed to make feasibility and engineering studies of the new route. In the gas-producing areas, representatives of Williams Brothers and the Katy Railroad began pressuring propane producers to sign Letters of Intent that they would use the new pipeline if certain conditions were met. The financial experts at White, Weld and Bear, Stearns began putting together details of a financing plan, and lawyers representing everybody remotely concerned started to draw up their legal documents. By early December, 1959, the promoters were ready to approach the Prudential Insurance Company of America in the hope of getting a $42,000,000 first-mortgage loan.

The presentation to Prudential was made by Frank Kernan and Joe Smith, the latter a personable financial analyst who had been assigned to carry the ball for Bear, Stearns in the pipeline promotion. Mr. Smith, a Senior Vice President of the Singer Company at the time of this writing, recalls the presentation to Prudential as follows: "Frank and I went over to Newark and had lunch with a guy named [Monroe] Chappelear, who ran the investment part of the company. We told Chappelear what we wanted to do and I spent maybe a couple of afternoons over there with their analyst, discussing the whole project. They kept horsing back and forth about the lack of contracts. Finally, when things looked pretty grim, Frank [Kernan] went over to Newark by himself and put it to bed. I think one reason why Prudential went along with the deal was their respect for Frank Kernan."

At least, by mid-December, 1959, Prudential's Bond Department management was sufficiently interested to agree to send two representatives—Norman Mansfield, head of the company's Public Utilities Department, and Robert Poindexter, an analyst—to a three-day meeting that Bob Thomas had arranged in Tulsa during Christmas week of that year. The purpose was for Prudential's representatives and some bankers to hear firsthand from representatives of the thirteen liquid petroleum gas companies who had signed Letters of Intent as to what use their companies expected to make of the proposed pipeline. At this writing—16 years later —everyone who attended the Tulsa meeting retains certain vivid memories of it. One reason was that it interrupted everybody's Christmas holiday. But Robert E. Thomas has never been one to allow relaxation to interfere with business.

Felix ("Gus") Mulgrew, a Vice President of Dean Witter and Company, Inc., of New York City in 1975, had been a Vice President of Bankers Trust Company of New York in 1959. Bankers Trust was one of three banks from which Bob Thomas hoped to borrow a total of $15,000,000 dollars in temporary construction funds, pending receipt of the $42,000,000 loan from Prudential— in case, of course, Prudential decided to make it. "Bob Thomas, a representative of the Chemical National Bank of New York, a man from White, Weld and Company and myself met at the airport in New York the day after Christmas and flew out to Tulsa," Mr. Mulgrew recalls. "When we got to Tulsa, we held some conversations about the pipeline at the Mayo Hotel, where we were all staying, and Bob told us that during the next couple of days we were going to meet at the Williams Brothers office there in Tulsa.

He would bring into the meeting a number of propane shippers and producers who would tell us how much propane they could, or would, ship through the line. This was very important, because if we were going to make loans—that is, Bankers Trust, the Chemical National Bank and the Republic National Bank of Dallas, Texas—and if White, Weld and Bear, Stearns were going to underwrite the issuance of the necessary securities—it was vital for us to know that the business was there. No contracts existed at the time with producers to ship any certain quantities. But Bob had worked out a most interesting discussion in which the shippers told us what their production would be and how much of it they would ship over the pipeline. Their principal reason for using the pipeline was economic. They could ship by pipeline much cheaper than by railroad.

"As a result of these meetings," Mr. Mulgrew went on, "I agreed verbally on the part of Bankers Trust to loan $5,000,000 to the pipeline project, provided Prudential signed a bond-purchase agreement. Our money would be available to the pipeline company immediately upon the signing of the bond-purchase agreement by Prudential. The idea of the bank loans was to get the company started in construction, although it was never necessary for the pipeline company to borrow any of the $5,000,000 from us because the Prudential made its funds available in time. As I recall, neither Chemical nor Republic made a commitment at the time of the Tulsa meeting, although later I know that Chemical has loaned the Mid-America Pipeline Company substantial sums from time to time. Early in 1960 Bankers Trust was appointed trustee of the first-mortgage bonds issued by Mid-America Pipeline Company, which Prudential bought."

The only major distraction during the Tulsa conclave was the antics of one hard-drinking Texas banker, who appeared to have the notion that he was attending a Christmas party instead of a series of business conferences. This phase of the affair was recently recalled by Horace C. ("Nick") Bailey, a Vice President of Kidder, Peabody and Company, Inc., of New York City, who was a Vice President of the Chemical National Bank in 1959 and who attended the Tulsa meeting as that bank's representative. He tells of landing at the Tulsa airport with Robert Thomas and the New York party and being met by "this banker from Texas who was quite a character. He had two of his young assistants along with him, and he was already about six sheets to the wind. We all lived at the Mayo Hotel in Tulsa. Bob had a big suite down at the end of the hall, and there was considerable socializing in the evening. This Texas banker, though, became such a disruptive force that Bob finally had to ask one of his young assistants to take the man home."

Joe Smith, then of Bear, Stearns, recalls the situation in

more colorful terms: "This dizzy banker kept showing up at the meetings loaded, and here was everybody with their big charts and all trying to make a sound case out for the pipeline. And this banker kept hollering, 'I've heard enough. Let's give them the money. Let's go have a drink.' He wanted no bothersome details. It was a typical banker's group meeting, all pretty stuffy—and here was this guy sitting over in the corner raising hell."

Unfortunately, the drinking banker took an intense dislike to young Robert Poindexter, one of the two Prudential men in attendance. And it was especially important to Robert E. Thomas to impress favorably the people from Prudential. "I finally took one of this banker's young associates aside," Mr. Thomas recalls, "and told him to take his boss to his suite and *keep him there.* I would send up a case of Scotch to keep him entertained.

"I could just see $42,000,000 floating slowly out the window," Bob Thomas recalls nowadays—a remark that he generally accompanies with a flapping motion of his hands, like a bird in flight.

Everything considered, though, the Tulsa meeting achieved its objective. "I was quite encouraged by it," Frank Kernan says these days. "It was a smart move on Thomas' part to set up those meetings out there between the money people and the producers, after being assured that the producers were going to talk the way they did talk. From then on, I had a feeling of confidence that somehow or other we were going to get it done. The Tulsa meeting gave the entire promotion a feeling of team play as far as I was concerned."

Sure enough, the deal with Prudential *did* go through. Bob Thomas likes to recall that day—only a little more than a month after the sessions at Tulsa. "We had been given assurance that we were going to get the $42,000,000," he says, "but until the Finance Committee of Prudential met, it wasn't definite. Sometimes the Finance Committee says 'No.' Well, when Norm Mansfield telephoned me from Newark, there were maybe ten or twelve lawyers in the room with me in New York City, and we all knew that the Finance Committee had been meeting that day and if we got a 'No' answer, we were done for. We would all break up and go home. So when the telephone rang in that conference room, we all knew who the call was from. I tell you, you could have heard a pin drop. So I got on the phone and all Norm said was: 'Well, Bob, you got your money.' And I said, 'Fine, Norm, why don't we just simplify this and get rid of all this paperwork and you send me over the check this afternoon?' "

But finance is not that simple. The pipeline promoters would have to burn a jillion gallons of midnight oil and go through many tons of paperwork before laying their hands on one penny of Prudential's money. And the first—and most important by far—item on the program was to come up with a plan of financing that would make the Mid-America Pipeline Company's securities sufficiently desirable to investors to raise $28,628,250 in equity. Prudential's $42,000,000 mortgage loan was contingent upon that.

Prudential Makes a "Hairy Deal"

6

The Mid-America Pipeline Company really came into existence on Ground Hog Day (February 2, 1960) when the Prudential Insurance Company of America agreed to a $42,000,000 mortgage loan to Robert E. Thomas and his associates. And Prudential made the loan without much hesitation, even though most of its officials concerned considered the matter a "hairy deal"—a colloquialism in the trade meaning a very risky proposition, indeed.

"The gist of the problem," according to Gordon S. Kerr, a Vice President in Prudential's Bond and Commercial Department, "was that here we had a proposed common carrier that had nothing, really, but an idea. It had no suppliers; it had no customers. All its backers could show us were just some so-called Letters of Intent from, I believe, thirteen potential suppliers. These producing companies said they would like to use such a pipeline—provided a long list of conditions was met. Legally, these Letters of Intent were not worth the paper they were written on.

"We made a study of the economics of the proposed line. Were the supplies of the product adequate? Did a sufficient market exist at the other end to make the enterprise profitable? Could this pipeline operate at a better than competitive rate with the other carriers? Our studies and a report by Stone and Webster Engineering Company gave affirmative answers.

"But, in my opinion, lending money is primarily a 'people business.' What about the reliability and professional capabilities of the people behind this project? This brought very much to our attention Robert E. Thomas, who was going to be the Chief Executive Officer, and William N. Deramus, President of the Katy Railroad, and others, including George Bennett, President of the State Street Investment Corporation of Boston and Treasurer of Harvard College. These were solid and able men. And so we at Prudential made the loan—but it was still a unique and highly imaginative investment."

There was also another extremely important factor—to be precise, nine of them—in the background that caused the officers of Prudential to think, in the first place, in terms of "hairy deals" that might produce higher returns than investments in blue-chip securities. These background factors are very real, entirely physical and quite impressive—and you can see one of them any day you care to go to any one of nine cities and take a look:

In Boston, the 52-story Prudential Tower rises high above all the other steeples and pinnacles of Beantown, and is visible for 25 miles or so away. It is the main structure of Prudential Center, containing also a hotel, department store, shops, plazas and other such installations on the order of Rockefeller Center in New York City. Boston's Prudential Center is one of those background factors that caused Prudential's people in charge of making loans to think favorably of "hairy deals."

Or there is the 41-story Prudential Building on Chicago's lakefront. Built in 1955, it was the first major commercial structure erected in downtown Windy City since before the 1930's depression, and it was hailed there with great civic enthusiasm. The others are: the 10-story Prudential Western Home Office in Los Angeles, the 22-story Canadian Head Office in Toronto, the 21-story Southwestern Home Office in Houston, the 22-story South-central Home Office in Jacksonville, Florida, the 10-story Prudential North-central Home Office in Minneapolis, the 18-story Prudential Eastern Home Office in Newark, New Jersey, and the sprawling complex of the Prudential Central Atlantic Home Office at Fort Washington, Pennsylvania.

Monroe Chappelear, Vice President in charge of Prudential's Bond Department at the time of the Mid-America loan, explained in the summer of 1975 how this group of impressive structures, their personnel and contents had a very real effect upon Prudential's "imaginative attitude," which dominated its investment thinking during the latter 1950's and early 1960's:

"Mr. [Carroll] Shanks, President of Prudential at the time, had put through this policy of decentralizing the company, from having all of top management at Newark, by constructing these large and impressive Home Office Buildings, which would be headquarters for the company's operations in various areas of North America," Mr. Chappelear relates. "Our President started off first by constructing the big office building out in Los Angeles in 1948. Then he built the Prudential Buildings in Toronto, Houston, Jacksonville and Chicago. This last was an especially impressive structure and the only one in which Prudential did not occupy the entire building. Those Home Offices had all been completed by 1955 and Mr. Shanks was planning to go ahead with constructing the big Prudential Center in Boston and the other structures in the building program." [These impressive area "Home Office" structures replaced what had been mere agencies in these various cities. The big Prudential installations gave the company greater local status and were fine for public relations—but . . .]

"It was all working out fine," Mr. Chappelear says, "except

for one flaw. The program was *extremely* costly. By the end of 1955, Prudential already had $125,000,000 tied up in buildings alone—and more were to come. Besides, this meant a duplication of personnel in all of these 'Home Offices' around the country. That, too, was quite costly. Prudential's cost of insuring all of these fine buildings was far higher than that being paid by any rival insurance company on its real estate properties. So one day Mr. Shanks came down to see Pete and me about it. [Pete was Caleb Stone, then Vice President in charge of the Bond Department.] The President said to us, 'We've got to do something about all these expenses—and do it right quick. And the only way I can see is for the Investment Department to get more income—more rate. No more triple-A bonds for us. (As I recall, blue chip securities were bringing at the time around four percent.) Mr. Shanks went on: 'We want to get five percent on our money at least and that means participation in profits—a *kicker.*'

"Well, this sort of policy didn't appeal too much to Pete, who was basically quite conservative. But Mr. Shanks said, 'That's the way it's going to be. I've been reading about some of these oil companies. Some insurance companies down there in Texas have been putting money into them and—first thing you know—they're making 10, 15, even 20 percent on their money. Now that is what I want you fellas to do.'

"When Mr. Shanks had finished, I got hold of our investment contacts in New York City and told them the story—no more triple-A stuff for us. 'If you've got something where we can make some real money,' I told them, 'bring it over to us.' Well, those guys just loved that because they could then peddle their real good stuff to other companies. And they brought to us the kind of deals Mr. Shanks was looking for.

"When the Mid-America thing came along, that was right down our alley. It promised a very good yield, and had a nice kicker attached to it. But it was risky, though. Any company that doesn't have a record and is trying to launch a new enterprise is risky. I don't think Metropolitan Life would even have looked at it. And New York Life! They wouldn't have touched the deal with a ten-foot pole! Shanks realized that going into these things meant some risk—but it also meant some good profits, too. So we went ahead with Mr. Shanks' policy of looking for big profits on somewhat risky deals. That doesn't mean that we took *all* those risky deals. We looked thoroughly into each one of them. We examined the Mid-America proposal most carefully—especially the people behind it, to determine what sort of management we could expect from them—and we liked what we saw. My predecessor, Pete Stone, used to say, 'We don't lend to a company—we follow J. P. Morgan's advice and lend to people.'

"The Mid-America proposal was brought to us by Frank Kernan of White, Weld and Company about the middle of December, 1959. [Actually, the first Mid-America memo in the Prudential General Operation File is dated December 18, 1959.] We knew Frank Kernan and had great respect for his ability and integrity. That was in Mid-America's favor from the start. But we needed to know about the people who would actually operate this proposed pipeline. And the best way to do this was to call our good friends who knew the people in question and ask them. I checked with several New York bankers who knew Robert Thomas and they all spoke highly of his ability. I believe I also checked with some railroads. It soon became apparent that Mr. Thomas knew his way around Wall Street, and his record was good in railroad management. You don't find many people with his caliber and background. I'd say that Bob Thomas was the strongest asset that Mid-America had. If it had not been for Thomas, we probably never would have made the deal. I did not meet Mr. Thomas until after the deal was closed, but when we did meet I was quite impressed with his appearance and manner—but I had already made up my mind about him from the checking we had done."

Norman Mansfield, Head of Prudential's Public Utilities Department, carried on from there. He studied at length a feasibility report by the Stone and Webster Service Corporation and projections furnished by Williams Brothers, and did further checking. "I remember," he said, "that one of the thirteen suppliers who had signed Letters of Intent to use the line was the Sid Richardson Gasoline Company. We had a very knowledgeable lawyer named Henry Brock who knew Sid Richardson. Brock telephoned Richardson down in Texas and learned from him that the supply situation was about the way it had been represented to us by Stone and Webster, Williams Brothers and representatives of Mid-America.

"After much arguing and negotiating between Prudential and Mid-America and its underwriters," according to one Prudential spokesman, "we finally came up with a number. We agreed to submit to the Prudential Finance Committee the following proposal: Mid-America Pipeline Company would issue $42,000,000 worth of first-mortgage 6 percent pipeline bonds, due November 1, 1975, plus $3,000,000 worth of convertible 6 percent notes, due also November 1, 1975. These would be offered directly to Prudential through Bear, Stearns and Company and White, Weld and Company for a combined price of $42,000,000 to yield approximately 6.70 percent to maturity. Semiannual level interest and sinking fund payments of $2,350,000, commencing May 1, 1963, would retire the first-mortgage bonds by maturity. The notes would have no sinking fund and would be convertible to maturity into 300,000 shares of common stock in Mid-America at $10 a share after May 1, 1961.

"As a condition precedent to disbursement by Prudential of the $42,000,000, the same underwriters would offer for public sale

$30,300,000 worth of Mid-America's securities. Proceeds from this financing would be used to build a petroleum products pipeline approximately 2,100 miles long from deep in west Texas into Minnesota and Wisconsin at an estimated cost of $72,152,000."

Even though some risk was involved, this was a very fat deal for Prudential, which was getting, in effect, credit for lending $45,-000,000, while actually disbursing only $42,000,000. The $3,000,-000 in convertible notes—for which Prudential paid nothing—was the desired "kicker," which became a nice piece of change for Prudential. The insurance company sold half of those convertible notes in May, 1965, for $3,300,000. It sold the balance in May, 1968, for $4,516,000. In other words, Prudential realized $7,846,-000 on the "kicker," which amounted to a gift, and, in Bob Thomas' words, "they earned every penny of it."

The interest rate on the $42,000,000 loaned was also substantially higher than the going interest on ordinary investments at the time. It was listed at 6 percent on $45,000,000. But, since Prudential actually loaned only $42,000,000, the interest rate amounted to 6.7 percent. According to Monroe Chappelear, "this was at least a point and a half higher than we would have gotten on a standard deal.

Even Bob Thomas, the militant positive thinker, was somewhat appalled at first when he heard how high the interest rate had been proposed. Hugh Robinson recalls it this way: "I remember one day early in 1960 when Bob came back to New York from a meeting in Newark with the Prudential people and he was looking rather grim. He said they were going to charge an extraordinarily high interest rate of 6.7 percent. Beyond that, they were demanding a gift of $3,000,000 worth of convertible notes. It was one of the few times I've seen Bob need somebody to speak to in order to clarify his own decision. He said, 'What do we do about that?' I said, 'I can't see that we have much choice,' and he said, 'Well that's the way it's going to be.' And then Bob went out to confer with Frank Kernan and Cy Lewis as though there was absolutely no problem on his mind about getting the loan or the amount of interest. When they asked how the meeting went at Prudential, Bob said, 'Fine. We got their commitment—their oral commitment. They decided that this line really does have merit.' "

The report of Prudential's investigations into the Mid-America Pipeline proposal, prepared by Norman Mansfield, was presented on February 2, 1960, to the insurance company's Finance Committee by Gordon S. Kerr. In summary, Mr. Mansfield reported the following:

"The Mid-America Pipeline Company, with headquarters at Tulsa, Oklahoma, was incorporated in 1958 in Delaware by the Missouri-Kansas-Texas Railroad Company, which will own 29 percent of the common stock (later reduced to 18 percent in order to give the public a better deal). The company proposes to build a common carrier petroleum products pipeline of about 2,300 miles in length to move propane, natural gasoline and butane from gasoline plants located in the Permian Basin (in the general area of Midland, Texas) and the Texas Panhandle, which are now moved primarily by railroad tank cars. The system would carry propane to a point near the Twin Cities in Minnesota and Madison, Wisconsin. Butane and natural gasoline would be carried to McPherson, Kansas, for use in refineries. The system will include six rail-truck-loading terminals for the distribution of propane. . . . In addition, a number of shippers propose to invest an aggregate of over $3,000,000 in terminal loading and storage facilities at various takeoff points on the pipeline.

"The pipe sizes will be eight inches in diameter from west Texas to the Panhandle—10 inches in diameter from the Panhandle to McPherson—eight-inch pipe, McPherson to the Twin Cities, eight-inch pipe, McPherson to Ottumwa, Iowa, and six-inch pipe from Ottumwa to Madison. Initial pump capacity will be 50,000 barrels per day to McPherson and about 30,000 barrels per day for each of the eight-inch lines. To bring the pipeline to full capacity of about 80,000 barrels per day to McPherson and 45,000 barrels per day over the eight-inch line will require additional financing of about $3,000,000.

"Stone and Webster Service Corporation," the report went on, "has estimated the total cash requirement for the entire project at approximately $72,152,000, including construction funds, financing costs, line fill, supplies and working capital. . . . Construction costs of approximately $23,000,000 will be under a contract with Williams Brothers at a fixed cost per foot of pipe installed with a possible refund for excess profits. Other costs of $24,300,000 for steel pipe and about $11,000,000 for other materials will be fixed when construction is actually started. The company has Letters of Intent from thirteen of the major shippers of LP Gas . . . to use the pipeline . . . so long as the pipeline tariffs are competitive. It is believed that the pipeline can attract substantially more business than the estimates show," the report went on, "provided that rail-tank-car rates are not reduced. . . . The direct railroad shipping cost for a barrel of propane (at present) to Minneapolis is $1.68, whereas the proposed tariff for the pipeline will be $.80 per barrel." Basing its estimates on a load factor of 50 percent, Stone and Webster projected that the Mid-America Pipeline's gross income would be $6,151,000 by 1961, $9,279,000 in 1962, $11,286,000 in 1963, $12,527,000 in 1964, and $12,909,000 in 1965.

Mr. Mansfield's report ended as follows: "We recommend and request authority to purchase $42,000,000 Mid-America Pipeline Company first-mortgage 6 percent bonds, due November 1,

1975, and $3,000,000 convertible 6 percent notes, due November 1, 1975, for $42,000,000." The deal was approved by Prudential's Finance Committee the same day that the report was submitted.

When the Mid-America Pipeline was completed and began operations, its performance was substantially better than the Stone and Webster estimates. In the first place, costs of building the pipeline and putting it into operation were about $6,000,000 lower than the $72,152,000 estimated by Stone and Webster. This gave the fledgling company a comfortable operating cushion.

The average throughput of LP Gas in 1961 was 27,040 barrels per day, as contrasted with the estimate of a 22,000-barrel daily average made before the line began operating. The company's gross income for 1961 totaled $7,119,660, as contrasted with the predicted $6,151,000 gross. During its second year of operation, Mid-America Pipeline carried a daily average of 44,900 barrels of LP Gas, and its gross income totaled $11,987,515, as contrasted with the predicted $9,279,000. By 1965, the pipeline's daily average throughput had risen to 66,247 barrels as contrasted with the 41,-570 barrels estimated for that year back in 1960. Instead of the predicted gross income of $12,909,000, Mid-America realized from all divisions a total income in 1965 of $48,769,751. But by this time, the company had branched into the fields of oil and gas production and had just acquired the Thermogas Company as its gas retailing and wholesaling division.

This impressive progress gradually elevated the financial status of Mid-America—later MAPCO—in Prudential's book, although in 1963 Prudential turned down the company's request for a loan of about $11,280,000 to purchase natural gas liquid rights under 234,000 productive acres in the West Panhandle gas fields in Texas, known as WestPan Hydrocarbons. Mid-America financed this purchase through a group of banks, which also provided the funds for the company to acquire a gasoline plant and interest in oil and gas properties in Colorado, Kansas, Louisiana, Nebraska, New Mexico, Oklahoma, Texas and Wyoming.

"I think we made a mistake in failing to finance that deal," Gordon Kerr says. "We looked over the proposition quite carefully, but our engineer at the time who investigated the feasibility made a mistake, in my view, in not recommending the loan. This man was quite good technically, but he'd had very little experience in negotiating the lending of money.

"The next piece of major financing we did for Mid-America," Mr. Kerr recalls, "was around 1967 when Bob approached us for a loan of about $11,700,000 to build the first anhydrous ammonia pipeline in the United States. By now we'd had some maturity from our investment in his company's LP Gas Pipeline and were favorably impressed by its performance in general. Our main concern was whether the ammonia pipeline would blow up or cause some sort of ecological problem. But Mid-America already had the right-of-way for this new line and it was a good deal generally for us; so we financed it. The old mortgage we held over Mid-America's original LP Gas line was extended to include this $11,700,000 in new financing.

"Then in 1972," Mr. Kerr went on, "we made another loan to MAPCO—a $60,000,000 deal. We took the old debt dating back to 1960, and rolled it into a new package. You might call it a refunding of an expansion of the old loan. The old dollars were kept intact, and we added something in the order of $29,000,000-odd in new money for MAPCO to extend its pipeline. By now, MAPCO's performance figures were excellent. And I would say that Bob Thomas has a great talent for dealing with a lender. He has always been realistic in his projections, and his accuracy and integrity are admirable. Beyond that, Bob never lets the lender be surprised by bad news. If there is anything a lender hates, it is to pick up the New York *Times* or the *Wall Street Journal* and read that one of his customers is in trouble. Bob always kept us informed of any significant development—but, I must add, mighty little bad news has ever come out of MAPCO."

The 1972 loan and refunding had unusual significance for Bob Thomas and MAPCO, because in this deal Prudential canceled its mortgage and made all of its MAPCO investments unsecured loans. "The mortgage had been necessary back in 1960," Gordon Kerr says. "If the pipeline had gotten into financial trouble and had to be foreclosed, we wanted protection—to be ahead of anyone else with a lien on the assets of the company. But, with the passing years and MAPCO's growing prosperity, the mortgage was becoming more of a nuisance than a protection. It was a pain in the neck administratively, because every piece of property the company acquired had to go under that mortgage. This meant a lot of legal paperwork every time. It would enhance MAPCO's credit generally to be an unsecured borrower. MAPCO's numbers were excellent, so we made the new loan and gave up our mortgage. Prudential now has MAPCO's notes, but no longer a lien on any of its properties. Of course, we deny MAPCO the right to allow anyone else to put a lien on the company's properties—but what we actually have now in the way of legal security amounted to nothing more than an IOU. Removing that mortgage amounts to giving MAPCO and Bob Thomas a vote of confidence by Prudential. We were glad to do it—and I think Bob was quite pleased by this action on the part of Prudential."

Bob was—but he never figured that Prudential canceled the mortgage for entirely altruistic reasons. "Gordon Kerr wanted to make that loan so bad he could taste it," Mr. Thomas says these days. "The people at Prudential knew that we now had alternate ways of raising the money we needed. We could easily have sold public debt, for instance. And Gordon knew that I wanted badly to get rid of that mortgage. So he did his best to accommodate *us* in order to make that loan."

Donald B. Ross, MAPCO's Financial Vice President, recalls: "Gordon Kerr made a big thing of that closing. He brought the mortgage over to the offices of White and Case, attorneys for Prudential, in New York City, and we had a 'mortgage burning ceremony.'

"A year later, in 1973, when we wanted to borrow from Prudential another $30,000,000 on top of the existing $60,000,000 debt, it was more or less mechanical. Gordon Kerr said there was no problem; the present loan agreement was fine—we'd just change the dates and amounts on it. We had reached a point of financial affluence where borrowing large sums of money had become a mere formality. Bob Thomas didn't even attend that $30,000,000 closing."

In a brief fifteen years, MAPCO's rating with one of the world's richest lending agencies had advanced from "hairy deal" to "preferred customer."

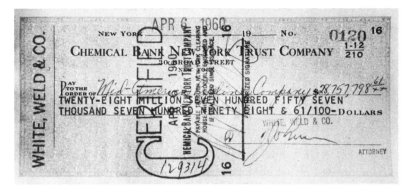

This certified check put Mid-America in business. The $28,757,798.61 represents, less underwriters' commissions, the public sale of 410,000 Mid-America securities units (3½ shares of common stock and one $50 debenture) at $73.50 each. The Prudential Insurance Company's $42 million mortgage loan to Mid-America, which had been contingent upon the success of this public financing, was soon forthcoming.

Robert E. Thomas receives first Prudential checks in April 1960. Norman Mansfield (left), Robert E. Thomas (center), Henry Brock (right).

Birth Pangs of an Enterprise 7

The Mid-America Pipeline got its name during the period between mid-December, 1959, when application for a $42,000,000 mortgage loan was made to the Prudential Insurance Company of America, and early February, 1960, when the loan was approved. Prior to that, the project had been called the "Midcontinent Eastern Pipeline Corporation." But that name was too long and unwieldy, in Robert E. Thomas' opinion. Besides, it was no longer strictly applicable since abandonment of the original idea of building the pipeline from the Southwestern oil-gas fields into New York State.

"I was visiting at the Prudential Headquarters in Newark, New Jersey, one day that winter," Mr. Thomas recalls, "and in the office of the President, Carroll Shanks, there were some big mural photographs of Prudential's regional office buildings about the country. One was of their headquarters in Chicago, and it was captioned: 'The Mid-America Region.' I said to myself, 'Well, there is a good name—Mid-America Pipeline.' I asked if there would be any technical problems in changing our name at this late date, and the people at Prudential said, 'No.' So we changed it."

For several months during latter 1959 and early 1960, Bob Thomas and his legal and financial associates worked 16 hours a day and longer, sometimes seven days a week, putting together the information, drawing up the legal papers, writing prospectuses and preparing the other necessary documents for the loan application they hoped to get from Prudential and later for forming a syndicate of investment houses to market to the public the Mid-America securities. The MAPCO President these days has an especially warm spot in his memory for Joe Smith, then an employee of Bear, Stearns and for James W. Needham who did the spade work for White, Weld. Mr. Smith has described his function during those times as follows: "In terms of getting the work done in the trenches, I did most of it. But none of it would have been worth a damn unless Frank Kernan and Bob Thomas had tipped the scales in our favor at Prudential."

"During those months of preparation, I had six to eight

lawyers and financial people as dinner guests every night at a restaurant in downtown New York," Mr. Thomas reminisces. "My expense account was horrendous. They all had to have a couple of drinks before dinner, because we were working at such a pace. And this fellow, Joe Smith! I never saw anyone like him. He could have two or three double martinis and then go back and make sense until four A.M. And Joe has a very nice personality. When the arguing got really hot and heavy at times, he was generally able to inject some sort of a pertinent, amusing remark that would suddenly relax everybody. There would be a howl of laughter, and then we would go back to work."

Fifteen years afterward, in his imposing office in the Singer Company suite on a lofty floor of the RCA Building in New York City, Joe Smith reminisced about the problems involved in putting together the Mid-America Pipeline financing:

"To understand our problem in trying to set up that pipeline to carry liquefied petroleum gases, you have got to understand the relationship of liquid products pipelines to the major oil companies," Mr. Smith explained. "These pipelines have always been the oil companies' device for controlling the producers. The natural gas business was a little different. After World War II, the Federal Power Commission became very active, and the major oil companies could see plainly that they would be highly regulated if they went into natural gas pipelines. So they said, 'To hell with natural gas,' and they didn't fight the Texas Eastern Pipeline, which was a conversion of the Big Inch and the Little Inch Crude Products Pipelines to carry natural gas. Nor did the majors fight the Tennessee Gas Transmission Company or the Transcontinental Natural Gas Pipeline. Both of these were promotions, like Mid-America. By 'promotion,' I mean you just start off with an idea and get the dough. The big oil companies were not behind the natural gas pipelines, but they were not opposing them, either. But with existing or proposed crude or any liquid products pipelines, it was a different story. By controlling the pipelines carrying liquid product, the big oil companies controlled the producers; they controlled the distribution of the product; they controlled the whole deal. And they were not about to surrender any part of this control without a fight.

"Those of us who were involved will probably never forget those interminable sessions when the lawyers and financial people got together trying to set up the Mid-America deal so it would work," Joe Smith continued to reminisce. "First, we had to document what we were trying to do. And, since Mid-America was a rather unique situation, it presented a whole series of problems. In the first place, we were trying to build a pipeline and get it financed with no contracts at either end—especially at the delivery end. In the second place, we were going to build a pipeline under a contract with Williams Brothers Company, where the specifications, in fact, were going to be written as the pipeline was built.

"I give a lot of credit for the success of this deal to John Williams and his company," Joe Smith says. "Williams Brothers were more than just a general contractor. They really did a package job all the way from acquiring the right-of-way to physically installing the pipeline and putting it into operation. Apparently, acquiring the right-of-way—even without eminent domain in some places—did not present too big a problem to them. I have always admired John Williams' policy of doing away with the red tape. His pitch was: 'Nobody ever wants to build a pipeline without a great big contract and all that nonsense and spend an awful lot of time and dough on legal technicalities about who will pay for what. . . . I'll tell you that I'm going to build the pipeline as cheap as I can and make a fair amount of dough for ourselves, and to hell with all the nit-picking.' And we bought that approach, and it worked. I think John will tell you the reason that they were able to stay within the budget in time and money was because we had bought his approach. So, on matters of river crossings, for example, we did not have to put a lot of crap in the contract that wasn't needed about who was going to pay for what and who was going to do what. He and his people simply did it the best way they could for the least amount of money to turn out a good job. Conversely, if they had to spend more money, they spent it. And so, we didn't have to keep going back to restatements of the contract and examining it and all that stuff. Williams just kept on going—just kept on laying the pipe."

In this connection, Bob Thomas says: "The construction contract between Williams Brothers and our company was one of the most unusual ever written. When we signed that contract, which we had to have for registration purposes with the Securities and Exchange Commission, we did not even know for sure where the line was going, except the general direction. We used to make minor changes in the route of that pipeline practically every day, just by taking those little narrow plastic, colored tapes from where they had been on the map and lifting them up and putting them down to show where we now wanted the line to go. A few days later, we would change them again. We were not even sure where all the terminals were going to be, or exactly how many we would have. So, when we negotiated this contract with Williams Brothers, we merely spelled out how much would be paid per foot for laying pipe of a certain size under certain conditions—that Williams Brothers would receive so much a foot for a river crossing, for example. But we didn't know how many feet of river crossing we would have. Williams would receive so much for rock excavation, although we didn't know how many feet of rock we would have to go through. When the pipeline was all laid, I had one session with John Williams in my office and we smoothed out all the remaining rough spots between ourselves—and when it was all over, we were still friends."

"Actually," Joe Smith says, "we never got as much active opposition to the Mid-America Pipeline from the major oil companies as we had anticipated, but we got considerable. I've always felt that Gulf Oil Company, which had bought out the Warren Petroleum Company, may have turned Bill Warren against us. He was very enthusiastic about our pipeline at first, talking about putting 100,000 barrels of LP Gas a day through it. And then he cooled off. Maybe the folks of Gulf in Pittsburgh told him, 'No way.' " (Parenthetically, one New York banker reports that William K. Warren told him privately that, "He didn't think this Mid-America Pipeline would ever be built—and if it was, it would not be successful.")

"To me," Joe Smith reflected 15 years after the pipeline was completed, "the most striking thing about the success of MAPCO is that this original pipeline got built in the first place, and was able to start delivering product to the Twin Cities. It is amazing that it ever got going. When we started on the project, I had my doubts. Yeah, yeah, it *did* give me a lot of personal satisfaction to see that line finished and successful. I remained at Bear, Stearns for a while after the pipeline started operating. And I remember going out there to Tulsa to see Bob. And here he was in a big, fine office in the Skelly Building, and they had people running all around the place operating the pipeline, and here was this big room full of controls and equipment to operate the pipeline all the way up to Minneapolis and St. Paul, and here was a big telephone switchboard and all that crap. There it all *was,* you know.

"But I don't think any of this would have happened if we hadn't gotten that loan from Prudential. The other big lending companies probably wouldn't have touched it. And, after we *did* get Prudential's commitment, that proved to be a heavy persuader —not only in lining up the potential customers for the pipeline, but when it came to selling Mid-America's securities to the public."

After Prudential agreed to the mortgage loan, the financial people at Bear, Stearns and White, Weld concentrated on devising some securities that the public would find attractive enough to buy. They decided not to attempt to sell common stock or bonds separately, but to put the two together and sell them as units. The Mid-America Pipeline Company issued $6\frac{1}{2}$ percent subordinated debentures, due in 1980, in the principal amount of $20,500,000. It also issued 1,435,000 shares of common stock without par value. These were put together to make 410,000 units, each consisting of one $50 debenture and $3\frac{1}{2}$ shares of common stock. Each unit sold for $73.50. The unit plan of selling securities was considered something of a novelty, although this was not the first time it had been used. The plan had been devised back in 1948 by Frank Kernan in financing the Transcontinental Gas Pipeline. But in the case of Mid-America, the financial experts gave a great deal of time and thought to the price that would give each unit the widest public appeal and what proportion of each unit should be debenture and how much common stock.

The unit plan was adopted because it was not realistic to expect to sell common stock in an enterprise that wasn't even in existence at the time. The units were offered for sale March 30, 1960, and the company did not receive its first money from Prudential until June 1, 1960. At the time the offering was made, there was no pipeline. The public could not be expected to buy either debentures or common stock separately in a venture that was still on paper. But the combination of the two made an interesting package: The $3\frac{1}{2}$ shares of common stock contained in each unit gave the investor a speculative ride and the hope that this would be a profitable enterprise and he would make money on it. At the same time, the debenture portion of the unit gave him a chance to get interest during the early years of the company's operation when there was little likelihood he would receive dividends from his common stock. And so, by holding his debentures, the investor could get his money back—or most of it—through interest. If the company proved to be profitable, he stood to make money on his common stock.

As managers of the issue, Bear, Stearns and White, Weld now sent out invitations to investment banking houses throughout the nation to form a syndicate for marketing the Mid-America securities. This turned out to be a tougher job than the managers had anticipated—and they had known all along it wasn't going to be easy. "It's always difficult, even during the best of market conditions, to sell securities at the start of a venture, when you don't have an operating record to go on," according to James W. Needham. "You are asking investors to buy securities on the basis of engineering projections and a prospectus that has a lot of gloom and doom in it. This is quite different from selling securities in an established company with a record of earnings and sales over the years. A prospectus for a company like MAPCO can't be too encouraging because it must be constructed to comply with the securities laws, which are such that a prospectus tends to emphasize the risks rather than the possibilities. Beyond that, the MAPCO project faced peculiar difficulties of its own—mainly the known hostility of large oil companies and the possibility of overwhelming competition from other carriers."

Jim Needham, Executive Vice President of White, Weld at this writing, was an Associate in that company's Corporate Finance Department at the time MAPCO was organized, and it fell to him to do most of the work in the trenches for White, Weld in lining up the syndicate. "For a period of several weeks, I spent most of my time talking on the telephone and in person to prospective under-

70

writers of the transaction," he recalls. "I would come to my office in the morning and talk to underwriters on the East Coast, then move on into the Midwest as the day progressed, and I would still be in my office at seven o'clock that night telling the same story to underwriters on the West Coast.

"There was quite a lot of resistance to the MAPCO securities. A good many underwriters were concerned about competition from the railroads. They were worried about whether the railroads might respond by cutting rates or improving service so as to make the pipeline unable to attract sufficient traffic. And the prospective underwriters knew that, under rules of the SEC and the various state utilities commissions, they would have to inform their customers that these were not suitable securities for a widow who would depend on income from them for a living. They had to make it clear that there was a degree of speculation here. In fact, in Illinois, we had to stamp right on the face of the prospectus, 'These Are Speculative Securities.' But in the end we were able to put together a fairly respectable group of underwriters. We had 135 investment banking houses in the MAPCO syndicate, about average size, including some of Wall Street's majors, such as Goldman, Sachs and Company, Bache and Company, Hornblower and Weeks, Carl M. Loeb, Rhoades and Company, and Paine, Webber, Jackson and Curtis."

The only advertising an underwriter can use in selling securities is the issue's prospectus, and putting the MAPCO prospectus together was, according to Needham, "the most complex and time-consuming one I've ever worked on. There was an enormous amount of documentation associated with the transaction, and the terms of all those documents had to be interrelated so as not to conflict with each other. A great deal of time was spent by myself and representatives of Bear, Stearns and the various lawyers involved in putting all this documentation together.

"We would assemble at nine-thirty or so in the morning, and we would generally be there until midnight, week after week. During the day it was hard to keep the group together. We'd get everybody assembled at nine-thirty, and by ten o'clock all the members would be in different phone booths, talking to somebody about some new wrinkle that had appeared and confused the transaction. We were at it every working day and every Saturday and several Sundays for the better part of two months.

"One problem was that the business terms of the deal kept changing as we went along, and when you change the business terms, you have to change the documentation to reflect that. I recall one time when a lawyer worked all night to modify one of the indentures to incorporate the latest provision. The printer showed up early next morning with a box full of fresh proofs containing the printed version of the lawyer's night's work. But by the time the proofs arrived, the deal had been changed again, and we never even opened that box, because everything in it was already out of date and had to be rewritten."

Frank Kernan recalls: "We had a hell of a time putting that syndicate together. If we'd had a contract for the purchase of a minimum amount of propane that we proposed to put through that pipeline, it would have been much simpler. But we didn't have any such contract. This is probably the first successful pipeline promotion ever made without one. That is what distinguished this deal from anything I know of. I'm sure it has never been done before. So we knew from the first it was going to be a tough job. We had the Stone and Webster estimate of future business to show the prospective syndicate members, but, even assuming that the producers would live up to their intentions as expressed in their Letters of Intent, it still didn't appear that the common stock was going to bring anybody up to the top of Mount Everest."

At that, the Stone and Webster Feasibility Report that was published was considerably more positive in tone than its preliminary report had been. "The first draft of that Stone and Webster report was so discouraging," Robert E. Thomas says, "that I quickly made a special trip to New York to try, as my wife says, 'to take the Stone out of Stone and Webster.' I was able to persuade them that their preliminary report had underestimated our potential, and the report that finally came out and was published, was, I'd say, about twice as favorable as that first draft."

The next blow came from the Northern Natural Gas Pipeline. "The Mid-America Pipeline was going right into their territory," Frank Kernan points out, "and the Northern Natural people apparently were upset because they should have thought of building an LP Gas pipeline, and they hadn't. So they ordered their principal underwriter, Blyth, Eastman, Dillon, to get out of our syndicate. This set us back considerably, both actually and psychologically, because Blyth was a major, and in the past they had been very strong at selling pipeline securities."

Robert Thomas was especially incensed when the two managing companies of the syndicate—Bear, Stearns and White, Weld —each received a telegram from the Sante Fe Railroad, which attempted to discourage them from going on with the deal. "Sante Fe had a lot of tank cars built for hauling propane, and they were trying to kill our company," Mr. Thomas recalls. "I remember that the Sante Fe people brought up the idea at that time of building new jumbo tank cars for hauling larger amounts of propane more cheaply than they currently were able to do. At that point, I decided I was going to sue the Sante Fe for a hundred million dollars if our deal failed to go through."

The market was not especially favorable for pipeline securities at the time of the Mid-America offering, according to Gus Mulgrew, then a Vice President of Bankers Trust Company. "There had been two recent offerings of pipeline securities before Mid-

America," he recalls. "One was the Houston Company, a holding company for the Texas Oil and Gas, which later became Florida Gas Company. They ran into difficulties around 1960. We had to get a moratorium and reorganize the company. They are very successful today, but the company did require refinancing because the cash flow was not sufficient to make the amortization payments on the first-mortgage bonds. And then a second pipeline, Transwestern, had taken an awful lot of money out of the market for this type of security. The Transwestern securities sold at a fairly high price, and Mid-America came along three or four months later when the market for that type of investment was a little bit shaky. However, it changed and got better and they were eventually able to sell the Mid-America securities."

"One of our strongest assets at this point," Bob Thomas says, "was Cy Lewis, who is one of the greatest salesmen I have ever known. Cy telephoned his friends—some wealthy friends—and said, 'By God, you've got to buy half a million or a million of this . . .'" Mr. Lewis commented, "I don't know much about pipelines, but I *am* a pretty good salesman. I made up my mind that if these two guys [Thomas and Kernan] felt as strongly about the situation as they did, I was going to bend my back to try to help get the job done."

At the most critical phase of the efforts to move the issue, Bob Thomas' close friend William N. Deramus, Senior, President of the Kansas City Southern Railway, made a heavy purchase of Mid-America units and thus helped—both financially and psychologically—sale of the remaining units. His son, Bill Deramus, Jr., recently recalled the occasion:

"At the time both White, Weld and Bear, Stearns were having trouble making these units attractive in the marketplace. Bob and I were in my father's office one day talking to him, which we frequently did, and, of course, both of us were extremely enthusiastic at the time about the prospects for the pipeline. But we were worried about moving the securities. My father on that day said to Bob, 'To help you out, the Kansas City Southern Railway Company will take $1,000,000 worth of debentures and stock in your pipeline, and I, personally, will take $500,000 worth.' And my father added that if the issue still had trouble getting moving, come back and he would buy some more. That provided a real shot in the arm. Everybody who'd had anything to do with railroads and transportation over the years knew my father and knew his integrity. His purchase was damn helpful as far as the New York financial boys were concerned. This allowed them to say, 'Well, here is one guy who has committed himself to $1,500,000 worth.'"

"At White, Weld, we'd had a hard time back in 1948 organizing the first syndicate we put together to finance a gas pipeline," Frank Kernan recalls. "But we had done four or five of them since that time, before the Mid-America deal, and they had all been wows—all huge successes. We had made a great deal of money for all those people [the investment banking firms participating in these syndicates] and for their clients on those pipelines such as Transcontinental, Texas-Illinois, Trans-Canada, Piedmont Natural Gas. . . . You could get more of a spread on this type of speculative securities than other types more conservative. Although their customers had made a lot of money on previous deals of pipelines we had handled, the boys didn't fall in line on this one for Mid-America. When we telephoned some of the investment banking houses about Mid-America, they would want to have meetings and explanations as to why this pipeline was going to work. 'But you haven't got anybody agreeing to take on the other end,' they'd tell us. Or, 'Suppose the railroads lower their rates by two or three cents—even if they lose money doing it—what happens to the pipeline then?'

"But the point is that we *did* put the syndicate together," Mr. Kernan adds, "and we *did* sell the issue, and Mid-America's securities have proven to be just about the best investment anybody who bought them had ever made. But, I tell you, I realized later that the underwriters had taken a little more risk in handling them than I had anticipated in the first place. They got away with it but I'm not sure I would recommend such a deal again for the underwriters."

During the latter months of 1959 and throughout all of 1960 —while the Mid-America deal was being put together, the mortgage loan arranged, the syndicate of investment banking houses organized and the public issue of securities sold, and then throughout the period of construction of the pipeline—Bob Thomas worked inhuman hours. He now looks back fondly on those times of stress, and enjoys recalling them. This is natural because, during those months, Mr. Thomas rescued his own career and in so doing created a business organization that was highly profitable to all concerned. By the mid-1970's it had become generally admired in business and financial circles as one of the best-managed and most promising young enterprises in the nation.

"Bob is a great optimist," his wife, Barbara, reports. "I don't think he could have put Mid-America together if he hadn't been an optimist. During those months of organizing the company and getting it going, his hours were terrible. He was working until eleven or twelve at night and sometimes later. We were living in New Jersey at the time and when winter came on, I told him just to stay in New York at night after he got through working. At least, that way I wouldn't have to worry about him driving home through the sleet and snow. Once I cut out a full-page ad from *The New York Times* that had a caption in big type saying: 'Mommie, Why Can't Daddy Work Like the Man in the Grocery Store and Come Home Every Night at Six?' I stuck it on the door of our dressing room one day, so that he would see it first thing when he came home late that night. Bob got in around eleven and I am sure he was dead tired, but when he saw it, he just stood there and roared. You have to find some humor at times like this.

"And there were a lot of discouraging times," Mrs. Thomas went on. "Things would start to fall apart, but then somehow he would work on them until he got them back together again. I remember one time we got away for a weekend in Florida and about the time we arrived there, some crisis happened and after that, Bob was burning up the telephones until we suddenly packed up and went back to New York to try to get things straightened out.

"I don't think Bob ever let himself get discouraged at any of these times. I never heard him express any sort of feeling about giving up. But it had to be a great physical strain on him. When we were getting ready to move our home from New Jersey out to Tulsa, I flew out to look at houses. Bob was staying in Tulsa by then, living in a hotel. And the first night I was there, he fell asleep at the table in the restaurant where we were having dinner. He was just exhausted. There hadn't been any letup for a long time. He just worked constantly."

But then, so did the others who helped put together the Mid-America Pipeline Company, among them, Jim Needham, the young analyst of White, Weld. "Jim was engaged to be married," Bob Thomas recalls. "But he was constantly having to break dates with his fiancée because of the 16-hour-a-day sessions that went on every day, sometimes including Saturdays and Sundays. His young lady friend just couldn't believe anybody would work that long and hard, so she broke the engagement.

"After the company was finally put together and the securities were sold, I gave a dinner at the Hotel Pierre in New York for all of the lawyers and investment bankers and everybody connected with our enterprise. And I made a little talk in which I referred to those long hours of labor and those times when we worked practically all night. I told how Jim Needham had lost a prospective wife—he had pretty well gotten over it by then. And then, referring to the entire group, I added that God alone knew how many babies didn't come into the world because the Mid-America Pipeline was being born."

Pioneer with a Briefcase   8

"In my professional career, I've had four or five high points—projects in which I was especially glad to have been involved. My part in helping in the formation of the Mid-America Pipeline Company was one of these."

Joseph Auerbach, a partner in the staid and solid Boston legal firm of Sullivan and Worcester, thus reminisced one day in 1975 about the time 15 years earlier when he served as Chief Legal Adviser for the concept that was to become the world's first long-distance liquefied petroleum gas pipeline.

"The Mid-America project," Mr. Auerbach went on, "was outstanding for several reasons: From an intellectual standpoint, I thought its financing was in the finest tradition of private enterprise. The principal figures were Bob Thomas, himself a man of finance, along with Frank Kernan, Senior Partner in White, Weld and Company, and Salim ("Cy") Lewis, Senior Partner of Bear, Stearns and Company, both prominent New York City investment houses. These three principals, with the help of a number of us subordinates, took what was nothing but a dream and—with literally no financial foundation but with great ingenuity and traditional American business perception—financed this project, had it built, and made a success of it. And this happened during a period of time when—if you compare it, say, with Governmental activities—the accomplishment is absolutely astounding.

"Then, a second satisfaction was to see the high quality of workmanship that went into the physical construction of the pipeline. I was extremely impressed by the personnel of Williams Brothers Company. Here a major pipeline was being put into the ground in eight months—faster than any pipeline of comparable length had ever been built or is ever likely to be again. It *had* to be completed on schedule in order for its founders to fulfill their commitments to their potential shippers. And Williams Brothers *did* meet their deadline—and yet, we had no money in hand to pay for this work ahead of time. The prime lenders, Prudential Insurance Company of America, released the monies to pay for this work in installments of about eight to ten million dollars a month—*but only after* we could show at the end of each period that we had actually put eight or ten million dollars worth of materials into the ground. This required a prodigious amount of daily deadline accounting and documentation. And all this while a pipeline was being built. Steel was being delivered. Other things were being done. Men were digging trenches in the ground. Great machines were thundering about the landscape. Pipes were being laid. Things were moving on. The Mid-America Pipeline was really built on faith, belief and magnificent imagination and energy that swiftly transformed the fabric of a dream into a productive and profitable reality.

"To me," Joseph Auerbach went on, "the Mid-America Pipeline project was very much like railroading of a century ago, in the days of the Iron Horse and the Golden Spike. We think back to the year 1859—a century before Mid-America Pipeline was built—when railroading was young, vigorous, imaginative, spreading out in all directions, experimenting with new ideas. Mid-America represented an important innovation in the early days of privately financed pipelining. Nobody had built a products transportation system of this kind. LP Gas had been transported before, of course, in batches through pipelines that carried mainly other petroleum products. But here was something new—a common carrier with instant delivery. Instead of a shipper putting his product in a railroad tank car and having it delivered 2,000 miles away ten days later, the shipper could put his product into the pipeline today and have product exactly like it taken out at the other end 2,000 miles away at practically the same time his product was given to the line. The shipper doesn't care whether the product taken out at the other end is exactly what he put in so long as all products accepted by the pipeline management meets certain standards. The Mid-America Pipeline was actually pioneering in the finest tradition—and it came during this modern computer age when 'pioneering' of such a hearty sort is generally regarded as a thing of nostalgic memories of covered wagons and savage Indians. Sometimes even *I* felt like a pioneer while working on this project."

Joseph Auerbach rolled out his colorful phrases while striding up and down his office, gesturing and posturing as he might have done before a jury. From the wide windows of his corner office one can look out through the surrounding financial towers of downtown Boston and out over the piers and old stone warehouses at that area of Boston Harbor where Colonial patriots of 200 years ago held their celebrated Boston Tea Party. Mr. Auerbach little resembles the image of the old-time pioneer, either physically or in dress, which runs to conservative gray flannels. He is a slightly built, balding man of early middle-age with a wide mouth and a square jaw, a solemnly pleasant expression and quick, intelligent eyes peering through large horn-rimmed glasses. Instead of a Winchester and six-shooter, his weapon is the briefcase.

For it is the nature of the lawyer's calling to do his "pioneering" with paperwork.

In the offices of Sullivan and Worcester are seven thick volumes known there as "The Bible." These contain the actual documentation of the financing arrangements for building the Mid-America Pipeline. "The Bible" is actually a condensation of several filing cases filled with working papers, each set of which was drafted several times, some volume-length within themselves. All of this required the efforts of a large number of lawyers and financial people, each of whom had his own ideas of how each document should be framed and worded.

"The Bible's" two largest volumes, I and II, are called The Registration Statement and contain the papers necessary for the public financing—the sale of Mid-America's securities, in the form of common stock and debentures, through 135 investment houses throughout the United States. The five smaller volumes concern the financial arrangements for issuance of first-mortgage bonds to the Prudential Insurance Company of America, the private lender of $42,000,000. Between June 2 and September 1, 1960, there were five separate closings, or "takedowns," of construction funds from Prudential, ranging from six to ten million dollars each. Before each of these takedowns of funds was made, it was necessary for Mid-America to certify exactly how much construction had been completed since the last payment, along with the current status of the entire project. The necessary documentation for each of these five takedowns required a volume from an inch and a quarter to an inch and a half thick.

As counsel for Mid-America, it was also necessary for Sullivan and Worcester to inform Prudential of the various bodies of law relating to acquisitions of rights-of-way and the operation of the proposed pipeline in each of ten states involved: New Mexico, Texas, Oklahoma, Kansas, Nebraska, Iowa, Minnesota, Missouri, Illinois and Wisconsin. Each state had its own laws relating to whether Mid-America had the right of eminent domain (the right to condemn private property for pipeline purposes), what regulations had to be observed for the pipeline to exist in each state, what certificates were required to operate it, what special accounting procedures might be involved, and on and on. Before the mortgage bonds were issued, the Mid-America lawyers had to provide the insurance company with opinions concerning these laws and regulations so that Prudential could satisfy itself that, once begun, construction of the pipeline could not be legally blocked and, when completed, the pipeline would be able to operate without legal interference.

"And so," Mr. Auerbach says, "it became necessary for our legal firm to have every foot of that right-of-way covered by some lawyer who would study all the laws and regulations relating to the proposed pipeline in each area and write legal opinions for the information of the lending insurance company. For this we employed local counsel in places like Des Moines, Chicago, Kansas City, St. Paul, Liberty, Missouri, Omaha, New Mexico, Tulsa, and in Texas and Wisconsin. We held meetings with our associate counsel in various areas and provided them with lengthy lists of the kind of information we wanted them to check. These are all first-rate law firms, but what they didn't know was how all the pieces of this complicated mosaic were being put together. It was necessary for us at Sullivan and Worcester to know the entire picture in order to give them proper guidance. Each of these local law firms was given a narrow segment of the problem as its responsibility. In addition to the widely varying types of regulations in the individual states—in one or two we could not exercise the law of eminent domain to condemn property—we also had to consider the United States Army Corps of Engineers, which dictates the regulations and requirements for pipelines crossing navigable rivers. All of this mass of information and legal opinions had to be provided the Prudential Insurance Company.

"As the private and principal lender, of course, Prudential required that Mid-America itself own some equity. It happened that this offering constituted *very ingenious financing* through pairing common stock and a debenture together as a unit. The underwriting companies deserve real praise that the offering went as well as it did. The two individuals mainly responsible for devising the plan of financing and for selling the units successfully, Francis Kernan, of White, Weld, and Cy Lewis, of Bear, Stearns and Company, are most interesting as individuals—most experienced, innovative and great personalities on Wall Street as members of a generation of financiers that is now dwindling. Cy Lewis, long known as one of the great securities salesmen on The Street, deserved much credit for moving these units. The unit plan itself was largely devised by Mr. Kernan, who is regarded as the nation's leading expert on pipeline financing—a fairly recent development in corporate financial history, which goes back really not much further than World War II. I think it especially significant that two financiers of the stature of Mr. Kernan and Mr. Lewis had the kind of vision necessary to put their names on that prospectus. And, bear in mind that no history existed for this kind of pipeline, and the amount of money involved was quite a big sum for 1960."

"It is impossible for a person on the outside to appreciate the long hours of hard work and the large numbers of legal and financial experts required to organize Mid-America and make it into an operating business," Joseph Auerbach says. "At one point we had employed—or were otherwise associated with—so many attorneys in the East and throughout the Midwest that we became known as 'The Sullivan and Worcester Bar Association.' In addition to the lawyers employed from outside our firm, we had two of our own people, say, working on the mortgage and indenture phase of Mid-America. At the same time two others were working on the Registration Statement for the SEC, and two more of our lawyers were working on the construction contract. One lawyer in our firm was handling the liaison with all the lawyers we had employed from other states, and somebody else in the firm was doing liaison with the investment bankers. As for Bob Thomas, he was attending meetings with all of these—constantly.

"One reason for all this effort in our law firm was that we had to put together an organization for Bob. He didn't have one; *we* were his organization. He was on the go literally every minute. As the Chief Executive and only employee of Mid-America, Bob had to make decisions on all these things that I have mentioned. So he would have a meeting in New York City today with the bankers or somebody; then he would have a session next day with some potential shipper out West, and that was followed by a meeting with some lawyers on how to write up some letter or other. Some of these letters were especially tricky, especially relating to how the pipeline management was going to get producers to put their products through the pipeline once it was built. The potential shippers were not about to give us legally binding throughput agreements, so we had to devise statements that we could legitimately file with the SEC that had the characteristics of a good-faith promise. After all, we were proposing to sell these securities to the public with nothing underlying them except faith.

"One day there would be a problem with the SEC, and Bob and some of us would have to meet with some of the SEC staff," Joseph Auerbach went on. "Next day there might be a problem with some accountants. And so there was for a period, I would say, from late 1959 to about four months into 1960 when we literally had constant meetings and needs for decisions. In almost every instance, Bob Thomas was involved personally. It was something like a military operation and he was the general, operating from a floating headquarters. Of course, Bob had a place to hang his hat in Tulsa, but Tulsa was not where most of the action was. Bob had the final say and decisions were being required of him practically daily. There were perhaps fifty people with functions to perform, all of which required some sort of an answer from Bob every few days. And at the same time he was recruiting staff. It was really quite an amazing performance that he put on.

"During the period of construction," Mr. Auerbach says, "I spent a week out of every month in Tulsa preparing this documentation of progress. I received wonderful help from two young fellows employed to keep track of the materials as they arrived and were put into the ground—Joseph Williams, who is John Williams' first cousin and is now President of the Williams Companies —and Wilbur Holleman, Jr., son of the Chief Counsel for Williams Brothers Company. These youngsters literally ran their legs off seeing to it that things got done. Joe Williams was quite a young fellow then, hardly out of college. Webby Holleman was about the same age. They tore up and down that 2,000-odd miles of right-of-way, counting the stacks of pipe, making sure things were where they were supposed to be, seeing to it that the certificates were ready. They realized how essential all this was. Williams Brothers wanted to get that pipeline built on schedule and they needed the money for it. But that money was available only from Prudential, the mortgagee, and Prudential wasn't going to give us that money until we had provided them with the necessary documentation. But these two young fellows, with me looking over their shoulders, got it done. We have all these volumes of paperwork to show for it, but paperwork merely evidences the physical work that had to take place to put the pipeline in the ground.

"And I must mention Vincent Butler, who was the straw boss of the entire construction project in every traditional sense. He is one of the most reliable men that I ever met. If Vince Butler said to you, 'This will be done on Friday,' that part of the job *was* done on Friday—not Saturday. He got it done. So, in addition to the intellectual satisfaction of this job, there was this—to use the cliché—'teamplay' in a way that I had never run into before. The laying of the Mid-America Pipeline was a most satisfying thing. It was done efficiently, quickly, expertly and when it was all over, the thing worked."

During the laying of the pipeline, Joseph Auerbach spent most of his time in New York City, where the financing work—both public and private—was done. New York was the most convenient location because Prudential was just across the river in Newark, New Jersey, and the public financing was being done on Wall Street. And so Sullivan and Worcester sent a team of lawyers down to New York to work with the people at White, Weld and Bear, Stearns and Company, with the Prudential lawyers, with the lawyers representing Bankers Trust Company, who were trustees for the bonds, and with the law firm of Winthrop, Stimson, Putnam and Robinson, attorneys for the underwriters.

"We literally lived in that big conference room of Winthrop Stimson, on Wall Street," Mr. Auerbach recalls. "We were closeted there days on end. People were constantly going in and out. When somebody got hungry sandwiches and coffee were brought in. This went on literally for weeks at a time. We would have some of our people over at the printers' waiting for new proofs. Maybe one section of our work might require three or four different sets of proofs. We used several different printing firms. Sometimes we had somebody waiting all night over at one of the printers' establishments. A group of analysts representing the underwriters might show up early in the morning accompanied by their counsel and they might be around most of the day. And we would all labor for hours trying to sweat out a paragraph that properly described some important phase of the project.

"Let me illustrate a typical problem that we might have on a given day. Here," and Joseph Auerbach indicated a portion of the prospectus as it was finally completed, "are about thirty lines in a prospectus that is forty pages long. These lines are on pages sixteen and seventeen under the caption, 'Regulation.' I can't tell you how many hours went into writing those lines in order to be certain that they were wholly correct, contained every material fact needed to make them correct and to protect the underwriters and the company against liability for failure not to state correctly all material facts. And you see, this deals simply with the jurisdiction of the Interstate Commerce Commission and what the company would have to be subject to under the ICC and under state regulations.

"I referred earlier to the power of eminent domain. You see, we did not have that power in the states of Minnesota, Wisconsin and Illinois. What did we do where we did not have such power? What were our special problems in New Mexico, Texas and Oklahoma? A simple sentence—a sentence of this sort—often involved consultation and meetings that might have to go on for days until everyone was satisfied that what we finally wrote correctly stated every material fact in a style that was readable. Oh yes, we had to be something of English scholars with it all. The style had to be readable in order to sell the securities covered by this prospectus and we had to know that when we sold the securities, no one was going to have any liability because of any misstatement.

"And look at this section entitled, 'Shipper's Letters of Intent.' We have already mentioned the problem that none of these shippers gave us legally binding throughput agreements. But how did we state it on this page, one of forty pages in the prospectus? These pages, twelve and thirteen, contain a summary of what those letters state in general. Can you realize how much work and how much time went into that page? When you read it carefully, you may be able to realize to a degree how much we compressed into those few lines and yet tried to make it readable. The lines involve not only an analysis of the thirteen letters that Bob had secured from producers such as Skelly, Sinclair, Texas Natural and others, and each of the letters had its own variances. How were we to make it clear that these letters were not legally binding throughput agreements and yet show that they carried far more weight than a casual, 'Yes, Mr. Thomas, we will be glad to help you if we can.' We had to show in legal words that these letters really meant something, because the whole future of the pipeline depended on a fine choice of wording.

"The Securities Act of 1933," Joseph Auerbach continued, "under which this registration was filed provides very substantial consequences for failure to state properly material facts concerning an issue of securities. Thus, what we wrote had to provide protection for the underwriters. And, of course, these underwriters had their own counsel and their own experts sitting in. If they, the underwriters, were not protected, they wouldn't go on with the deal; they wouldn't sell the securities. We had to find for them a sound basis for every statement—a factual basis for any claim in the prospectus, which is basically sales literature. In fact, the prospectus is the *only* sales literature permitted for securities by the SEC. And so, while the prospectus had to make the securities sound attractive, it had to provide protection for everybody concerned on every point. That is why every portion, literally, of this prospectus represents meeting after meeting after meeting: Who was going to prepare the map? Who was going to describe this or that? Who was going to describe the markets? How about the reports on the markets? How about those Letters of Intent and what did they mean and what could we say about them? When you go to write a stock, a bond agreement, a note agreement, any kind of underwriting agreement, this means meetings upon meetings. Every one of the pages in that prospectus involves meetings . . . meetings . . . meetings!

"Our only relaxations were late dinners at Delmonico's. Lunch was always out of a paper bag, but practically every night Bob would take half a dozen or so lawyers to Delmonico's, or Oscar's, as it is also called. That is the only good restaurant in downtown Manhattan, in the financial district, that remains open until late in the evening. We would go over to Oscar's and have a couple of drinks and a fine dinner. But the arguing would continue to go on—not arguing in the sense of opposition, but the kind of arguing that strives to find a solution: 'Can we say it this way?' 'No, no you can't say it that way.' 'How about this?' 'Bob, do you think . . . ?' 'If you say it that way, you'll *ruin it;* that's not the way to deal with this situation.' 'Well, how . . . ?' 'This way—this is the way you've got to get it across . . .' 'How *do* you get it across?' 'Oh, you can't do it that way . . .' 'After all, when you're talking about eminent domain, you've got to say it a different way . . .'

"What we were doing was giving solidarity and reality to dreams. The reason that all that hard work was so necessary is almost impossible to explain now. The Mid-America Pipeline has gone on and become an immense success—a sensation of Wall Street. And we lawyers are left with these volumes of final documents.

"Call it 'shuffling papers' if you like—but you can't pioneer a thing like the Mid-America Pipeline in these times without 'shuffling papers.' "

The "Mona Lisa" of Pipelining

9

"The Mid-America job was the 'Mona Lisa' of pipelining. There never had been—and never will be—another like it. What we did was complete a two-year project in nine months."

Vincent Butler, the Mid-America Project Manager for the Williams Brothers Company, which built it, says that the achievement of laying some 2,000 miles of pipeline in record time was "just one of those things when the timing was right and the right people happened to be involved—Bob Thomas, in particular. What you might call a 'spirit of adventure' seemed to pervade the entire operation—a fine enthusiasm to turn out a memorable result, which caused our people to work until they literally dropped in some cases. And then, we had some luck.

"We *had* to finish this project in record time. Our client, Mid-America Pipeline Company, had some rather flimsy agreements with LP Gas suppliers that depended upon the line starting operation by December 1, 1960. Beyond that, this particular pipeline had been conceived originally by Williams Brothers, which was still a rather young company at the time—and it was a matter of pride with us to show that we could finish a big, unique sort of job like that in record time and turn it over to the new owners on schedule in full operational condition. We began laying the pipe on April 8, 1960, and were scheduled to complete the line on December 1, 1960. We made it right on time.

"This was a 24-hour-a-day job, and our people out there laying the line had instructions to telephone me day or night if necessary, which they often did. The big thing was to get the materials delivered on time in the right way at the right place, so the crews would have no delay. And we finished the job without anyone having to lose a day of work for any reason, including those frequent annoyances in any pipeline job of materials arriving late and because of difficulties in securing rights-of-way. But we did have some mighty close calls.

"A mini-recession was going on at the time, and Westinghouse, which was building the motors, transformers, motor controls and switch gears, was reluctant to proceed full speed with the manufacturing by paying workers overtime. The Westinghouse management preferred to string the work out over a longer period of time and thus keep more of their people busy. At one point the whole plant went on vacation, which threatened to interrupt our time schedule and possibly destroy the project. But I went to their plants several times and made personal appeals to the management that we just *had* to have this equipment. And I think those appeals were effective.

"The railroads," Vincent Butler went on, "did a great job getting our material delivered to us—especially the Katy, which, of course, had quite a stake in the new pipeline. And I can't say enough for the people associated with me who did such dedicated work day and night, getting those pumping stations and electrical designs drawn up and the materials ordered and on the ground. One person who is certainly due tremendous credit in that area is Charlie Ward, who was Chief Engineer on the job and is now back with the Williams Engineering Company. Another was J. D. Mullen, in charge of purchasing and expediting the delivery of materials. He literally worked day and night. Joe Williams, now President of the Williams Companies, was my strong right arm. He did a fabulous job of supervising the handling of materials and the reporting necessary to prepare the documentation required before we could take down the money paid in various installments by the Prudential Insurance Company.

"And then there was the problem of getting the right-of-way in a hurry. Most of the landowners were quite cooperative, but we ran into some people, especially in Kansas, who gave us a hard time. And yet, under the existing condemnation laws—or in cases where such laws did not exist, we made out pretty well. But there were many times when we got a right-of-way agreement only twelve hours ahead of the pipe-laying crew. In the states that had no condemnation laws, we just sort of lucked out—that's all I can say. The agents in charge of acquiring the right-of-way handled it very well.

"In at least two instances, we sent an airplane with a lawyer and a right-of-way agent aboard to land in a farmer's pasture-lot and complete negotiations to go through his land, while a pipeline-laying crew was approaching from just beyond the hill. And there were several successful negotiations conducted on the steps of the courthouse, where we were ready to file condemnation papers, but then we achieved a compromise settlement with the landowners at the last minute.

"And so we were able to go right along putting the pipeline into the ground in record time. We had to reach the point where we were laying over a hundred miles of pipe a week—otherwise we never would have made it. One week we laid 137 miles of pipe. That's some kind of a record. I remember at one point, Charlie Keane, Chief Engineer of the Great Lakes Pipeline Company, telephoned me and said he would like to get some idea about when the Mid-America Pipeline was going to cross the Great Lakes right of way. I said, 'Charlie, we crossed your line a week ago.' He just couldn't believe it."

Psychologically, the success of the Mid-America Pipeline project, according to Vincent Butler, depended upon the good faith existing between the Mid-America people—namely, Robert Thomas and Dave Roach—and the Williams Brothers Company. "I had to represent both of them in a way," he says, "and that often presented me with a difficult situation. Bob Thomas was depending on me to be sure that we did the project within the financial estimate and on schedule and in the best technical, engineering manner. At the same time, I was working for John Williams, whose main interest, obviously, was to make as much money as possible for Williams Brothers, but he was also anxious to get the job done on schedule, within the contract estimate we had agreed upon and in the best working condition possible. So, in many cases, I had to be judge and jury. I was pretty harsh with some of the Williams construction people about certain things they wanted to do. I also had to be quite firm with the Mid-America people as to when we were going to do other things and why we were going to do them. I had to maintain the confidence of both. It really wasn't easy.

"And speaking of Bob Thomas: I have great admiration for him. He is dedicated and he is fair. I think his main quality that made this project go through was tenacity. Without that, Mid-America never would have succeeded. The oil, gas and pipeline industries never welcomed Bob Thomas and his project. I think many of the individuals and the companies did what they could to discourage him and to block the pipeline. But he was bound and determined that this dream was going to become a reality. (I think the story of Mid-America should be called 'The Impossible Dream.') Bob just refused to be discouraged. Let's put it this way: He put the thing together and caused it to happen, and I don't think anyone else should have the main credit—especially when you consider that when he started Bob Thomas didn't know a pipeline from a can of beans. I consider him one of the best executives that I have ever known—if not *the* best. Bob is the kind of guy who will make a decision and then stand behind you when you go to carry it out. In today's world, executives like that are at a premium."

Vincent Butler says that throughout the nine-month construction period practically every day was a crisis. "But I think," he added, "that the toughest part of the job came in late November, when we were nearly done, and most of our people were tired and exhausted. We, in management, had to strive constantly to prevent these people from just coming apart from exhaustion, and to keep their morale up. It was quite a job to stop tempers from flaring and just see that everyone stayed on an even keel and got this job done on schedule.

"And then right at the end, we almost had a terrible foul-up. Bob Thomas had set up a big picture-taking session for loading the first truck of propane at the terminal near Minneapolis. We had gotten everything pretty well set up mechanically, and I went to the terminal the day before the opening to check the system and make sure everything was working right. We started up the pumps and they began performing beautifully. And then, for some reason, the system shut itself down. We started the pumps again; they shut themselves down again, the machinery just kept on doing this. We fought that thing until three o'clock the next morning trying to find the problem and it began to look like we just weren't going to be able to. Finally, it occurred to me to check the manifold. We did, and found it had been set up backward. Once we got the valves in the right sequence, the machinery just kicked off beautifully and everything worked fine.

"Next morning, when they were getting set up for all the picture-taking, somebody from Mid-America telephoned me to come on out to the terminal and be in the photographs. But I had been up all night. I was tired. I told them thanks a lot, but I'd rather sleep."

Vincent Butler was born in Panama, where his father, Thomas J. Butler, was an engineer who helped to build the Panama Canal. After the canal was finished, the elder Butler went into the contracting business and, in fact, made the first survey of the Barko Concession, which became the first major oil find in Colombia. Vincent left Panama when he was sixteen to go to school in the United States. After graduation, he worked on pipeline jobs in Minnesota, Alaska and in South America as an employee of the (old) Williams Company, which was then operated by the generation ahead of the present management. He left the present Williams Companies in 1968 and organized his own enterprise, Butler Engineering Company of Tulsa, now a leading builder of pipelines that operates in the United States, the Near East, offshore and throughout the world. Vincent Butler, however, still regards the Mid-America Pipeline as the most remarkable job with which he has ever been connected. And that is saying a great deal, when one considers some of the colorful and spectacular adventures, especially of the (old) Williams Brothers, in the laying of pipelines in wild places.

The original Williams Brothers Company began in 1908 when two brothers, David R. Williams Sr., and S. Miller Williams, Jr., then barely out of their teens, left their employer, a paving contractor in Fort Smith, Arkansas, and launched out on their own in the contracting business with physical assets consisting of one cement mixer. Williams Brothers built their first pipeline in 1915. The oil boom in the Southwest had made it obvious that pipelines were the best way to transport crude to refineries from the fields of Texas, Oklahoma and Kansas. Williams Brothers convinced the oil company managements that they could do a better job building pipelines than the producers could. From then on to the end of their business careers, the original two Williams Brothers and their company remained at the head of their profession. Many of the early large-diameter, high-pressure, long-distance gas transmission lines built in this country during the 1920's and 1930's were Williams Brothers projects—Panhandle, Eastern Pipeline, Northern Natural, Colorado Interstate, Southern Natural, and Natural Gas Pipeline of America.

The ingenuity of Williams Brothers and other early-day pipeliners is responsible for the development of such modern equipment as the backhoe, the bulldozer, the side-boom tractor and self-propelled coating and wrapping machines. The lifespan of the (old) Williams Brothers Company saw pipelining develop from the old-time man- and horsepower method to the era of specialized machines. In the old days, the ditching was laboriously done by sweating pick and shovel gangs and great Percheron horses. These were replaced by tractors with caterpillar treads, and the ditching gangs gave way to the backhoe. Tomahawk crews that used to cut rights-of-way with axes and brush-hooks were superseded by power-saws and bulldozers. The labor gangs that once used block and tackle to lower the pipe into the ditch were replaced by side-boom tractors. And welders, with their hot spark, replaced the colorful tongmen, the stabbers, the jackmen, the ropemen, the growler boardmen and the collar pounders, who screwed the old-fashioned pipe together, or joined it with steel collars.

During World War II, Williams Brothers built the water crossings for the Government's war emergency pipeline, "The Big Inch"—the largest line in existence up to that time. Another Williams Brothers wartime job was pushing four pipelines across the Isthmus of Panama to serve tankers of the Pacific fleet. They built the first international line over the White Mountains from Portland, Maine, to Montreal, and Williams constructed a waterline to the submarine base at Key West, Florida. Williams laid a sea line off the coast of Africa and built underground storage tanks beneath the desert, while Rommel's guns were thundering beyond the horizon. By the time the original Williams Brothers retired from business in 1950, their company had laid about 40,000 miles of the approximately 400,000 miles of trunk gas, oil and water lines that form a web of steel under these United States.

After World War II, pipelining began to boom throughout the world. Williams Brothers built the giant 26-inch crude line in Venezuela, the first pipeline across the Andes in South America, the 30-inch Trans-Arabian pipeline, a large part of the original Trans-Canada system, the world's first 42-inch pipeline in Iran, and various other pipeline projects in foreign countries.

88

Harold H. Martin, one of the best writers on such subjects in the business, has described the old Williams Brothers Company as "a bullheaded, mule-muscle outfit which has laid pipe over every mountain range in the United States, spanned every major river except the Hudson, from the Rio Grande to the St. Lawrence, plus laying one-thousand odd miles through the jungles of Panama and Africa, the mountains of Mexico and the turbulent shallows of Coro Gulf in Venezuela."

During one South America pipeline job, Williams Brothers' workers had to weather a local revolution and withstand the inroads of thieves. They were harassed from time to time by hostile native truck drivers who tried to nudge the Williams Brothers' pipeline trucks off the precipices of the high mountain roads; they were frequently exposed to semihostile Indians, as well as to the various tantrums of the weather. And yet, according to Vincent Butler, the laying of the Mid-America Pipeline through the heartland of the U.S. was a more memorable job than any of the Williams' foreign enterprises, even the South American heroics. Of course, an irate Kansas farmer is hardly as formidable as an armed and drunken revolutionary, and the plains of the Midwest are not as frightening as the heights of the Andes. What made the Mid-America job so memorable was that it was built in about one-third of the time that ordinarily would have been required. And in the world of pipelining, speed is far more important than local color.

After the original Williams Brothers and their two partners retired from business in 1950, the next generation of the family organized a new Williams Brothers Company. Its incorporators were John Williams, the present Chairman of the Board of the Williams Companies; his brother, Charlie, and their first cousin, David Williams, along with six other men who had been middle-management people in the original Williams Company. "Each of us three young Williams boys took a 20 percent share in the new company," according to John Williams. "I put $5,000 into it. In fact, I had only $3,000 to my name at the time, but I borrowed the other $2,000. We started our company with a total of $25,000 as initial capital. All we got from the original company was the Williams' reputation and the opportunity to buy the old company's equipment on liberal terms. We purchased this construction machinery from the four individuals making up the original firm for around $3,000,000. We put no money down but gave them a demand note saying merely we would pay for the equipment when we could. And one big thing they did for us: They permitted us to go to a local bank here and borrow $1,000,000 by subordinating this equipment note to the bank loan. That gave us an artificial financial statement.

"We immediately went out and began bidding on some work. Our new company was the successful low bidder on a fairly big project—the Plantation Pipeline—a $7,735,000 enterprise, going from Baton Rouge, Louisiana, to Greensboro, North Carolina. We worked like dogs to build it, and we did build it and in the process lost $800,000, which we didn't have. That is when we really started growing up. I was thirty-two years old at the time, and I began taking a more realistic view of things. Fortunately, before we finished that Plantation job, we had taken on some other work, which turned out to be profitable. We were able to pay off the note for our equipment in four and a half years, which was late in 1954.

"At the time we began the Mid-America Pipeline job, our company probably had a net worth of about $5,000,000, but every penny of it was tied up in equipment. We had no free cash. We had perhaps 2,000 employees and about half of them, I would say, made up the three spreads of pipeliners and the three station gangs who built Mid-America. That job constituted probably about half of our activities at the time.

"The Mid-America enterprise originated as part of our program of beating the bushes in search of new business. An earlier example of the same sort of thing," John Williams says, "is this one: In our studies, we determined that the City of Las Vegas, which was getting all of its supplies of gasoline and jet fuel brought in by railroads, really needed a pipeline from the refinery. But we quickly ran into the fact that the Union Pacific Railroad, which was handling these liquids, didn't like the idea of somebody competing with them. So we went to Union Pacific and said, 'Why don't we join together and build a pipeline?'—and that is what happened. We operated the Las Vegas Pipeline jointly for half a dozen years and then we sold our interest to Union Pacific, which now owns all of it. It was a good transaction for us both."

John Williams thinks it possible that his new company's association with Union Pacific in the Las Vegas Pipeline may have encouraged the Williams' idea of using railroad rights-of-way to build an LP Gas line from the Texas–New Mexico area into the East. "We learned, of course, before the line ever became a reality, that using railroad rights-of-way was not feasible, nor was the idea of building an LP Gas line into the East," he says. "But our original idea gradually reformed itself into what became the Mid-America Pipeline, which resulted because we were an organization looking for a customer—and we found the right customer. We said, in effect, 'Here is a great idea; we think it will work and we will do the work of installing the pipeline.' At that time we didn't have the foggiest notion of how to finance such a line. We were babes in the woods on how to go about that—how to promote the deal into becoming a reality. We talked to the New York Central Railroad and we talked to the Missouri-Pacific Railroad, casting about for somebody to take hold of it.

"Then, finally, the Katy Railroad came into the picture, and the idea struck a spark. Bob Thomas and Bill Deramus were there to fan the spark. They were aggressive, ambitious, intelligent, and—especially Bob—poised and ready. He needed a project for the Katy Railroad, and he jumped on this one. It's true that he didn't have any idea of what a pipeline was all about when he started. But he learned real fast, even though he had no background at all in such things. But Bob is a financial man; his heritage was all in finance and he knew how to go about getting the money for such a project. He had the energy to jump right in; he got Frank Kernan interested, and the project began to roll from then on. But, in my opinion, Bob Thomas, without question, deserves the great credit for breathing life into this thing. He called on a lot of people for help, but he quarterbacked the whole show. A lot of times, I'm sure, he got pretty discouraged, but he never gave up.

"Actually though," John Williams went on, "I think what he has done with MAPCO since the original LP pipeline was completed is probably more spectacular than starting the line in the first place. I'm quite familiar with MAPCO's progress because our company has gone along pretty much the same way. You build up an organization with some capability, but then you've got to go forward with that and use it as a stepping-stone to other things. Bob has done that by going into the oil business, with the ammonia pipeline, into his coal activities—and now MAPCO is a well-rounded major operation that is becoming an ever more important factor in the business scheme of this area. More importantly, it is performing a useful function.

"In the early stages of trying to make reality of the idea of the Mid-America Pipeline, though, it was touch and go at times. The Katy Railroad had some front money for the early organizational expenses, but Bob took a hell of a risk in pushing this project through before his financing was entirely arranged. That was the only way, though, he ever would have succeeded. And we took quite some risks ourselves. After forming this association with the Katy Railroad, we, at Williams Brothers, went ahead pretty much on speculation that this project would succeed. We completed most of the design work and actually got started on some of the construction work before the whole project was entirely financed. That's damned unusual for us. We never did it for anybody else. But we had sort of grown up with this project. We believed in it and we thought it was going to succeed and it did and the reward was commensurate. It was a good contract, and we made a good return on it. The whole project turned out well for us and, obviously, from the story of MAPCO, it turned out great for them. But I can't think of another engineering company that would have gone as far as we did before it was totally financed.

"We had done larger jobs than Mid-America," John Williams says, "but we never did a job of greater significance for us. It was important for us to get it done because this gave us greater stature in the industry as to our ability to perform all the functions on a large job. We had done a bigger job in Alaska for the U.S. Corps of Engineers, building a pipeline into Fairbanks. But that was a bid job, and we didn't have any question about getting paid. The Mid-America concept showed that we had the organization to do the total turnkey job. At the time Bob had a staff of maybe two or three people and we did *everything* completely from designing to laying the line on through every aspect. We bought all the materials, expedited their delivery, handled all the construction, put the pipeline into operation and did all the testing. That built an enviable image for us. It said if somebody wanted a difficult job done, maybe they should come and talk to Williams."

Aside from increasing the stature of Williams Brothers in the industry, the Mid-America Pipeline job brought John Williams and his organization into contact with people associated with Bob Thomas, who later became important to the Williams organization. Joseph Auerbach, the Mid-America attorney during formation of that company, is now a Director of the Williams Companies, successor to the Williams Brothers Company. And Frank Kernan, who was extremely important to Bob Thomas in financing Mid-America, later helped Williams Brothers finance the purchase for $287,000,000 of the Great Lakes Pipeline system. Ironically, Mid-America was the second-highest bidder for this expensive transportation network.

In 1964, Williams Brothers got out of the construction business in the United States in favor of pipeline construction in foreign countries and offshore. The organization then went into oil and gas exploration, fertilizer and real estate. Between 1966 and 1975, the Williams Companies grew from a $30,000,000 contractor to a diversified operation with assets of $1,200,000,000 and annual revenues exceeding $900,000,000. John H. Williams, who was fifty-six in 1975, is Chairman of the Board. President is Joseph H. Williams, forty-one, the same who "literally ran up and down" the 2,000-mile ditch keeping track of supplies while Mid-America was being built.

The people at Williams Brothers who were there at the time now look back with fond nostalgia to the days when Mid-America was being built as an important milestone in the progress of the Williams Companies. "It came along in a period of the financial evolution of our nation when it was possible to finance a dream," John Williams says these days. "You wouldn't even talk about trying to do such a thing today, with OPEC and the financial crisis of tight money and high interest and all those things. But those were the days of low interest. In Mid-America you had the whole evolution of an idea and how it was possible to breathe life into it and create something of value by the joint effort of so many people. We started the idea and were willing to share in some of the risk. But I would be the first to tell you that we couldn't have done it ourselves. We had no idea of doing it by ourselves.

"It is difficult now," John Williams went on, "to convey the excitement we felt for this project. Sometimes it seems that something more profound than 'chance' brought the proper people together at the proper time so that it was possible to develop this dream into an important reality."

David A. Roach (standing, left) was the first, and Gilbert V. Rohleder (standing beside him) was the second employee hired by Robert E. Thomas in 1960 when the Mid-America Pipeline Company was preparing to begin operations. Mr. Roach is now the Senior Vice President in charge of MAPCO's Pipeline Division, and Mr. Rohleder is the MAPCO Vice President in direct charge of pipeline operations. They are watching the flashing electronic figures and symbols in the Pipeline Dispatcher's Room in Tulsa that tell how the entire system is functioning at any given instant. From this room the Dispatcher (seated) can regulate valves, pumps, and the flow of LP gas and ammonia along the entire 5,000-mile system that serves the Midwest from deep in the heart of Texas northward to Minnesota and Wisconsin.

The first stage of actual pipeline construction is ditching and stringing the sections of pipe along a 50-foot-wide right of way, preparatory to welding the joints together, sealing the pipe in a plastic sheath and burying it. The Williams Brothers Company probably set an all-time speed record while building the Mid-America line by laying 137 miles of pipe in one week.

Mid-America's most impressive looking storage tanks are the sphere-shaped type, gleaming white in the sun, as this one does at the Iowa City, Iowa terminal. The spherical and the more common cylindrically-shaped above ground storage tanks hold from 30,000 to 70,000 gallons of natural gas liquids.

When a LP gas pipeline system is completed, it consists of a complicated system of pumps, valves, gauges, computers, control panels, communications networks and batteries of storage tanks, towers and acres of glistening pipes at each terminal or pumping station along the way. Here at the Iowa City, Iowa terminal, a maintenance man checks a gauge on a tower. Spread out in the distance are the bullet-shaped storage tanks, towers and sections of pipeline emerging out of the ground.

On October 25, 1963, Robert E. Thomas pushed the button that loaded the first propane-carrying truck to fill up at Farmington, Illinois—the last truck-loading terminal opened on the completed Mid-America Pipeline. The company invited all its shippers and other interested parties to an open house celebration in connection with the terminal's opening. Since Skelly Oil Company was Mid-America's biggest customer, a Skelgas truck was given the honor of hauling out the first load.

A two-year job was completed in only eight months—April 8th to December 1st, 1960—when Mid-America's more than 2,000 miles of pipeline was ready to operate along its entire length with the opening of its furtherest north terminal at Pine Bend, Minnesota, near the Twin Cities. Robert E. Thomas and four of the shippers who attended the open house here inspect the pumping assembly. From left: Robert E. Thomas; George Eppley, Union Texas Petroleum; Dick Wenner, Suburban Propane; O. C. Murray, Farmer's Union Central Exchange; Frank Carpenter, United Petroleum Gas.

The Show
Hits the Road

10

The Mid-America Pipeline Company began to look like a going business in October, 1960, when Robert E. Thomas moved his group of newly hired employees and their brand-new office equipment into the company's new headquarters—about one-third of the eighth floor of the new Skelly Building at Boulder Avenue and Fifteenth Street in Tulsa. The most impressive installation in the place, which distinguished the headquarters from just another collection of offices, was a "Dispatcher's Room," with a "Big Board" that resembled somewhat a segment of the NASA Control Room in Houston, Texas, familiar to most TV viewers, that manipulates by remote control the rockets in the Space Program.

For its part, Mid-America's "Dispatcher's Room" manipulated by remote control the valves, pumps and flow of liquid petroleum gas all the way from the west Texas–New Mexico border to the Twin Cities in Minnesota and to Janesville, Wisconsin. A panel some four feet high extending perhaps 30 feet in a semicircle against the wall of a round-shaped room flashed with red, yellow and green lights, indicating what pumps were working along the 2,180-mile main line and gathering systems, what terminals were taking product, what refineries were pumping product into the pipeline and the conditions in general along the entire system. A control board facing the panel allowed a dispatcher in Tulsa to start and stop the total of fifteen pumping stations along the entire route of the line that produced a combined force of 13,600 horsepower. This forced the liquefied petroleum gas through the pipeline, which varied from four to 10 inches in diameter, at a maximum speed of six miles an hour. The fact that the pipeline remained full of product—of standard quality—at all times meant, however, that as soon as a barrel of LP Gas was put into the line at Hobbs, New Mexico, a barrel of propane just like it was pushed out, in effect, at the other ends, either at the Pine Bend, Minnesota, or the Janesville, Wisconsin, terminals, some 1,600 miles to the north or at unloading points along the way. In short, the Mid-America Pipeline was providing what amounted to instantaneous transportation.

Mid-America's new and unique service was prominently reported in the oil and gas trade journals, local newspapers, especially throughout the Midwest, and nationally by the Associated Press, which began its article as follows: "From a chair on the eighth floor of the Skelly Oil Company Building in Tulsa, one man can deliver 100,000 barrels of liquefied petroleum gas a day from Conway, Kansas, to Pine Bend, Minnesota, or Janesville, Wisconsin. He does it by pushing buttons, watching lights and dials and pushing more buttons. This is automation in the pipeline industry . . ."

During the next fifteen years, Mid-America was to more than double its pipeline capacity by adding over 3,000 miles of new pipe and more and larger pumping units. Even the wondrous "Big Board" was replaced by a much smaller, computerized, telemetering system, said to bring in about fifty times as much information as the old board did with its impressive display of flashing lights and massive read-out screens. The new equipment requires only 15 seconds to interrogate every location along the more than 5,000 miles of pipeline, including the fourteen terminals. The pipeline opened in 1960 with only seven terminals, under the general control of the "Big Board" in Tulsa, a relay-type key system, made by the Union Signal and Switch Company and similar to the equipment employed by railroads in switching and dispatching trains. It became obsolete a dozen years later, but when Mid-America opened, it was the latest thing, a prestigious and, for then, efficient installation that commanded considerable news value.

The pipeline began to pump liquefied petroleum gas through part of its system and dispense it through some of its terminals on October 24, 1960. The entire system was functioning by December 8, 1960. Throughput averaged 3,420 barrels a day in November, 1960, the first month of partial operation. It had increased to an average of 18,700 barrels per day in December and to 26,050 barrels per day during January and February, 1961. The daily average throughput for that first entire year of operation was 35,-828 barrels. Within a year after the pipeline began operating, the thirteen original shippers of LP Gas had grown to more than thirty.

By the end of 1960, the company had 151 employees, which was exactly 150 more than had been on the payroll a year earlier. Robert E. Thomas had been the one and only employee of Mid-America Pipeline Company from the time it was incorporated on October 1, 1958, until the spring of 1960, when Mr. Thomas employed David A. Roach to be directly in charge of the pipeline operation. Mr. Roach still holds that position under the title of Senior Vice President in charge of the Pipeline System.

"I first met Bob Thomas when he came to see us at the Phillips Petroleum Company offices in Bartlesville, Oklahoma, where I was employed by the Phillips pipeline operation," Dave

Roach recalls. "Mr. Thomas and some of the people from Williams Brothers were making trips around the petroleum-producing area trying to interest various LP Gas producers in using their new pipeline. Phillips wasn't interested because they had their own pipeline. In fact, they probably viewed Mid-America as competition. At the time, Mr. Thomas was also looking for somebody with pipeline experience to head up the actual operation of the Mid-America Pipeline. A few days after his visit to Phillips, he telephoned me and offered me a job. That's how I happened to go to work for Mid-America.

"Not long after that, I hired Gil [Gilbert V.] Rohleder as the Technical Head of the Pipeline Operation, and Gil hired four superintendents during 1960. At the time all the major oil companies were cutting back on personnel, and we were fortunate in being able to pick up men of outstanding ability and experience to run our pipeline. They were mostly young men, willing to take a chance, who were low in seniority in their old jobs. They could see cuts coming in personnel where they were and that influenced some of them to join us. The oil companies do this every once in a while; they overbuild their staffs, then clean house."

"The thing that impressed me most from the very beginning of Mid-America was the high caliber of people they had operating the pipeline," John O'Donnell, retired Pipeline Editor of *The Oil and Gas Journal,* commented in 1975. "Dave Roach is one of the most respected men in the business. And just nobody knows more about pipelines than Gil Rohleder. One of his early accomplishments, while working for the Okan Pipeline, was to develop, with Ernie Slade, the gas turbine for powering pipeline pumps."

The third employee hired by Bob Thomas back in 1960 was his secretary, Mrs. Helen Jones, who has held the job ever since. "When we moved into the Skelly Building that fall, it wasn't yet completed," Mrs. Jones recalls. "We took over part of the eighth floor, then we expanded to all of the eighth floor. Next we took over the entire seventh floor and now, when the company is fifteen years old, we also have part of the eleventh floor and we are still crowded. We will soon be moving into our own building."

After a few years, President Thomas hired a second secretary, Mrs. Helen Malone, who has since shared Mrs. Jones' duties. And today, Mr. Thomas has an Assistant—Robert J. Swain—to help with many of his duties and responsibilities. But in those early days, every Mid-America employee was turning out as much work in a day as two or three people ordinarily do.

"We had to start everything from scratch—files, the whole bit," Mrs. Jones says. "The first time I talked to Mr. Thomas, he told me, 'I have certain ways of handling my desk and papers— you may not think it's a neat way to do it—but it's just the way I like to do it. You may find my system different from that of anybody you've worked for and a little hard to understand.' I told him, 'Fine, whatever you want to do—we'll try to do.' I don't know what his system is to this day. It's his—and it works for him.

"It quickly became apparent to all of us that Mr. Thomas was *very much* the boss of the company—the head of it—and he makes everyone aware of this fact. He's very confident, very sharp and it's almost uncanny how he can pick out things. He's very brilliant." By "picking out things," Mrs. Jones says she refers to a whole range of capacities from her employer's ability to spot weaknesses in contracts, to seeing opportunities for profitable expansion in fields that most others could not at the time—all the way down to finding misplaced commas in a letter. Her boss is such a rapid reader that he once decided not to take a speed-reading course because he could already read faster than the course promised it could teach him.

Another of Mid-America's early employees is Dean Cosgrove, who began as a general accountant at age twenty-six when the company moved into its new offices in the Skelly Building in the Fall of 1960. Mr. Cosgrove, who was elected Treasurer of MAPCO in 1967 and has continued in that position ever since, recalls:

"Keeping an accounting of the pipeline during construction was wild. That first year was hectic, but a lot of fun when you look back at it. From an accounting standpoint, we had to start from nowhere. We didn't have a piece of paper; we didn't have a thing to record the history of the company accounting-wise; we had no charts of accounts, which are the numbers assigned to various items for filing in the computer. In fact, we didn't have a computer at the time sophisticated enough to run our 'deals' when we bought properties. We had to work these out with pencil and paper. Nowadays, through the use of input sheets, the computer will work out a deal for you by doing the multiplication, division, compute the taxes, determine the amount of cash that is going to come back to you and, in effect, tell you how much you're going to get back for every dollar you put in. All that used to take us three or four days to do by hand, the computer now does in thirty minutes.

"Back at the time I started, we had to set up the entire accounting system. Tony Skodlar—he was the Director of Accounting then—and I set up our chart of accounts. [In 1975, Mr. Skodlar had been Controller of MAPCO for a number of years.] It has always amazed me that we were able to get so much done with so few people back then." Mr. Cosgrove went on. "Back in those early days our Accounting Department had maybe 14 people in it. The entire Tulsa office had no more than 35 or 40 people. Now we have over 200 people in the Tulsa office alone. But when you consider the growth of the company's assets and revenues, the increase in numbers of people working here really hasn't been so great in proportion. This indicates to me that we still get some mighty good mileage out of our people. From my standpoint as an accountant, I think back to the time when we did things for the first time. Generally when an accountant goes to an organization, they already have their ways of doing things —an established procedure for accounting. But at MAPCO it was a fresh start. You had to pick somebody's brains to find out what was needed and how, for example, to put together our first Annual Report in 1960. The whole report was quite short then. Mr. Thomas really did most of the work on it.

"We started with a fine bunch of energetic guys who had been with other companies. They were looking for an opportunity for themselves to grow with a new, growing company. We found Mr. Thomas to be a very demanding individual, but very fair. And he set an example that made us rather glad to work nights, weekends and holidays when we had something that needed to be done."

At the time the company was just beginning to function in 1960, however, the two all-important problems at hand were (1) to hire enough competent technical people, and (2) to fill the pipeline with liquefied petroleum gas and get the operation going physically. And the individual who was in overall charge out in the field was Gil Rohleder. He is a native of Hays, Kansas, an old railroad town founded by Buffalo Bill Cody, who made it his headquarters for hunting buffalo back when the Union Pacific Railroad was being built across Kansas. Gil went from Hays into World War II, was wounded on Omaha Beach during the invasion of Europe, returned to the United States and took a degree from Massachusetts Institute of Technology. He married a girl from Wisconsin, came to Tulsa in 1948 and has been there ever since, eight years with the Service Pipeline and the rest of the time with the Warren Petroleum Company until he joined Mid-America.

"When the Katy Railroad people and the Williams Brothers representatives started this pipeline, everybody in the oil business around Tulsa said, 'Well, it will never make it,'" Mr. Rohleder recalls. "In fact, when I left Warren for Mid-America, everybody there wanted to know why I was going to join up with a bankrupt outfit. I guess they thought Mid-America wouldn't make it because it was a new concept, and most people are afraid of change. They probably figured we didn't have enough talent and know-how in the organization to bring it off. But I had worked on some LP Gas marketing research when I was with Warren and, having made essentially the same sort of economic study I imagine the Katy people and Williams Brothers had, I saw the possibilities in a propane pineline, and I'm glad Bob offered me the job. It has been very profitable for me ever since. And it has been good for the industry. The tank cars and trucks were just not taking care of the business. They were always getting hung up in various marshalling yards. The customer would then be out of propane and the economics of the situation were driving propane out of the fuel market. I think MAPCO reversed that trend and really provided the services that were needed—and that is the reason the company has been so successful.

"While Williams Brothers were building the pipeline, the three of us—Mr. Thomas, Dave and I—were getting people together and forming an organization to operate it. We spent six months hiring a staff—finding men, then interviewing them. Then, after the construction phase, there was a cleanup of the line we had to do and what we call the initial line fill. That means getting liquefied petroleum gas and filling the pipeline with it all the way from west Texas to Minneapolis and to Janesville, Wisconsin, and that is a lot more difficult and complicated job than most people would imagine.

"When you get all through building a pipeline, all you've got is a piece of pipe in the ground containing nothing but air and waste material. So you have to displace the air and debris by running through the line what we call 'pipeline pigs.' A 'pig' is a shaft supporting some rubber cups that fit closely within the pipeline walls and are rimmed with metal scrapers which clean the inside walls of the pipe as they move along. Even after the pipeline is in operation, we run pigs through it about once each six months to scrape the inside." But the most demanding operation is that first cleaning and filling the pipeline with product. When filling a pipeline, the pig that cleans out the debris fits so tightly within the pipe that sufficient pressure is maintained behind it to keep the propane following along in a liquid state. In fact, the rubber cups on the pig fit so tightly and the pressure behind it reaches such a degree that the pig sometimes shoots out the end of a section of pipeline like a champagne cork.

Bob Hunter, one of the pipeline's early employees who worked on the line fill, likes to tell about the time "on the Missouri River, I never will forget. There was a bunch of Indians below us fishing from the river bank. Billy Hunter (another early Mid-America employee, who is still with the company) went down there and told them, 'Ya'll better get back out of the way. We're gonna run a pig out of this pipe in a few minutes.' Them Indians didn't pay any attention and kept on fishing. And pretty soon that pig blowed out into the river like a volcano, and ole Billy, he scattered Indians all up and down that part of the country. They left their fishing poles, buckets and all."

"Yeah, that pig comes out of there with a big rush and a lot of brown dirt and rust and it makes a hell of a noise," Billy Hunter added. "Hell, them Indians didn't know what it was. Hell, they took off running up that river bank and they didn't fish around that part of the river for two or three days. We sure scattered 'em—Winnebago Indians, they was . . ."

"We didn't have our telemetering equipment installed during this time," Gil Rohleder says, "so we had no central communications point in Tulsa. We had to communicate along the pipeline using radio and telephone. People at various points along the pipeline were putting product in, regulating the flow, while other crews along the way kept track of those pigs as they moved along by listening for them and reporting when one passed their position. You 'listen' for a pig by putting your ear on the pipe, and you hear its scratching noise maybe 40 miles away, like kids used to listen to a coming train by putting their ears on the railroad track.

"When a pig didn't arrive on schedule, we would raise the pressure. If that didn't get it moving, chances were the pig had hit a place where too much water had been left in the pipeline and it had frozen. We would then probably have to bore a hole in the pipeline, put a nipple on it and use alcohol to thaw out the water, then seal up the hole in the pipeline. That is the way we worked 24 hours a day. I mean it was just one of those times when if something happened to delay you, you stayed with it until you got the problem corrected and then moved on. We started in August and we had the West Leg filled to Pine Bend, Minnesota, near the Twin Cities, on December 1. We had the East Leg filled to Janesville, Wisconsin, on December 8.

"It took us 150 days just to fill that pipeline," Mr. Rohleder says. "At the time we had probably ten to fifteen LP Gas producing plants connected in west Texas and Oklahoma. Each of these could pump into the line, say, about 200 barrels an hour and we might have ten of these plants operating into the line on a given day. This would mean 20,000 barrels a day. That much LP Gas would fill about 30 miles of 8-inch pipe. We had roughly 2,000 miles of pipeline to fill, and we were doing this at the rate of 30 to 40 miles a day. That means 50 days if we didn't have any trouble and assuming that all those plants could always come in. But they were also supplying local markets and they couldn't give us product every day. And then we were taking product out of part of the pipeline already filled during the latter stages and distributing it to customers.

"The original line ran some 2,200 miles," Mr. Rohleder went on. "Now we have about 5,000 miles, including the offshoots into Illinois, through New Mexico and other places. We have also built a 10-inch second line parallel to the old main line to double the capacity in the most important areas. That original LP Gas Pipeline in 1960 had a capability of pumping 30,000 barrels a day from Conway, Kansas, to Pine Bend, Minnesota. Now we have a capability over that leg of pumping 84,000 barrels a day. We started the East Leg to Janesville with a capability of pumping 30,000 barrels a day and now it has the capacity to pump 118,-000 barrels a day.

"We started our line down south from Hobbs, New Mexico,

to Conway, with a capability of pumping 50,000 barrels a day and we can now pump 140,000 barrels a day over that segment. We have pumping stations about every 50 miles along the line and at last count, there were about sixty of these stations, totaling some 100,000 horsepower. Some of the pumps are driven by electric motors but a good majority are driven by gas turbines. Of course, everything is remotely controlled from our Central Dispatcher's office in Tulsa. At present, we can draw product out of the line from fourteen company terminals and there are also five or six independent terminals. Besides, we make deliveries to various refineries and chemical plants, including an SNG Plant in Morris, Illinois. So we have about thirty places where we can take product out of our LP Gas Pipeline."

What you can see above the ground's surface of MAPCO's pipeline are mainly the various terminals, each built around a flat-roofed one-story brick building. At the larger, more important terminals, the main room in this building is filled with various dials, controls and communications equipment. You look through a picture-type window at a line of eight and 10-inch pipes, shining white in color, with their accompaniment of valves. These pipes slant up out of the ground and are visible for 100 feet or so before disappearing back into the earth. The arrangement allows the pigs to be put into or taken out of a section of line during cleansing times. The powerful pumps, each in its blue-painted metal housing, flank the display of valves and pipes, and out in the distance great shining, white-painted steel storage tanks are mounted in parallel formation on their metal frameworks. The dispensing terminals north of Conway are also equipped with a row of pumps where the big trucks fill up with propane for distribution to customers over a wide radius where the pipeline doesn't go.

The most impressive installation along the entire system is the fractionating plant that MAPCO completed building in 1973 at its Conway terminal—a glistening complex of steel towers, each a dozen feet in diameter and some reaching 170 feet into the air. These are used to separate, or fractionate, a mixture of all types of LP Gas into the five separate principal components. Many of the liquefied natural gas producers that use the Mid-America system put a "raw" stream into the line, meaning it is an unrefined mixture of all the LP Gases after they are separated from the natural gas. MAPCO has another fractionating plant at Fritch, Texas, but the installation at Conway is the big one.

According to Gene Grounds, Foreman, the Conway fractionator can process a mixed natural gas liquids stream of 52,000 barrels per day. This stream can be separated into five purity products, ethane-propane, propane, isobutane, normal butane, and natural gasoline. The fractionator can make 15,000 barrels per day of ethane-propane, 15,000 barrels per day of propane, 4,000 barrels per day of isobutane, 8,000 barrels per day of normal butane, and 10,000 barrels per day of natural gasoline.

The mixed natural gas liquids stream is heated and moves through a series of towers to produce the needed purity products. An immense furnace produces the heat required for the process and in BTUs per day is equivalent to heating 7,000 homes for a period of one month. There are five principal towers in the installation, one for separating each of the five products. Each product is boiled off in a given tower and leaves the top part of the tower in a pure or specification state and it is then condensed back into a liquid under pressure for further movement to storage or the pipeline. The fractionator provides an economic service for the pipeline customers in that it allows them to reduce their investment in field plants that strip the liquids from gas and oil.

In 1975, some 200 shippers were using MAPCO's LP Gas Pipeline, although only about 20 of the larger ones provided 85 percent of the business. Customers range from the big producers such as Skelly, to small independent brokers. As a common carrier, the Mid-America line publishes a tariff of charges, on file with the Interstate Commerce Commission. The rate is the same for all customers, although charges have increased somewhat over the years. In mid-1975, it cost about 56 cents to transport one barrel of propane from Hobbs, New Mexico, to Conway. The line will take no less than 5,000 barrels of product in a batch, and it is necessary to plan shipments a month ahead so that on a given hour of a given day each customer will know when and how much of what product to put into the pipeline.

The sophisticated, computerized control system in Tulsa, which is manned 24 hours a day, allows the dispatcher on duty to know what is happening anywhere along the system. He can tell how many pumps are working, the pressure at any given point, what installations are putting how much of what product into the line and which are taking out how much of what product. The batches of the different products flow along inside the pipeline behind each other like cars, each loaded with a different product, in a freight train.

The dispatcher pays particular attention to pressure readings. If the pressure begins to get too high at some point, this may indicate some sort of blockage and danger of rupturing the pipe. If that happens, the dispatcher shuts down pumps up stream from the pressure build-up and thus begins lowering the pressure.

If he notes a dramatic fall in pressure, this could indicate a break in the pipeline. The Tulsa dispatcher immediately shuts off the pumps south of the apparent break, and closes the nearest valve north of it. This confines the escaping gas to a relatively short segment of the pipeline. The dispatcher notifies the nearest MAPCO emergency crew and state and local police, who seal off the area and, if necessary, evacuate people in the vicinity, while the emergency crew speeds to the scene and repairs the pipeline. That sort of quick, effective action has kept injuries and fatalities to a minimum from pipeline mishaps. In 98 percent of the relatively few breaks in the Mid-America Pipeline over the past fifteen years, there have been no injuries at all.

The pipeline began operating in 1960 by transporting propane only, and, although transportation of the other LP Gas products has increased in considerable degree, propane still constitutes 60 percent of the pipeline's throughput. For a number of years the system has operated at 100 percent capacity during the heating and crop-drying seasons. During the warm months, business is more erratic. In the gathering areas, south of Conway, the pipeline probably averages operating at 75 to 80 percent capacity the year round. But in the consuming area, business falls off rather dramatically during the summer, sometimes as low as 15 to 20 percent of capacity.

The efforts of Robert E. Thomas and the company's Board of Directors to offset this summer-declining income were mainly responsible for transforming Mid-America from a pipelining operation only to "a broad-based, integrated energy business," in words of MAPCO's 1972 Annual Report. By then, in addition to operating its LP Gas and ammonia pipelines, MAPCO had become a producer and merchandiser of liquefied petroleum gas and liquid fertilizers and was also into the production of natural gas, oil and coal.

Considering the fact that Mid-America had begun its life back in 1960 with only 7 percent equity in its property and 93 percent debt, it has required some imaginative and unique financing for the company to acquire such widespread and profitable holdings and, in the space of a short fifteen years, develop into one of the most highly regarded investments on Wall Street.

During construction of its original liquefied petroleum gas pipeline in 1960, Mid-America loaded more than 500 country weekly newspapers throughout the Middle West with advertisements, selling the LP Gas idea to farmers and residents of small towns. "We used every trick in the book," says Benton Ferguson, whose company was Mid-America's first ad agency. "Comic page-type ads were especially popular. In a small town weekly, an ad like that stood out like a walrus in a goldfish bowl."

Keep Your Pipeline Off My Place!

11

Without much question, the most sensitive operation in the Mid-America Pipeline's setup is its Right-of-Way Department, which is sometimes beset by verbal and written abuse, damage suits, threats of physical violence and other expressions of passionate emotions by enraged human beings.

It is the duty of the Right-of-Way Department to conduct the delicate negotiations with farmers and other owners of property through which Mid-America wishes to run its pipelines. And when you start dealing with a man about crossing his land with a pipeline that he fears may blow up at any time and cause bodily injury—or, almost as bad, despoil his crop of alfalfa—you encounter tensions and strains that make the Arab-Israeli peace negotiations seem calm and friendly.

Fortunately, such emotion-laden confrontations are the exception. Senior Vice President David A. Roach, top executive in the pipeline operation, reports: "In MAPCO's experience, about 99 percent of the property owners with whom we negotiate for rights of way turn out to be fair, honest, and accommodating people, when they are properly approached and informed."

While negotiating with Mid-America buyers, however, a few irate landowners have pounded on the tables so hard that they have fallen out of their chairs and lain exhausted on the floor. Groups of farmers, armed with shotguns, have confronted advancing pipeline crews now and then. On infrequent occasions, enraged landowners have physically assaulted the right-of-way procurers, and, of course, there have been many confrontations in the courts of law. And yet, it has been necessary for Mid-America officials to resort to legal condemnation to get rights-of-way in less than 5 percent of its acquisitions. One reason, as previously pointed out by Mr. Roach, is that most people are reasonable—in the long run, at least. Beyond that, the pipeliners over the years have learned a great deal about human nature in general and land negotiations in particular, and they have become quite expert.

"People give various reasons as to why they don't want us to put a pipeline across their land," according to Grover C. Denison, Manager of Mid-America's Right-of-Way and Claims Department. "Some act like they are afraid of the product we're shipping through the line. They try to make out like it is a terribly dangerous thing to have going under the ground near them. I don't really believe most of them actually think that—but that's one of the excuses they give. Most of these people have a big tank sitting on their farm right outside their home filled with the same product that is in the pipeline—so they couldn't be *too* afraid of it. And then they come up with all the inconvenience they are going to experience in farming on the land above the pipeline for the next four or five years. Some will try to claim that we reduce the productivity of their land by bringing up subsoil and mixing it with the good topsoil. You think you have reached a point where you have heard all the reasons—and then a new one will come up.

"We had one lady in Texas who said we caused an influx of rattlesnakes on her place by building a pipeline through it. Her explanation was that the soil out there is so hard-packed in the range country that the groundhogs can't come in and bore down through it. But when we opened up this hardpan with a pipeline ditch, we made a good soft place where the groundhogs could tunnel down into the ground to water. And when the groundhogs dig a den, the rattlesnakes then come along and occupy it and the rattlesnakes take care of the groundhogs. But groundhogs reproduce rather rapidly, so you always have groundhogs and you always have rattlesnakes. Anyway, this was her theory. I don't know if there was any truth in it. But it was just another way to say, 'I don't want your pipeline on my place.' "

Mr. Denison is a large-framed, easy-drawling Texan, who resembles physically somewhat the late President Lyndon B. Johnson. He possesses great diplomatic finesse, which is an extremely important quality for a man in his line of work. "Even though we pay good money for rights-of-way, we don't have any people coming up to us and saying, 'Here, come over and lay your pipeline on my property,' " he reports. "They had rather you put it somewhere else; so it's an uphill fight for us all the way. Most people have built up in their minds that a pipeline reduces the value of their property for resale purposes. Studies have proven this a fallacy, but that is difficult to convince the landowner trying to keep you off; he won't accept the word of the people who made the survey. And, to be truthful, a pipeline does put some restrictions, I guess, on the use you can make of land. We wouldn't want a building over our pipeline right-of-way, for instance."

Perhaps the most spectacular imbroglio between representatives of Mid-America and an irate landowner occurred in 1960 at Ashland, Kansas, during the construction of the original LP Gas Pipeline. The combatants were Robert M. Baker, an Ashland attorney representing Mid-America, and David S. Santee, a farmer of the area noted for his erratic behavior and temper tantrums and father of Wes Santee, the famed miler of the University of Kansas. The elder Santee refused to deal directly with Mid-America, and became enraged when the court condemned a strip of his land for pipeline right-of-way and awarded him only $734.86 damages. Santee demanded $75,000 damages.

When some Mid-America officials came to look over the strip of right-of-way, Attorney Baker reported in writing, Mr. Santee showed up and told the intruders, "how he would make a lot of them drop like flies at his feet," that "they might get me, but I will take a lot of them with me," and that he had "a lot of holes on his place that he had just as soon fill up with pipeliners." A few days later when a Mid-America pipe-laying crew actually came on his property, according to Attorney Baker, "Santee came driving up to the corner through the pasture in a terrible rage and pulled up about half a dozen stakes that the crew had driven in preparation for their work, cursing everyone around. We all stood in the middle of the road and never said a word. Santee then made known his intention of assaulting me personally, and commenced to climb over the fence. As Santee came across the ditch, I told him that if he laid a hand on me I would sue him for all he had. This didn't faze him, and I told him I would have him arrested for assault, but he kept coming, so I defended myself.

"He tried many times to hit me with his fists and after I caught one blow on my arm, I commenced to try to unbuckle my wristwatch. He then tried to kick me a number of times, and succeeded in kicking me on the left leg and right groin. However, I stepped back and he only grazed me in the groin. I then kicked him good—right in the family jewels! This stopped him. Apparently he had enough."

A day or so later, Mr. Santee was arrested on charges of assault and released on $500 bond. Later he was found in contempt of court for defying the condemnation order. The court, however, suspended sentence with the admonition that if there was "any more foolishness" Mr. Santee would be placed under a heavy peace bond or committed to jail. No more violence has erupted in the area since then, and at last reports, Mr. Santee and the Mid-America people were on quite friendly terms.

A pipeline right-of-way is generally 50 feet wide to accommodate a ditch 24 inches wide and not less than 36 inches deep that holds a steel pipe usually ranging from four to 10 inches in diameter. The 50-foot width is needed to store dirt and for all the construction activities. The ditch is generally dug 15 feet from the left boundary of the right of way and 35 feet from the right. A 24-x-36-inch ditch displaces a great deal of dirt, and that occupies almost all of the 15-foot-wide side of the right of way. The 35-foot width of right-of-way is needed as space for the pipeline crew to bring in pipe, string it and lay it on skids, occupying a width of five or six feet. The rest of the space is needed for equipment room, for welders, for the inspectors and for crews stringing pipe. Room is also required for two vehicles to pass and turn around, plus working space to get the pipe coated with a plastic jacket and welded. In any event, farmers can cultivate over the pipeline, which doesn't interfere with farming of the land after it has been buried for a short time.

Like other pipeline companies, Mid-America pays for its rights-of-way, generally on a per rod basis, which is generally $2 a rod in the lonely spaces of Texas and New Mexico with somewhat higher prices in the rich farmlands or the industrial areas of Iowa and Illinois. The pipeline companies keep in contact with one another as to the "going rate" for rights-of-way in the various areas, and they try to stay within these price ranges. Even so, the charges are rising steadily, and negotiations with landowners become increasingly difficult as time goes on.

"Thirty or forty years ago, putting down a pipeline was much simpler than now—from a right-of-way standpoint," Grover Denison says. "The pipeline companies back then seldom ever had to buy an easement. They'd just go out and start digging a ditch. If the fellow who owned the land came along and said, 'Hey, what are you doing there?' They would say, 'Why, we are building a pipeline.' And if the landowner didn't like it, the pipeline people would buy an easement from him. I have heard the old-timers talk about those days, although, personally, I wasn't fortunate enough to be involved with such relaxed attitudes. But even when I started, people were not as well educated as now; they understood very little about how to negotiate prices upward. They are becoming more skillful every day. Each time we do some new construction in an area, we encounter more opposition than we did the last time through.

"Twenty years ago landowners figured that pipelines just didn't bother anything. It was just out there in the field, buried, out of the way, out of sight, out of mind. Times were not so good, and farmers were glad to get that $1 a rod back then, which seemed like more money than $10 a rod does now. These days a lot of landowners don't want a pipeline through their property because they have big plans for industrial facilities to go there—or at least, they'll tell us they have such plans. Another big objection that they hit you with now is that everybody seems to think his property is potential subdivision land and, naturally, we all know that a pipeline through a subdivision would spoil a number of building lots. Aside from all these things and the matter of price," Mr. Denison went on, "we are faced with many unexpected or concealed reasons why landowners don't want to sell rights-of-way. One of these is the problem of heirs. Some landowners are afraid that the deal is going to end up in a family squabble. I remember trying to negotiate a right-of-way with one elderly lady and I was never able to get out of her the real reason she was reluctant to sell. Finally, we learned through her banker that she was afraid she would end up in an argument with her son over all that money we wanted to pay her. These are some of the unknowns that you have to dig out."

The most difficult types to deal with are people who are well fixed financially and don't need the money. It takes the right-of-way buyer longer to get to see them, and to finally consummate the deal. One of the most exasperating wealthy landowners in Grover Denison's experience was a resident of Lubbock, Texas, whom he calls "the Cat Lady." Mid-America wanted to buy a right-of-way through seven miles of her land, but the woman refused to see him for weeks. When he finally did get to see her it was only for a moment and the woman said, "I'll call you when I want to. I don't want a thing from you. So you just wait for my call." When she didn't call, Denison went out to her home. Nobody was there but the gardener, and he said she owned three houses in a row and lived in the middle one. "If you have a strong stomach, I'll show you through," the gardener volunteered. Denison said he had a reasonably strong stomach.

"He took me in the back door of one of those houses," Mr. Denison recalls, "and here were hundreds of cats with sandboxes everywhere and electric fans blowing to keep the air stirred up. This house was furnished—it wasn't any vacant house—and the cats were all over the chairs and tables and sofas and beds. Everywhere there were cats. The gardener said, 'The house on the corner is just like this. The one she lives in has got eighteen cats in it.' The gardener told me that the woman spent $5,000 a year buying meat to cook for those cats."

Denison had the bright idea of buying a cat and giving it to the woman as a sort of peace offering, but the gardener told him, "She don't want anybody giving her cats. She picks her own." Later, Denison gave the woman's secretary $50 to try to get him in her front door, but the "Cat Lady" flew into a rage and threatened to fire the secretary if she ever did such a thing again. "Finally we just wore her down," Denison says. "After months and months she finally agreed to see us. The last time Mid-America ran a pipeline through her property *we never did* get to see her. We finally managed to get her to tell us the name of her lawyer and we negotiated the deal through him. But she held back *his* name from us for three months. Said she didn't want us bothering him.

"Normally," Grover Denison says, "people are pretty receptive, although we do find some parts of the country where they will make you stand out on the porch and they will talk to you only through the screen door. They won't open that door. We encounter that every now and then, especially in Iowa and Illinois. That has always been their way on their farm. These people just don't seem to want strangers in their house. They are especially suspicious of Southerners. It's obvious to them when I open my mouth that I am a Southerner and a lot of them are very reluctant to talk to me for that reason. This comes under the heading of emotional dislike. Sometimes a landowner will take a personal dislike to you because he doesn't like the way you part your hair or some other trivial thing that upsets him. When that happens, it makes no difference what you do, you will not be able to get a deal with that owner. In this business, you learn that if one person can't buy from the owner, perhaps another agent can. So you send in somebody else to negotiate the deal."

One of Mid-America's most effective right-of-way buyers was the late Bob Coleman, but even Mr. Coleman was occasionally stymied because somebody did not like his personality. Sometimes these dislikes can arise because of simple, innocent error. "One time we were negotiating with a landowner in the Midwest whose name was Rhea," Grover Denison recalls. "We were virtually in agreement with him, but a couple of small items had to be ironed out, so we sent Bob Coleman in to finish up the deal. Unfortunately, the mapmakers had misspelled Mr. Rhea's name on the map Bob Coleman had; they had spelled it Phea. The only way to pronounce that was 'Pee.' When Bob addressed the landowner as 'Mr. Pee,' the latter flew into a rage and said, 'You did that purposely to put me on the defensive. I won't even talk to you. Send somebody else.' "

Rights-of-way are procured by professional Right-of-Way Buyers, who usually work as independent contractors. On a 100-mile project, Mid-America generally employs four buyers—one for every 25 miles. In most parts of the Middle West, there are an average of three separately owned tracts of land for every mile. Thus, a single buyer will negotiate with about 75 separate people or groups on this particular job. Right-of-way buyers are often retired people, or younger men who like to be independent. Most of them have worked for oil companies or in real estate or perhaps with insurance companies.

One of the greatest "salesmen" to work for the Mid-America Right of Way Department was no professional land acquirer but a young fellow named Bill Geis, attached to the company's Ad Valorem Tax Department. Mid-America had reached an impasse in trying to acquire rights-of-way on properties lying between the Mississippi River and Farmington, Illinois. Gene Bell, MAPCO's Chief Legal Counsel, Grover Denison, and six experienced right-of-way men flew to the area to try to get things moving. Bill Geis went along to do whatever he could. He was assigned a segment containing twenty-two separately owned tracts, and to everybody's astonishment the taxman secured rights-of-way on all twenty-two tracts in less than two weeks, while the six veteran right-of-way experts made no progress at all.

Dave Roach, Senior Vice President in charge of Pipeline

Operations, has speculated that, being inexperienced, the taxman didn't realize how difficult acquiring rights-of-way was—so he just went ahead and did it. Several weeks later, Grover Denison learned from the wife of one of the landowners signed by Bill Geis that the young taxman possessed salesmanship and an even greater degree of charisma than anyone had yet suspected.

"Prior to construction," Mr. Denison says, "I went back through McDonough County to distribute drafts to landowners our taxman had signed. At one house, when I told the lady of the house why I was there, she started laughing and said, 'So, that's what it was all about.' The lady then told me that her husband is stone deaf. He had told her about some young man who had shown him a map of something and had waved his arms in the air for a while, then handed her husband a document and a pen. The husband said, because of the friendly nature of this young man and the enthusiasm he exhibited, the landowner got the feeling that whatever it was the young man wanted must be all right, so he signed the paper."

Bob Coleman, who worked for Mid-America practically full time, was by far the company's most celebrated and spectacular right-of-way acquirer. Since his death in 1972, he has become something of a legendary character in the annals of Mid-America and MAPCO. "His initials were O. R. C.," according to Grover Denison. "The middle initial stood for Robert and we called him Bob. He would never tell us what the O. stood for. In writing reports, most professional right-of-way buyers are brief and businesslike—but not Bob Coleman, who penned his reports colorfully *and at great length*. Some of these have become classics in our departmental file. I think one reason Bob was so loquacious was that he got lonely in those motel rooms at night, and writing those long, folksy reports gave him something interesting to do. But he was also very sincere in wanting to give us the entire picture."

One of Bob Coleman's reports gives some interesting insights into a confrontation between pipeliners and railroad men. In this case, Mid-America was building its pipeline, in 1968, to carry anhydrous ammonia from Texas for use as fertilizer in the wheat and corn belt to the north. All the railroads in the area were strenuously opposed to the line, which would take from them valuable tank-car traffic. The confrontation Bob Coleman reported occurred at a point where Mid-America wanted to bore under tracks of the Chicago and Northwestern Railroad near Schaller, Iowa. The Chicago and Northwestern people had absolutely refused to grant a crossing right. At this point, the railroad had only an easement to run through the property. Rather than resort to a long court proceeding to get a permit, the Mid-America pipeliners secretly bought an acre of land on either side of the railroad tracks and made their plans to bore away without a permit. Bob Coleman's *drastically cut* report gives a colorful picture from the pipeliners' standpoint of what went on when Mid-America started to bore:

"When I arrived at the scene, our company inspector told me that some railroad men had ordered our people away and then they had left, indicating that they were going after either the sheriff or some high railroad official to stop us from boring. I told the inspector to have the contractor continue rounding up all the necessary equipment and if we all got thrown in jail, it would at least be a change of scenery. We brought all our equipment alongside the track and here came two railroad men in a car wanting to know what we thought we were doing. I told them I was glad they asked that question and I was going to answer it in a loud, clear and sharp manner so that there would be no doubt whatsoever. I then proceeded to explain how one goes about boring under a railroad, saying that we would dig a deep hole on the southside of the railroad track and come out on the other side. Then we would insert the casing and inside that the pipeline, joining the ends by welding and then we would start pumping anhydrous ammonia through the line to the tank area to the north.

"The railroad men said we had no permit. I informed them that we not only did not have one—that we did not want one—that I was standing on land owned by Mid-America and that the land across the tracks was likewise owned by Mid-America and that the land where the railroad was, was also owned by Mid-America subject only to the railroad's prior rights to an easement. . . . I also suggested that they should convey my personal beliefs to the railroad company that it ought to spend some time and money in cleaning up the surface of the railroad right-of-way, especially of the obnoxious weeds and thistles growing thereon, so that said weeds and thistles did not blow over on Mid-America lands outside the railroad right-of-way and spoil the beauty of our lands. . . . At this point, the supervisor of the division, a Mr. Davis, arrived. I told him practically the same thing I'd told the others and he said he was under orders to observe what we were doing. I said we would welcome that as we always enjoyed watchers and observers. . . . All was peaceful and quiet and the work was proceeding when I left."

A somewhat different type of problem occasionally encountered by pipeline right-of-way buyers is described in this report by O. R. Coleman from Kansas in 1971:

"The trouble with this landowner is that he is slightly off his rocker, has bats in his belfry, has lost part of his marbles—and besides that, he is a real ornery old coot. . . . When I knocked, he came to the door with tobacco juice running down four sides of his mouth, right through his chin whiskers and all, and he ordered me off the place. 'Git off and stay off . . . and git going . . .' I started to leave and he hollered at me and demanded to know, 'Where you from?'

"I told him I was from Claremore, Oklahoma. The man said come back and talk to him. I stood out there in a downpour of rain, much preferring the rain to having to go into his lair . . . this fellow said all kinds of crooks and bums had been bothering him and that he had orders from his son, Bob, to run every one of them off. He said the crooks had sold him lightning rods . . . fake paint jobs on his barn and had stolen from him. He said he had too much income to get relief or social security and he couldn't find a rest home that would take him. He'd had trouble with his first wife and his second one was no good. Several children had moved in on him and taken possession of his home, so he had to live out in the chicken house. I didn't see any chicken house, but figured it couldn't be much worse than the place he was calling his regular home. Finally we agreed that I would take the papers to his son, Bob, and the old fella said he would sign if Bob said so. Bob is a machinist and he was agreeable . . ."

Perhaps Mr. Coleman's most difficult and frustrating type of encounters occurred occasionally when he had to deal with persons involved with the Occult. In one case he called on a man named Foster and his wife, Mable, who dwelt in a one-time schoolhouse on a small farm in Nebraska.

"I called for the first time today at the Foster home," Mr. Coleman reported, "and found only the husband there. He was quite a strange-looking man with a beard and the most cockeyed man I ever saw in my life . . . his only companion at the time was a large tomcat. Mr. Foster informed me that he knew all about 'protane,' because he was once connected with a natural gas company in Louisiana. He then informed me that natural resources did not belong to anyone, but belonged to the Creator. I agreed. He asked what method we used in dealing with people—by visits and talks or by force? I assured him we used friendly methods with no force. He said that was the right way. He then wanted to know what method we used in digging the line and I told him we used the trenching wheel and the steel tape method. Again he said that was the right way.

"Mr. Foster then told me in rapid order that the Fiftieth Psalm mentioned the words Foster, Foster and Foster. He next said he had been receiving messages from outer space and he had obtained bits of information concerning the God of all Gods. There were a few bits he had not received yet, but he is still in touch with the interplanetary forces and will eventually be able to get all the dope. At this point, I informed him I would call again when Mrs. Foster was at home . . .

"The man told me that the woman I would meet was only the representative of the true Mrs. Foster but that this representative would receive me and help me out. Meanwhile, the large tomcat had gotten up on the kitchen table and was going all out for all the food in sight. It was nearly noon and I figured that when

Mrs. Foster—or her representative—got home and found the table bare, she might be kind of put out. However, I enjoyed watching the cat. But I did not dare to take my eyes off Mr. Foster for too long a time, being afraid that he would try to take me into orbit with him. He went on with a lot of wild talk concerning things not of this world and about interplanetary messages. I gathered from it all that I was expected later to attend a seance where we would learn if the Creator and the stars favored him granting us this easement for our pipeline . . ."

Now and then Mr. Coleman regaled the Tulsa office with reports of the recent adventures, triumphs and mishaps of landowners with whom the company had dealt in the past. One such report concerns, a farmer near Mapleton, Iowa. At the time he signed his right-of-way agreement, the landowner had insisted on being paid in MAPCO stock. He was told he could take the money MAPCO paid him and buy the stock, but he insisted that the payment be made directly in securities. So Grover Denison's department bought several shares of MAPCO common and gave them to the man as his payment. A year or so later, Bob Coleman brought the Mid-America people up-to-date on how the landowner was doing:

"I regret to report," Mr. Coleman wrote, "that our friend has not been doing too well lately. On my last visit before this one he seemed hale and hearty and in quite good spirits. In fact, he saluted me with hand upraised exclaiming, 'Heil Hitler' and 'Heil Mussolini.' But this time when I went by his home, I found he had suffered a broken ankle, he said, 'in nine places.' His wife told me he had fallen out of the second-story window during the night. Apparently he had awakened and thought someone was chasing him so he ran out the window . . .

"I got the straight dope, though, the other day in Onawa. They tell me there that he had been imbibing large quantities of beer during the day and early evening. After retiring upstairs, he needed to go to the bathroom during the night. Since the bathroom was downstairs, it seemed needless to keep running up and down the steps. He decided to use the upstairs window as a substitute. During one of these exercises he slipped and fell out the window two stories to the ground below. This broke his ankle and, I should think, helped sober him up . . .

"I just thought you would want to keep informed about our friend, since he is part owner of your company . . ."

I'd Rather Have 12
a Bastard

Pipeliners—the men who operate the big ditching machines, transport the pipe to the site and put it into the ground, weld together the joints, and cover over the ditch and those who fill the line with product and later maintain it—are a rough and ready breed, akin to the roughnecks of the old oil-field days and a sort of throwback to the gold seekers of 1849.

A story that pipeliners enjoy telling about themselves concerns the plight of an innocent farmer's daughter, who· lived in an area where a pipeline had recently been built and who found herself pregnant shortly thereafter. When she tearfully informed her father about her condition, the old gentleman flew into a rage, grabbed up his shotgun and loudly demanded, "What son of a bitch is the father? Tell me and I'll make him marry you."

"It is one of those fellows with that pipeline crew that was working through here last summer," the maiden revealed. The father gave a sign of resignation, laid down his shotgun and said, "Oh well, let's just forget *him*. I'd rather have a bastard in the family any day than a pipeliner for a son-in-law."

Real-life motel owners often have somewhat similar reactions to pipeliners as did the fictional father of the girl in trouble, as Mid-America's pipeline men have discovered from time to time. "When we were filling the original pipeline back in 1960 between Conway, Kansas, and Pine Bend, Minnesota," Bob Hunter, one of Mid-America's first pipeline employees, recalls, "a number of times we had to settle for smaller, scrubbier motels and hotels because the better ones wouldn't let us in. I remember particularly when we were moving into Atcheson, Kansas, we tried to make reservations in the leading motel in town, but some other pipeliners had been there before we arrived, and they wouldn't let us in. Because of the rowdy reputation pipeliners have or because sometimes of the shortage of motel or hotel space in some of those little Midwestern towns, our people used all sorts of unusual accommodations. Hell, we had people living in onetime skating rinks, barbershops, old restaurants and everywhere. They'd just move in a bed and a little furniture and take up light housekeeping for a few weeks while we were working in the area."

"Actually, the guys who tear up motels, restaurants, beerhalls and such are a little different from us," according to Billy Hunter, MAPCO Pipeline Supervisor stationed at Hobbs, New Mexico. Billy is one of the pipeline's first employees and the Division's most gifted raconteur. "Those fellas are construction crews and they are generally rougher and rowdier than the men, such as we were, who have a regular job with a company. But that is not to say that we don't work hard, play hard and have a lot of fun." Billy Hunter describes pipeline construction crew members this way:

"Pipeline workers come from everywhere and they've done everything. But mainly they just follow pipelines. They are rough-living people, but good people if you know how to take them. I've always enjoyed being around them. They usually say what they think and work hard and live high and die young. Some of them look like they are seventy years old when they are just about half that age. The life they live takes a lot out of them. They all make a lot of money and spend it and have a good time. There is a lot of overtime on these jobs. Most of them know their stuff, and it is real good when you get on a job with experienced pipeliners. Boy, you've got it made. Everyone knows his job and does it. A lot of them own farms some place, where they go during the winter and spend the cold months drinking and enjoying themselves. Then when it gets warm again they start out to work on the pipelines. The pipeline-building season usually lasts from early spring until cold weather—except in the case of Mid-America. We are always in a hurry on our jobs, and we often put down pipe in frozen ground under several feet of snow."

Traditionally, the journeyman pipeliner will drop whatever he is doing and tear off to Timbuktu or some place when he hears that a big job is starting there. In this connection, Oral Trammell, Technical Supervisor for Mid-America at Hobbs Station, New Mexico, tells this yarn:

"This pipeliner died and went to Heaven, and when he saw St. Peter he said 'I'd like to get in here; I've got a lot of friends in here.' St. Peter said, 'We've got all the pipeliners we can handle in here now. We don't need you; we are overcrowded with pipeliners.'

"The pipeliner then said, 'Well, if you will let me in there for a few hours, I think I can make some room.' So St. Peter said, 'Okay, come on in.' The pipeliner got in there with his old friends and he started a rumor that the fire had gone out in Hell, and they were laying a big gas pipeline from west Texas into Hell to get the fire going again. He told them, 'This is the biggest job you ever saw.' And all those ole boys started going to St. Peter and saying, 'Let me out of here. I want to get down to that big job on that big new line.' It was just a big ole lie, of course, told to make a little room. And sure enough, first thing you know, all those pipeliners were gone.

"Finally, after a few days in Heaven, the pipeliner who had started this movement went to St. Peter and he said, 'You'd better let me out of here, too. There just *might be* something to that damn rumor I started.' "

When oldtime Mid-America pipeliners get together at divisional meetings and such, they like to reminisce, after the day's sessions are over, and talk about their adventures—especially on some of the more spectacular jobs, such as building the 400-mile spur in 1972 from the Four-Corners area in northwestern New Mexico, southeastward across the state to the Texas border. This job took them through rough, mountainous terrain during a bitter winter and included colorful contacts and confrontations with hippies, Indians and history. The original employees of the pipeline most especially like to recall, however, those days of filling the main line with propane during the fall and early winter of 1960, from Conway, Kansas, to Pine Bend, Minnesota, and to Janesville, Wisconsin. Three of Mid-America's early employees and biggest talespinners who are still with the company are Billy Hunter, Bob Hunter, Expediting Supervisor stationed at Tulsa, and Harvey Henderson, of Tulsa, who is Manager of Pipelines for the entire system. Harvey likes to tell about the day Billy Hunter came to work for Mid-America:

"I had gone up to Conway to work as the Pipeline Supervisor of the West Leg," he says, "but I didn't have anybody working with me when I got there at first. Mr. Rohleder telephoned me from Tulsa and said he had talked to a fella by the name of Billy Hunter down in Arkansas, and did I know him and would I be interested in hiring him as my equipment operator. I said yes, I knew Billy, and I would be happy to have him if he wanted to work with us. They hired him and told me that Billy would be arriving at Conway on a bus around four or five o'clock in the afternoon. I asked a couple of the construction pipeliners, Bob Crow and a fellow named Rusty Frick, if they would meet Billy when he got to the bus station. I said to them, 'When you guys go to pick up Billy, don't do any drinking around him because he is very religious and doesn't go in for that sort of thing at all.' In the meantime, I had talked to Billy on the telephone and told him the same thing about Mr. Crow and Mr. Frick.

"After Billy arrived that evening, I was kind of late getting to his motel. When I arrived there, the three of them were just sitting in Billy's motel room, visiting with one another as polite as could be. All of them were thinking to themselves, 'Boy, I sure could use a cold beer right now.' After I had sat around in the room a little while, I said, 'Well, I believe I'll have me a beer.' All of them looked at me like I had cussed out loud in church. And then they caught on. I expect that this was the longest time any three pipeliners had ever sat together in a motel room stone cold sober."

Bob Hunter says, "We all kind of met at Conway. That is where we started knowing each other. I kind of think of us when we started on this Mid-America job as being sort of like the Lewis and Clark expedition. All of this was new to us. Billy had been working down in Arkansas for a crude oil line. I had been with Williams Brothers. Harvey had been with the Service Pipeline Company. This was the first experience any of us had had handling liquefied petroleum gas. We didn't know really what to do, and we made a lot of mistakes. We didn't know about the pressure to keep propane under or exactly how to run the pigs in a propane line, or how much water was left in the line and how it was going to react to the propane and all that. We found out quick that water would freeze the damn line and get ice plugs in it when propane struck it, and we had to figure ways to get the ice out. We learned that you just couldn't let propane run down the pipeline like you could crude oil. You had to keep enough pressure behind those pigs so that they moved forward, but at the same time, you had to make the pigs provide enough resistance to hold the propane back under sufficient pressure to keep it in a liquid state. It is a delicate sort of balancing act. We worked from one valve to another, and they are about 25 miles apart. When the propane didn't arrive at the time it should, it generally had been stopped by an ice plug. Then we would have to bore a lot of holes up and down the line until we located the plug and thawed it out. Of course, we would have to seal up every hole. Nowadays, we know different and better ways of filling a pipeline with LP Gas without all that trouble—and a lot of other people have profited by our mistakes."

"And of course, we had leaks," Harvey Henderson says. "One of the orneriest leaks we ever had was close to the end when we were filling the pipeline up near the Pine Bend terminal. That was in December. One night some fella who lived near the pipeline down at Mankato called up and said he'd had an explosion in his basement and he thought it was a pipeline leak. We went down there in a hurry to see about it, arriving about dark. He had a mean dog and that damned old dog ran out and bit me.

"We had a horrible time locating that leak. It was right near a road crossing and the line was buried deep there. We jackhammered that ground for days. It was frozen, both from the weather and the escaping propane. The land around those parts is full of tile for draining water in wet weather and the propane had gotten into this tile and seeped a long way through the ground, making it difficult to locate where it had come from. But it was escaping into this fellow's basement and every time his furnace kicked on he had a little explosion. It took us a lot of time and two jackhammers. We dug on the north side of the road first, but it turned out the leak was on the south side when we finally did find and fix it."

"We didn't have an accident in our bunch during the whole job," Bob Hunter says. "Why we didn't I don't know. Several of our fellows lost their breath a time or two, damned near scared to death, but other than that. . . . I remember one time when we were working in Iowa some place, Harvey [Henderson] went four days and nights without any sleep. One time I was so sleepy I ran off the road in a pickup and dozed off and pretty soon Harvey came along and woke me up and we were on our way. We were out there in the snow wearing those heavy boots that made our feet so sore that we could hardly walk. Finally one night, Mr. Rohleder said, 'Hell, you all go and get some rest.' And boy, we did. We headed straight for the beer joint."

"We worked mighty hard but we had a lot of fun," Billy Hunter says. "Everybody had a good sense of humor. We got a pretty good working knowledge about places to eat throughout that part of the country and dance floors and especially beer joints. I remember one time we went into a place where a fellow and his wife had heard that the pipeline was coming and they opened up a beer tavern especially for us, I think. It was real small but the pipeline crews liked this couple. So at night and when we had a rainy day, everybody would go in there and drink beer and once a week, the man would give it away free. It got so crowded you couldn't get in. By the time the pipeline was finished, the man had paid for his bar. He said, 'I wish a pipeline would come through here every week and it would rain every other day.'

"I never will forget: We had two ole boys up there in Minnesota sitting out there in a pickup truck one night waiting for propane to arrive. The valve was open so they could see the gas when it started out. When propane starts coming out of a pipeline it settles on the ground like smoke. These two fellows had been working two or three days without any sleep, and they dozed off there in the pickup. While they were sleeping, a fog moved in. Hell, they waked up and saw the fog and thought it was a terrible lot of propane they had let get loose. They ran and shut off the valve and got to a phone and called up Harvey and told him there was a propane pall all over the bottoms in that part of Minnesota. We were down at Mankato and we looked out the window and it seemed like the escaping propane had gotten all the way to us. Finally we learned it was just fog. The fellas in the pickup were Frank Bray and a fellow named Piper. Ole Frank never did like much to be reminded of that night.

"Frank. He was a dandy. Ate apples all the way. And we had another guy named Howard May. He ate hamburgers all the time. We picked him up in Lincoln. Yeah, we'd eat them sardines and potted meat and canned beans and stuff at midnight just like it was midday. Bad as the food was in those restaurants all through that part of the country, it tasted pretty good after you had been living for several days on that canned stuff.

"The best eatin' I ever did on a pipeline job," Billy Hunter recalls wistfully, "was one time when I was inspecting the construction work while we were putting the pipeline across the Mississippi River from Iowa over into Illinois. Williams had a big dredge on a barge up from Louisiana. They had an old Cajun woman on there cooking for the hands—and boy, could that old lady cook. I had me a little old rented boat that I could go back and forth in, and I went over there to that barge right quick and got acquainted. Then I'd get there for breakfast every day and try to hit all the meals. That old lady would set out this trotline with plastic jugs as floats, and she would catch these big catfish and she would cook fish and I would go there and do some mighty big eating. She'd make them big ole cathead biscuits and with sorghum syrup, boy it was fine."

"We didn't eat bad on that first Mid-America job when we could get back from the pipeline to where some of our wives were staying," according to Bob Hunter, a man of large girth, denoting thousands of good meals over the years. "Several of us had brought our wives along. We would try to find apartments or rooms to rent that had kitchens because the restaurant food was so terrible in those little towns. We'd leave the ladies there while we went out a day or two or three on the pipeline, and we'd come back as often as we could. Before the weather got too cold, we did real well, had some fine cookouts. We made barbeque pits and cooked barbeque and a lot of beans. We took care of ourselves pretty good on food. We ate a lot of red beans, all of us being from places like Oklahoma, New Mexico, Texas and Arkansas. Anyway, pipeliners always eat a lot of red beans—just beans and cornbread are fine, but a little ham when you can get it makes it better."

"We had a two-story building we were living in at Lincoln, Nebraska," Billy Hunter recalls. "Harvey and I lived on the top floor. We had a kitchen up there. Bob and his wife and a fellow then working for us named Drummond and his wife lived on the bottom floor where there wasn't any kitchen. So the womenfolk would come up to our kitchen and do all this cooking. Harvey's wife was coming up from home to join us, but he didn't tell her about Bob's wife and Drummond's wife who were up there cooking in our kitchen, although he did tell her where we lived. So she came up there and found two other women in our place. It was kind of hard to explain. . . ."

"The ladies, who were all from down South, got along pretty well until the cold weather set in. Then they almost froze to death. They had some terrible times getting the cars started on cold mornings," Bob Hunter recalls. "You'd see three or four of them out in the street behind one of those cars, pushing, trying to start it, slipping and sliding and falling in the snow. I guess Billy's wife had the most traumatic experience with the cold. It was already wintertime when she moved up from Arkansas where we were in Sioux City. But it had been hot when she left home and she was wearing summer clothes. When Billy drove her into Sioux City, to the motel where we were staying, it was late at night, and they left her suitcases out on the car's luggage rack. That night it rained and froze hard, and the next morning they couldn't open the suitcases and they couldn't get them off the car. So Billy's wife showed up out there in zero weather wearing a pair of shorts with open-toed sandals and no socks on."

"Yeah," Billy Hunter says, "she got mad right then and she never got over it." A few days later when they were out on the pipeline, Billy got what his friends call "one of the shortest phone calls in history." According to Bob Hunter, "Billy said, over the phone, 'Hello. . . . O.K. . . . Good-by.' Then he turned around to me with the damndest look on his face and he said, 'She's gone.' Billy sat there a little while and then he said, 'I may just go with her.' But he stayed on with us."

"When we got up to Minnesota it was *really* cold," Billy Hunter says. "They had a big bunch of people working on the terminal up there—a lot of skilled folks doing a lot of little jobs. In other words, union help. They had a little house built out there where they stayed most of the time warming themselves beside a stove. These Minnesota people used to say to us, 'Boy, you Southern people are going to freeze to death up here.' Finally I told them if they didn't get to hell away from that damn stove, we sure enough were going to freeze to death. They were in there all the time taking up all the warm spots. Those natives up there got just as cold as we did, but they had learned more about how to crowd up to the stove."

What makes these MAPCO pipeliners willing to knock themselves out on the job on occasion, go for days without sleep—and enjoy it, they say—is the feeling that they are constantly doing something new that hasn't been done before, pioneering even in these overdeveloped times. Billy Hunter puts it this way:

"I think what sold me on this company to begin with was when they told me that they were gonna pump propane and stuff in a way that nobody had ever pumped it before. 'Hot damn,' I said, 'I want to get in on that.' I like MAPCO because it is the sort of company that figures, 'If there is a profit in this new thing, we'll try it.' In this company you don't use the word 'can't,' especially around Mr. Rohleder. It's not in our pipeline dictionary. This company is interested in progress and looking ahead; if it sounds possible, try it, do it—make it work. To me, working for Mid-America is kind of like those people flying those rockets up to the moon. Hell, practically everybody has got a pipeline—but we've got unusual ones. And it's getting more unusual all the time.

Every time you turn around something new is happening. That makes it pretty nice. Some people think about getting these jobs where they can just sit around and wait for retirement. Hot damn, you might as well let somebody take you out and shoot you. You lose ambition for just about everything. But with this outfit, you can take some pride in what you're doing—because so often it's what nobody has ever done before and there just ain't everybody who can do it.' "

Billy Hunter worked regularly in that "damned polar region" of Iowa, Minnesota and Nebraska for Mid-America until 1963. Then, he says, "I got a chance to come down here to Hobbs Station in the sun, and so I took it." As Pipeline Supervisor in the Hobbs area, Billy is in charge of the emergency crews that go out to fix the pipeline leaks. He spends many of his weekends driving 500 miles or more, putting out warning signs to other pipeline builders who are about to cross Mid-America's right-of-way, and he has charge of inspection of new construction.

The most colorful adventures in pipelining encountered by Billy Hunter or any of the other Mid-America employees who were involved resulted from the preparation and building of the 400-mile spur across New Mexico in 1971–72. About a year before construction began, Gene Bell, MAPCO's Secretary and General Counsel, was sent as a sort of special emissary to supervise acquiring of rights-of-way and to pacify and secure the cooperation, if possible, from four basically hostile groups—the Indians, the State administration, the ecologists, and the archeologists. "This was right at the beginning of industry's confrontations with the ecologists, so I had to worry about preserving the environment and historic sites," Mr. Bell reports.

"It was hard for me to see how just burying a pipeline through a lot of sand and rocks was going to hurt the desert, but the archeologists were set on preserving every piece of broken pottery left by forgotten tribes, and the ecologists were hollering especially loud about protecting the black-footed ferret and the American bald eagle. They absolutely refused to let us have any kind of construction going on where the bald eagle was nesting. We never did see a black-footed ferret, so far as I know."

Mr. Bell leased an airplane and flew members of the Sierra Club, the State Geological Society, and the Archeological Society over the proposed pipeline route. "We approached the matter in an attitude of cooperation, rather than confrontation," he says. "As a result of our meetings, MAPCO hired Curtis Schaafsma, an anthropologist, to survey the route ahead of construction and mark all the historical sites where ancient towns and villages had been and which contained buried artifacts."

The Indian tribes were suspicious and resentful of the pipeline project. "We were dealing with the Navajos, the Zia, and the

Santa Ana Pueblos," Gene Bell recounts. "I got along fine with the Zias. The Governor of that tribe was a fine young Indian and I enjoyed working with him. But we still had problems. The Indians have certain religious holidays, and when one of them arrives, nobody outside the tribe can get on their land. So we had to gear things up that none of our people or equipment moved on their reservations at these times. I was even afraid to let a jeep come on the reservation while we were making the survey, so our people had to walk the whole way across."

MAPCO's General Counsel also had his problems with officialdom, both Indian and the State's. The Governor of New Mexico didn't like the idea of a pipeline that would carry off the LP Gas, which he thought would be better used for consumption within the State. The problems of the Governor of the Santa Ana tribe of Indians were more basic; Mr. Bell's first task was to get the Governor to hold a council meeting.

The New Mexico pipeline construction began in the late Fall and was finished the following April, according to Billy Hunter, one of nine Mid-America inspectors who kept track of the contractor's expenditures and the quality of construction. "I don't know if you would call this a colorful job, but it sure was different," Mr. Hunter reminisces. "It would have been nice work if the weather hadn't been so miserable. You think of New Mexico as being warm. Hell, Cuba, New Mexico, is the North Pole of the U.S.A. It can be hot everywhere else, but they'll have snow in Cuba. One time I got stranded there for a couple of days and nights in the cold and snow. All the motels were full and the water even froze in the town water tank. Driving got so bad in those mountains from the snow that we had to use tractors for transportation instead of cars.

"And we ran into trouble with the hippies. There was a colony of about 3,000 of them around Placitas, between Albuquerque and Santa Fe. They didn't want anything modern coming through there. They said those little piñon trees had been striving for a hundred years to make it, and they didn't want us cutting them down. This was just destroying life, you know. And the Earth is their Mother, they said, and we were putting a big scar on their Mother by digging this pipeline. They didn't like that a bit. They would lie down in the road and try to block us. They would knock the glass windows out of our pickups. They would curse our machinery, and the contractor finally had to hire guards to protect it.

"They are kind of religious people, I guess, and they told me one time—they said, 'We're gonna have a little session with God. Come up and meet with us.' I thought, 'Damn, I need all the help I can get.' So I went to their meeting, but I hadn't been there more than fifteen minutes before I could tell that what they were doing was trying to pray me into Hell instead of Heaven. So I got out of there right quick.

"I liked the Indians pretty well," Billy Hunter says. "They are easier to deal with than a lot of the poor whites and certainly them hippies. But we got into some trouble with the Indians, too. When we were going through some Indian country there was a lot of snow, which we graded back off our right-of-way. The Indians kept three or four thousand ponies up in those mountains, and the ponies came out and started grazing where we had been scraping. They got over into some land owned by the Bureau of Land Management. The BLM people impounded those ponies at Cuba. The Indians got all excited and said we were responsible. If we hadn't moved the snow, the ponies would have stayed back in those draws, where they usually went in cold weather. But when we moved the snow, the sagebrush started sticking up out of the ground, and the ponies came out to eat.

"The BLM sold a few of them, but the Indians finally got back almost all of their ponies, and we didn't have to pay for them. The Indians came down from the reservation and sat around most of the night and got a little drunk, and they set fire to the corral and the ponies all got out and the Indians got 'em back. The Indians said later it was just an accident. They had built the fire a little too close to the corral fence.

"I made a lot of friends up in Indian country," Billy reports. "One time the Navajos invited all of us to their Squaw Dance, which is a colorful ceremony. Then the Zias had us to their Corn Dance, a big festival sort of like the Fourth of July with all kinds of things to eat. But I can't brag too much about Indian food. It's lamb mostly. Those little trading-post restaurants sell you Navajo tacco. If that don't kill you or cramp you too much, you can get by a whole day on one of them. And the food in some of those Spanish restaurants is full of red pepper. One morning I took one bite out of a green chile omelet—I thought 'green' meant it wasn't so hot— and God Almighty, I burned 'til noon. Everything in that part of the country tastes like chili. You get a doughnut; it tastes like chili. The damn water even tastes like chili.

"The Indians have some cars that are dandies—mostly old, old, old Buicks. They drive old-model pickups that are called Navajo Coupe de Villes. I was always fascinated by this: An Indian will drive up to a filling station out in the desert in an old rattletrap car. You can see for miles and miles and there ain't a thing worth mentioning between here and the horizon. But that sucker will have two gallons of gas put in his car and he will leave and I could never figure where in hell he goes. Why, you can see further than the two gallons of gas would take him.

"But I liked the Indians pretty well. We took the Zia tribe one of our MAPCO flags, white with a blue MAPCO insignia in the center. They put it in their Council Lodge right alongside the United States flag and the State flag of New Mexico. But I'm here to tell you, those Council meetings can get pretty rough," Billy says. "It's hot and tight in there and kind of smelly and half or more of 'em are drunk. They talk In-din most of the time, and you can't tell what they are saying. But occasionally they will come out with an English word or phrase.

"After a while, as the crowd got drunker and talked louder and longer, we would get to thinking, 'Well, we might as well leave. They are not talking about our problems any longer. They are off on something else by now.' And then, all of a sudden, we'd hear one of 'em holler out in English, *'Pipeline Son of a Bitch!'* And we'd know they were still talking about us."

The Saga of "Smoky" Billue

13

For the past quarter of a century, the most exotic and colorful character in the Liquefied Petroleum Gas Industry has been a large and loquacious gentleman by the name of "Smoky" Billue, of Webber's Falls, Oklahoma.

Gene Grounds, Superintendent of MAPCO's Fractionating Plant at Conway, Kansas, recalls his first meeting with Garrison Haines Billue as follows: "This great big fellow, weighing maybe 300 pounds and apparently in his latter fifties, whom I had never seen before, came stomping into my office like he owned the place. His hair was in a ponytail, under an immense sombrero, and he wore a red shirt and a fancy leather vest. A big Colt .45 was stuck in his beaded belt, and he carried a Bowie knife in a sheath sewn into his intricately tooled red-and-white Texas boots. I was trying to decide how to throw him out and not get scalped while doing it before realizing that here was one of the main men who had made it possible for the LPG Industry to become as large and profitable as it is today."

Gil Rohleder, MAPCO Vice President in charge of Pipeline Operations, tells of the day he took Smoky to luncheon in the crowded cafeteria of the Skelly Building in Tulsa, where MAPCO's general offices were located. "That day, Smoky was wearing a suit of fringed buckskin, like a plainsman of the Old West," Mr. Rohleder relates. "He was carrying an assortment of oldtime weapons and a large moose horn was hung around his neck by a buckskin thong. Right in the middle of lunch, Smoky raised the moose horn to his lips and said to me, 'I think I better blow on my horn and get these folks' attention and make a speech.' I finally dissuaded him, but with considerable difficulty."

Until his retirement in 1974, when he was 62 years old, the irrepressible and unpredictable Smoky Billue, in his colorful costumes, with his exotic artifacts and erratic behavior, was the most startlingly conspicuous figure in attendance at various LP Gas and other fuel conclaves. Actually, Smoky Billue is an intelligent, articulate and well-informed man—an original thinker and a millionaire several times over. His colorful costumes and peculiar behavior were just part of his robust sales campaign to promote and capitalize on his great idea, which has done as much as any other single development to put the distribution and sale of propane and other liquefied petroleum gases on a practical, commercial basis and elevate the LPG Industry into the category of big business.

For 40 years after commercial sales of LP Gas began in 1912, the principal drawback had been that the big demand for the product existed only during a few months of the year, namely the home heating season. Yet, the liquefied petroleum gases were being brought out of the ground constantly throughout the year. It was impractical to store surplus LP Gas during the warm months in any conventional facilities, such as aboveground pressurized steel tanks, because this storage was too expensive. And, without adequate storage facilities, it was impossible during the cold months to get enough propane to consumers to supply the demand. As a result, much of the valuable LP Gas products deriving from crude oil and natural gas was flared—wastefully burned at gasoline refineries and methane processing plants because the producers had no other way to dispose of the stuff.

Smoky Billue's solution to this problem rests, literally, in a bed of salt—specifically the great salt deposits left buried from ancient, forgotten seas. The deposits begin in Kansas and extend southwestward all the way to southern Texas and New Mexico, ranging from 100 to 200 feet thick. The salt layer is 700 feet below the surface in Kansas, then slants downward to a depth of about 2,700 feet in the Texas–New Mexico area. What Smoky did was drill a well down into the saltbed, then circulate through it thousands of barrels of fresh water. That gradually dissolved great caverns in the underground salt deposits, large enough to hold thousands of barrels of hydrocarbons in each cavern. This system was to provide almost unlimited areas of economical storage for propane, butane and natural gasoline and give the LP Gas Industry what it had been looking for in order to become a more viable enterprise.

Smoky began washing out salt caverns in the early 1950's. Thus, by the time Mid-America Pipeline was constructed, salt caverns were already plentiful, providing abundant, cheap storage. A few years earlier, such facilities wouldn't have been there—another example of the fortunate timing of the Mid-America Pipeline project that has had so much bearing on its remarkable success.

Over the years, Mid-America from time to time has leased storage space in the salt caverns Smoky Billue constructed and owned in the McPherson-Conway area. But MAPCO's Pipeline Division now uses principally salt caverns that it constructed and owns and in 1975, was operating 38 salt caverns, with eight under construction, around Conway, and nine at Hobbs, New Mexico. The largest, which is at Conway, holds 686,000 barrels of product, or 28,812,000 gallons. (The LP Gas Industry counts a barrel as 42 gallons.) The other Mid-America salt caverns range in capacity mainly between 100,000 and 200,000 barrels. Thus, in mid-1975, the company owned and operated salt caverns with total storage capacity of about 9,000,000 barrels, with caverns under construction that will contain probably a total of 1,200,000 barrels. The pipeline began operations in 1960 with only three salt caverns at Hobbs and three at Conway, plus some aboveground steel storage to the north —a combined storage capacity of less than 500,000 barrels.

"If we didn't have as much storage facilities as we do now, we could not serve our customers satisfactorily in critical times," Gil Rohleder says. "We use the storage mostly for propane, which has three times greater consumption during the five cold months— November through March—as during the seven warm months. Propane that is produced, but not consumed, in summer goes into storage. Our present storage capacity has allowed us to have adequate propane in the various consuming areas to meet the challenges of the coldest winters."

Throughout the winter, the storage caverns, which are drawn upon heavily during cold spells, are replenished with propane in times when the weather moderates. Butane, ethane, isobutane, butane-propane mix and natural gasoline are also stored in the caverns, which are used constantly as reservoirs to have ready at all times whatever type of product any customer might order. Otherwise, the customer might have to wait until the type of product he desired happened to be flowing north in the pipeline from the producing area. Its storage facilities permit Mid-America to schedule its shipments from producers a month in advance, and generally make for a smoother, more efficient operation.

At Greenwood, Nebraska and Farmington, Illinois, where there are no underground salt formations, Mid-America employs another type of underground storage, which is dug out like a mine. "We sink a shaft down to a formation of impervious rock—in this case, shale," Mr. Rohleder explains. "We have to work in a substance that will not allow LP Gas to pass through it and escape into the ground. We go down anywhere from 200 to 500 feet, using regular mining tools, and take out half of the shale in an area about the size of a city block and 25 feet high. We use the drift and pillar type of mine construction, leaving a pillar of shale 25 feet square to hold up the roof at intervals of every 25 feet of mined-out corridor. We pile the material dug from the mine on top of the cavern and sod it down so that you can't tell by looking aboveground that the storage cavern lies beneath.

"Our mined underground storage will hold 400,000 barrels of product each at Greenwood and Farmington. Mine storage is more expensive than salt caverns, but much cheaper than aboveground steel storage, which—at present, in 1975—costs about $40 for each barrel of storage capacity. Mined storage costs about $8 a barrel to build, and salt cavern storage costs about $2 per barrel of capacity."

The underground formation that makes possible the salt caverns is the same substance as table salt, except that it contains sand and other impurities and it is not granulated. The formation is crystalline, and looks something like a wall of dirty glass bricks. It takes from three to six months to leach, or wash, out enough salt from underground to form a cavern capable of holding 100,000 barrels of product. Gilbert Rohleder has described the process of leaching out the cavern, and later of storing and removing product from it, as follows:

"We drill down to the top of the salt formation and insert a piece of pipe anywhere from 13 to 20 inches in diameter, which we cement to the sides of the hole. This pipe becomes our access to the salt formation. On top of this pipe we put a wellhead, or "Chrismas Tree" in oil-field parlance. We put inside the Christmas Tree the top end of a pipe 8 inches in diameter that extends inside the larger pipe down into the salt. This serves as the channel to pump fresh water down to dissolve the salt and to bring out the brine. On the surface of the ground we dig a brine pit, capable of holding probably 300,000 barrels of brine, and line its inside with plastic to keep the brine from escaping into the ground and killing nearby vegetation. We use the brine from the pit to force the liquefied petroleum gas out of the salt caverns, when we need it.

"After we have washed out enough salt to form an underground cavern of the desired size—we know this by the amount of brine we have brought out—the cavern is ready for use. We pump propane, or another of the liquefied gases, down through the outer pipe—the portion between the outside of the 8-inch pipe and the inside of the larger pipe that surrounds it. The LP Gas must be pumped down under sufficient pressure to force up through the inner pipe and out into the brine pit as many barrels of brine as we put in of LP Gas. We can fill the cavern to capacity with LP Gas, or use only half of its capacity or any portion thereof. The remaining space continues to be filled with brine. The brine is two and a half times as heavy as, say, propane. Thus, brine remains in the bottom of the cavern and the LP Gas on top of it. Water and LP Gas will not mix; hence, it is not necessary to refine or purify the LP Gas after it comes out of storage.

"To remove the liquefied petroleum gas from the cavern, we simply pump as many barrels of brine down through the 8-inch center pipe into the cavern as we want to bring out of LP Gas. It is not necessary to pump the brine down under pressure. The much heavier brine easily forces the liquefied gas up through the outer pipe and into the pipeline.

"If you could see down there," Gil Rohleder says, "an underground salt cavern for storaging 100,000 barrels of liquefied petroleum gas would look something like a flat wheel lying on its side, about 100 feet thick and 200 feet in diameter. We keep the product stored down there under sufficient pressure for it to remain in liquid form, but not enough pressure to fracture the formation. This would cause the salt to crack so that the propane or other stored gases might end up in a farmer's well or some other place where we don't want it."

Gaines Harrison Billue, who with the help of several associates, originated this unique, remarkably practical and widely used system of storage, says he got his nickname back around 1948 while building a carbon plant at Odessa, Texas, for the Sid Richardson Gasoline Company. "A fellow named Benny Keeland, who worked for a supply company, came out to help me to get a regulator running right," Smoky reports. "There was a bunch of smoke all around where I'd been working for three or four days and nights, getting the plant started up, and I was pretty black with soot when he found me. Benny said, 'Well, here is Smoky the Bear.' So that's where I got the name Smoky."

In the summer of 1975, Smoky Billue was living in Webber's Falls, a small rural community some 70 miles southeast of Tulsa on the banks of the Arkansas River. A down-river dam has enlarged the Arkansas to the size of a lake at Webber's Falls, and a great deal of local thought is devoted to the art of catching catfish. Smoky rolls silently around the town in a battery-powered golf cart, accompanied by his ancient hounddog, Queenie. He says he bought the golf cart originally for his late father, after the old gentleman's automobile driving habits became too erratic for the community's peace of mind.

Smoky lives in a comfortable, not unattractive, structure of uncertain architecture that appears to have originated as a trailer-house that has been several times enlarged. In its spacious living room, filled with Western artifacts and mementos, Smoky talked one June day about how the idea of developing salt caverns for LP Gas storage had originated. Smoky was born in a "sharecropper's shack" five miles from Webber's Falls. He finished high school there and was graduated from junior college at Warner, Oklahoma. He worked first for the Oklahoma Public Service Company, then the Telephone Company and, having become something of a mechanical engineer, helped design Army camps during World War II. He was employed constructing gasoline refining plants for various companies and in 1947 became construction superintendent for the Sid Richardson Gasoline Company at Kermit, Texas.

"I hadn't been there long when I became aware of the problem of what to do with propane and butane," Smoky relates. "I got to thinking about the problem, and, after coming up with a couple of pretty wild and impractical concepts, I remembered that every time you drill an oil well in west Texas, you always hit a layer of salt at a certain depth. Then the drilling crew has to put salt in the drilling mud so it will not wash out a big hole by dissolving the salt layer. Well, I got to playing around with this idea: Why not set your pipe in the anhydrate just above the salt, and drill down into the salt, or practically through it. Then you could start pumping water down into the salt layer and wash out a big hole which we could use to store propane. Herb Jones, the Sid Richardson Chief Engineer, seemed to think the idea might work. We filed a patent application and I went out and tried to sell it to somebody."

Smoky found his man at a hearing called by the Texas Railroad Commission, at which various producers of natural gas and crude oil in the state were ordered to show cause why they were burning their propane and other LPG products instead of utilizing them. All of the major producers except one, according to Smoky, shut down their operations at the time of the hearing so their lawyers could get up before the commission and say, "We are not flaring or burning any propane or natural gasoline at our plants at this time." The one producer who refused to do this was John Oxley, President of the Texas Natural Gas Company, who told the hearing that his company *was* burning propane and natural gasoline to get rid of it, and that they were going to continue to burn these products as long as they didn't have any practical way to conserve them.

"As soon as the hearing was over," Smoky recalls, "I got hold of John Oxley and told him I had a way to build an economical storage that would hold propane and butane, and I would be glad to go ahead and develop it if he would pay for putting the first products into it. Mr. Oxley said he would think about it. A week later, he telephoned me and said they'd decided to try out my idea at a gasoline plant his company operated in west Texas. They wanted a cavern with 50,000-barrel capacity, and it took considerable time to dissolve that much salt. It requires six or seven barrels of water to dissolve one barrel of salt. While the process was going on, I wanted to try out the cavern to see if it worked. The Texas Natural people said no, they thought it would work all right, go ahead and wash out the entire capacity for 50,000 barrels.

"Meanwhile, the Sid Richardson Company had decided to put in a salt cavern. The management told me to wash out just a little cavern and try it out, and that's what we did at Kermit. We had a big opening for this event and invited all the gas companies to come and see it, along with the Defense Department. They sent some people from the Air Force and from the Army and some other branch of the service to see what happened when we put propane into that salt cavern that first time and then took it out. We put 30,000 gallons of propane into the cavern that morning and took it out that afternoon. We recovered practically all of it, and the quality of the product had not changed at all. The specifications of the propane when it came out of the cavern were just the same as when the product was put in. Our idea was a success.

"When we were preparing a lawsuit for patent infringement," Smoky went on, "we did a lot of experimental work to learn more about why salt would hold propane and other hydrocarbons. I drilled some holes down into the salt and plugged the front end with a packer, then put propane into the hole. It would leak out any hole that we drilled. But when we *washed* the hole, that did something to the salt that made it leakproof. The *dissolving* of the salt evidently glazed over its surface in such a way that it sealed the salt and gave it an impervious surface that prevented the escape of any hydrocarbons."

The patent infringement suit was brought by the Sid Richardson Company, which had filed for a patent on the salt cavern idea and formed a company to exploit construction of underground storage. Defendants were several natural gas and crude oil processors who had been washing out salt caverns, using Smoky's idea without permission of Sid Richardson. The case was settled out of court by the defendants' paying the Sid Richardson Company about $1,500,000, according to Smoky Billue, who says, however, he does not believe a patent was ever actually issued. In any event, by the time Mid-America Pipeline Company was formed, the process of washing out salt caverns had been declared in the public domain, so that anybody could do it, given the technical knowledge.

"I got a little money from the court settlement," Smoky says, "but I made most of my money by putting in storage myself and renting it out to companies, including Mid-America Pipeline Company several years ago. My first caverns were leased to the Army Air Force when the Shilling Air Base was operating at Salina, Kansas." After the base closed, Smoky converted his caverns from storage places for jet fuel to storing propane and other hydrocarbons. In all, he had about eighty caverns in the Conway area, capable of holding upward of 8,000,000 barrels of storage, which he rented to some thirty companies, including a number using Mid-America Pipeline.

In 1974, Smoky sold out all of his salt caverns to Home Oil Company for about $10,000,000. Since then he has been trying to spread his money around in gifts where it will do the most good and be most advantageous to him from a tax standpoint. Most of his gifts have been trusts to various schools, including the majority of his collection of about 100 antique cars, which he gave to the Community College at McPherson, Kansas, near Conway, where Smoky still has a home and trailer court. The school expects to have its students rebuild the antique cars in connection with courses in electricity, painting, woodwork, welding, upholstery, and fender and body work.

Smoky says that he seldom, if ever, wears any more the exotic clothing and Western equipment with which he has long been identified. "Those fancy clothes—and some of my goings-on—always were sort of an act," he claims. "If you got something to sell, you've got to let people know about you and it. People have got to know you and like you. And so I did some of those crazy things just to draw attention to myself. It was salesmanship."

The Scrappy Little Company

14

"I guess I am basically a scrapper," Robert E. Thomas sometimes muses when he looks back over the years of trying to create the Mid-America Pipeline Company and then make it profitable after the pipeline had begun operating. He is fond of the term "scrapper." Thus, during its early years especially, he liked to refer often—both verbally and in print—to the Mid-America organization as "The Scrappy Little Pipeline Company."

And, indeed, it had been necessary for the enterprise to struggle and "scrap" to survive and prosper. In order to get born in the first place, Mid-America had to overcome the opposition of some of the large oil companies, along with an absence of guaranteed business, a shortage of funds to pay for organizational expenses and finally a considerable reluctance by investment houses to undertake the marketing of its securities. And then, after the pipeline was in the ground and had begun operating, its management began to realize ever more emphatically that they were now faced with yet another formidable adversary—the weather.

By the time its fifteenth birthday arrived, MAPCO had become an extremely successful "integrated energy" business by broadening its endeavors from a pipeline operation only into coal, oil, natural gas and natural gas liquids production—the retailing and wholesaling of LP Gas and the production and distribution of liquid fertilizers. But the original motivation for all this expansion was to try to make the Mid-America Pipeline profitable on a year-round basis. It required nine years, however—from the time the pipeline operations began in 1960 until 1969—before MAPCO was able to show a profit for all four quarters.

During 1961—the pipeline's first complete year of operation—Mid-America lost, as expected, to the tune of $2,567,536. The next year, however, the new company came out of the red ahead of expectations, with a net income of $1,507,562 from gross revenues of $11,987,515. But all of that profit—in fact, 80 percent or more of the total revenues—was derived during the first and fourth quarters of the year. From October through March, the peak months of the heating season throughout the frigid upper Middle

West, business was great. But since 75 to 80 percent of propane sales in those days were for home heating, from April through September business was terrible.

And so, during the early years especially of Mid-America's existence, Bob Thomas and his people concentrated on leveling off the pipeline's income by increasing business during the warm months. The problem was attacked from several directions. The company built pipeline branches to petrochemical plants in Iowa and Illinois, which used LP Gas for making plastic feedstock and synthetic natural gas. These customers represented a steady, year-round demand for hydrocarbons, which were furnished through the pipeline. Mid-America also went into the transportation and merchandising of liquid plant foods. In 1968, it opened the nation's first pipeline to transport anhydrous ammonia—rich in nitrogen—into the wheat and corn belt. That same year, MAPCO acquired Indian Point Farm Supply, Inc., near Athens, Illinois, which manufactures and distributes mixed liquid plant foods. A sizable percentage of its production was soon being merchandised through MAPCO's Sales Division, Thermogas, another business acquired earlier by MAPCO for income-stabilizing purposes. Both anhydrous ammonia and mixed liquid fertilizers are in demand after the heating season has slacked off in the spring and before it starts booming in the fall.

In its first move to equalize income over the year, Mid-America set out in 1962, its second year of operation, to try to acquire some liquefied petroleum gas-producing properties of its own. The motivation was twofold. Not only did pipeline deliveries of LP Gas fall dismally at the end of the heating season, but some producers forsook the pipeline completely during warm months and shipped what propane they *could* sell in railroad tank cars, because the railroads offered them what amounted to a rebate on regular shipping tariffs. This was the situation: The greatest appeal of the pipeline to shippers during the rush season in cold weather was dependability. The pipeline provided practically instant delivery, regardless of the weather, and it was especially desirable at times when railroad tank cars were stalled and frozen in the icy yards. Thus, all producers wanted to use the pipeline during the cold weather. But come the warm season and a fall-off in propane demand, the railroads would deliver propane in a tank car leased by a producer, and pay the LP Gas producer mileage for the use of his car in delivering propane to customers of the railroad. A good percentage of the LP Gas producers took advantage of these favorable rates in slack season and let the Mid-America Pipeline people make out the best way they could. And so the first concern of Mid-America's thinkers was to acquire some liquefied petroleum gas-producing properties of their own that would make it possible for them to send their own product through their own pipeline at times when other producers were attracted by the blandishments of the railroads. Fortunately, as things turned out, the first LP Gas-producing property that Mid-America acquired developed into one of the most profitable deals it has ever made.

Situated in west Texas is the famous West Panhandle Gas Field, which over the years has supplied enormous amounts of natural gas and has been the source for a number of gas pipelines. One portion of these vast fields, Westpan Hydrocarbons, alone has inspired the formation of the Natural Gas Pipeline Company of America, Pioneer Natural Gas and the Colorado Interstate Gas Corporation. About 43 percent of Westpan Hydrocarbons was owned by Producing Properties, Inc. of Dallas, Texas. By the Autumn of 1962, Donald B. Ross, a man with wide experience at putting together deals for acquiring oil and gas properties, had become Assistant to the President of Mid-America. He was convinced that the owners of Westpan Hydrocarbons would soon have to sell out because of various financial complications. Ross set out to acquire these properties for Mid-America, and he worked on the deal for a year so strenuously that he very nearly wrecked his health. But in the end, Mid-America acquired rights to the liquefied natural gas products under some 230,000 productive acres, making up about half of Westpan Hydrocarbons. It was a so-called "ABC Deal," which allowed the buyer to make the purchase largely with pretax dollars—a method which has since been discontinued by the Internal Revenue Service.

Mid-America put $6,000,000 cash (borrowed from banks) into the deal and financed the remainder of the purchase price, $19,597,496, via the ABC method. This meant that a third party to the buyer and seller—in this case, the Republic National Bank of Dallas, Texas—paid the seller the $19,597,496 and then got its money back under Mid-America's agreement to dedicate 95 percent of the income from the gas field to the bank until the $19,597,496 and financing charges were repaid.

The Colorado Interstate Gas Corporation had the contract for processing the natural gas from these properties and stripping from it the natural gas liquids, which Mid-America had purchased. Don Ross surveyed the stripping processes in Colorado Interstate's plants, found them inefficient and made some strong recommendations for changes. Since then the fields have yielded a considerably higher ratio of liquefied petroleum gases.

Beyond that, the property turned out to contain about 19,000,000 more barrels of natural gas liquids than the Mid-America management thought it was getting at the time it purchased the property, in 1963. The returns of natural gas liquids under the 230,000 acres were then estimated at 53,000,000 barrels. On that basis, MAPCO's accountants figured that the company would be able to pay off the $19,000,000 loan and realize a net income of about $24,000,00 on its $6,000,000 investment in cash. But, with 19,000,000 additional barrels of product, which in 1975 was worth about $6 or more per barrel, the field should gross another $114,000,000. And that meant that the total natural gas liquids that could be taken from under the 230,000 acres would gross in all about $138,000,000, some two-thirds of which goes to MAPCO. The other third goes to the Colorado Interstate Gas Corporation for its service in processing the gas. In addition to that, starting in 1968, when Phillips Petroleum's contract to purchase a portion of the liquids expired, Mid-America began putting the entire natural gas liquids output of the field into its own line. This amounted to about 10,000 barrels a day, which went a long way toward helping to bring up the pipeline's income during those slow quarters of the year when the weather is warm.

The Westpan Hydrocarbons purchase, which was negotiated by Mid-America's wholly owned subsidiary, Mapco Production Company, also gave Mid-America a natural gasoline processing plant, then under construction, and interests in oil and gas properties in Colorado, Kansas, Louisiana, Nebraska, New Mexico, Oklahoma, Texas and Wyoming. But at the time, the liquefied petroleum products under the 230,000 acres were by far the most important to the company. In addition to the advantages already cited, the LP Gas from under the Westpan properties, plus similar products from the old Hugoton Plains Gas Field, which Mid-America acquired in 1964, has allowed MAPCO to supply its Marketing Division, Thermogas, with about 30 percent of the propane it sells.

Mid-America's acquisition of the Hugoton Plains properties involved perhaps the most interesting and unique piece of financing in the company's history of imaginative fiscal operations. This is the way it happened: The Hugoton Field, in Oklahoma and Kansas to the north of the West Panhandle properties, was the largest known gas field in the world until the relatively recent discoveries of immense natural gas deposits under the North Sea. In 1965, the MAPCO Production Company completed purchase from the Rock Creek Corporation, of Tulsa, of Hugoton Plains Properties, consisting of 180 gas wells in the Hugoton Field, plus a gas gathering system of 211 miles of pipeline and a gasoline plant. The purchase price was approximately $3,100,000 in cash, plus $17,000,000 in reserved production payments, meaning that the lender of the $17,000,000 received 94 percent of MAPCO's return from the field until the principal and interest of the loan were repaid. This purchase gave Mid-America natural gas reserves estimated at 367,000,000,000 cubic feet and about 5,000,000 barrels of natural gas liquids, which meant another 1,000 barrels of LP Gas per day that Mid-America would transport to its own pipeline.

Mid-America's method of raising most of the $3,100,000 cash payment for the Hugoton Plains Properties was what made this deal interesting to all investment bankers and especially on Wall Street, where it is still considered one of the most ingenious financing plans ever devised. Even though the method is generally regarded with great admiration by financiers, apparently it has never been tried again by anyone. MAPCO hasn't needed to, and as far as others are concerned, perhaps it was too unorthodox, since financiers, like most human beings, are cautious about something new and different.

At the time of the purchase, "Mid-America was quite small and we had borrowed up to our eyeballs," one officer of the company has explained. So it was not a propitious time to borrow more. Nor did Bob Thomas want to issue and sell more common stock. The relatively low price Mid-America common stock would have brought would have made it necessary to issue such a large number of shares that they would have diluted the existing holdings to an unacceptable degree at the time. Beyond that, Mr. Thomas did not want more shares that would count in the determination of the company's future earnings.

The solution, a product of the fertile financial mind of Frank Kernan, of White, Weld, was this: On March 17, 1964, the company offered its stockholders 306,450 warrants to purchase common stock on the basis of one warrant for each share held. Each warrant, which was good for half a share of stock (if not exercised by the expiration date, in 1972), was sold at the time for $9. (This would amount to two shares on today's market, when adjusted to the stock splits that have since been made.) A warrant entitled the purchaser to buy at any time through March 31, 1972, the other one-half of the share of common stock for another $9. (That half share is now equivalent to two full shares.)

Warrants, of course, were not new. A warrant simply entitles the investor to buy a share or a fraction of a share of common stock at a set price up to a certain date in the future. If the value of the stock represented by the warrant rises sufficiently for him to make a profit on it before the expiration date, the investor exercises his warrant by paying the stated price and gets his specified amount of stock. With the usual type of warrant, if the stock does not rise sufficiently, the investor does not exercise his warrant. It simply expires, and the investor loses whatever he had paid for the warrant in the first place.

The unusual feature about Mid-America's warrants, which financial students consider "brilliant," was that these warrants did not simply expire on the expiration date. The investor got a half share of Mid-America stock for his $9 regardless. If the stock went up to more than $18 per share during those eight years, the investor could pay another $9 and get a whole share. Thus, his chances of losing were rather remote. This arrangement made the Mid-America warrants especially attractive, and the issue was sold without difficulty. The investors who exercised their warrants in the Spring of 1972 more than quadrupled their money. From the company's standpoint, the warrants gave Mid-America the cash it needed at the time without diluting its equity until several years later. By then, the company was much stronger financially and the equity dilution was relatively insignificant.

"The $2,700,000 those warrants raised for us doesn't sound like a whole lot now," MAPCO Treasurer Dean Cosgrove says. "But we needed the money then. It helped us acquire an important producing property when we were not financially strong. These warrants were off-balance-sheet financing. The only time you reported them was when the warrant holder paid his additional $9 and got his entire share of stock or, after March 31, 1972, when any investor who had not exercised the warrant got his half share of stock anyway. Then we listed the warrants as equity. In this manner, the equity was built up gradually."

"It was a very ingenious device and it has never been used since," says one prominent investment banker with long experience in oil and gas pipeline financing. "I don't know why it hasn't been used because I think it was very smart and entirely ethical. In fact, the entire financing of MAPCO from the first has been unusually brilliant."

Bob Thomas recalls that he first heard of this warrant idea from Mr. Kernan when the two of them had met with Cy Lewis for luncheon. "After Frank outlined his idea," Mr. Thomas says, "I thought about it all afternoon. Then I telephoned Frank and told him, 'I think that warrant idea is positively ingenious. When did you think of it?' And Frank told me, 'It came to me just as I was walking into the dining room to have lunch with you and Cy. Most of my ideas come about four o'clock in the morning. This one arrived at a more comfortable time.'"

The pipeline company now expanded into the LP Gas sales field by acquiring the Thermogas Company of Des Moines, Iowa, in a merger, effective March 1, 1966. Mid-America had previously acquired about 23 percent ownership of Thermogas through purchase of stock for cash. The merger was effected after Mid-America issued 602,343 shares of newly authorized $1.12 convertible preferred stock, which it exchanged for 1,204,686 publicly held shares in Thermogas.

During 1965, the last year before the merger, Thermogas had sold at retail and wholesale 223,186,045 gallons of propane and butane through 140 directly owned and operated distribution plants and to 128 distribution plants operated by others, 32 of which were owned by the Thermogas Division and leased to franchised operators. Thermogas also had a substantial fleet of motor transports for delivering LP Gas to distribution points and about 1,000 employees—four times the number of people Mid-America then had. By 1974, Thermogas sales of LP Gas had increased the 1965 total by about one-third, following nine years of MAPCO operation.

By the end of 1965, Mid-America had acquired more than $50,000,000 worth of gas, oil and natural gas liquids properties, principally in Texas, Oklahoma and Kansas, for about $11,280,000 cash, subject to reserved production payments of approximately $38,785,000, which by that time had already been reduced to about $33,251,000. During 1965, the company began drilling in a modest way for oil—eight shallow wells and one dry hole in the Panhandle Field of Texas and one dry hole in the South Creek Field in Oklahoma. That year, Mid-America's total oil production was 208,775 barrels, or 572 barrels a day. From that time through 1974, the company had acquired net leased holdings totaling 410,880 acres in the United States, including Alaska, in Canada, Indonesia and the Philippines, and had drilled several hundred wells, some on its own, some as part of a syndicate. By late summer 1975, MAPCO's oil production was averaging more than 8,800 barrels a day.

Mid-America's securities had been bought and sold over the counter until August 10, 1966, when the company was listed on the New York Stock Exchange. At that time, Mid-America had 1,839,-908 shares of common stock and 645,684 shares of $1.12 convertible preferred stock outstanding. The company's 304,870 warrants to purchase common stock, issued to acquire the Hugoton Plains Properties, were still being traded over the counter. When the company was listed on the New York Stock Exchange, it had 6,500 stockholders residing in forty-nine states and the District of Columbia and in four foreign countries. Robert E. Thomas bought the first 100 shares of Mid-America common sold on the Exchange.

At the Annual Meeting in 1968, the company's new name, MAPCO, was approved. This name and the firm's new corporate symbol, in fact, had been in use for a year or more before they were approved officially. The MAPCO symbol consists of four arrows pointing in four directions and so situated that their bases come together to form an optical illusion of a capital M. This insignia now appears on all MAPCO installations, stationery, and uniforms, and for several years it has been displayed as a regular weekly one-column ad, four inches high, on the back page of *The Wall Street Journal.* The insignia is called "The Big M," and is intended to signify growth in all directions.

"The Big M" was designed by Bill Fritz, Executive Art Director of Creswell, Munsell, Schubert and Zirbel, Inc., of Cedar Rapids, Iowa, which has been the advertising agency for Thermogas for a number of years. Robert H. Schubert, the advertising firm's Executive Vice President, reports, "We got the Mid-America account after showing Mr. Thomas what we had done for Thermogas, telling him about our advertising philosophy and suggesting that Mid-America's Directors change the name of the company to MAPCO. In retrospect, I'm sure that they were already planning to change the name, because it wasn't long before we were working on a corporate identity program that would set MAPCO up as a young, growing, progressive company. In presenting our reasons for changing the company's name, we used a full-page newspaper ad

141

layout with a headline that read: 'Buy Your Mid-America Pipeline Overshoes Now.' This was intended to point out that it was confusing to have a corporate name concentrating on the pipeline when the company was also merchandising natural gas liquids and producing them along with oil and natural gas and would probably go into other lines later."

The same year that MAPCO officially became MAPCO, the company committed itself to a full-scale liquid fertilizer manufacturing and distribution program when it purchased Indian Point Farm Supply, Inc., for 100,000 shares of common stock. Indian Point, the country's largest independent manufacturer of liquid plant foods, solutions and suspensions, was marketing its product under the trade name "Hopcaid," through 29 independent franchised associate dealers and 120 independent dealers. In addition to this business, MAPCO made the Indian Point plant a supplier of liquid plant food marketed through its Thermogas Division.

On the company's tenth anniversary, MAPCO "expanded into another dimension of the energy business with the acquisition of the Webster County Coal Corporation through issuance of 500,000 MAPCO common shares," the Annual Report for 1970 stated.

In the company's tenth year, President Thomas reported to the shareholders: "MAPCO today, as reflected in the 1970 results, generates earnings by the production, transportation and marketing of propane, butane and natural gasoline; the transportation of refinery and petrochemical feed stocks; the production of oil and natural gas and manufacture and marketing of liquid plant foods. And of major significance, MAPCO has achieved an ability to operate in the black during all four calendar quarters, and has done so for the second year in a row."

When a young, publicly owned business enterprise begins to enjoy success, its management is sometimes threatened and occasionally ousted by envious outsiders who manage to accumulate enough stock to gain control. Some people in Mid-America's management thought they saw a threat of that happening to their company—once—when Mid-America was four years old.

"On December 10, 1964," the Mid-America Annual Report noted, "George F. Bennett and O. Guinn Smith resigned from the Board [Mid-America Board of Directors] and were replaced by Bernard H. Barnett of the [legal] firm of Greenbaum, Barnett, Wood and Doll of Louisville, Kentucky, and Mr. Stanley R. Yarmouth, President of National Industries, Inc., of Louisville, Kentucky. Mr. Barnett was also elected Chairman of the Executive Committee, replacing George F. Bennett."

The seating of Barnett and Yarmouth on the Board was cause for "a kind of a scary time" and considerable "tenseness" among some of Mid-America's top officers. Barnett and Yarmouth came on the Board, according to Bob Thomas, because they had bought the State Street Investment Corporation's 50 percent owner-ship of controlling interest in the Missouri-Kansas-Texas (Katy) Railroad. Barnett and Yarmouth were friends and business asso-ciates of Edward A. Merkle, Robert Thomas' former rival in the old Pennroad Corporation (now the Madison Fund) which owned the other 50 percent of controlling interest in the Katy. And the Katy Railroad, with about 18 percent of the common stock, was the largest shareholder in the Mid-America Pipeline Company. Thus, it looked to some observers as though Bob Thomas' old nemesis, the Katy Railroad, was about to rise up and kick him out of control of his new baby, the Mid-America Pipeline.

"At the time (Barnett and Yarmouth came on the Board) all was sweetness and light," Mr. Thomas recalls, "and I was given the usual verbal assurances that nothing was to be changed. But after the first few meetings, with these two new fellows on the Board, they began to show their teeth and acted as though they wanted to run matters. They had various ideas that differed from the thinking of the rest of us on the Board, and they threatened a proxy fight. I said, 'If you fellows want to have a proxy fight just go ahead; I have enough votes in my hip pocket to beat you.'"

Mr. Merkle said, in 1975, that Barnett and Yarmouth bought only part of the State Street's Katy holdings, and if they ever en-tertained any idea of trying to take over control of Mid-America, he (Merkle) didn't know anything about it. "It wasn't possible any-way for Barnett and Yarmouth to have gotten control of Mid-America," Mr. Merkle said, "because at the time they didn't have the money or the credit. And I would not have gone into it with them."

Nevertheless, Bob Thomas and the Mid-America manage-ment were convinced that an attempt to take over the company was in the wind. "Just to be sure we had enough votes, I went to see the people at the Prudential Insurance Company of America," Mr. Thomas recalls. "This was quite early in our history, and we still owed them about $42,000,000. I explained the situation and the Prudential people were quite alarmed because they didn't want to see any change in management. So we approached them with a proposal for buying half of that $3,000,000 convertible note, which we had given Prudential as a 'kicker' at the time we got our first mortgage loan. The $3,000,000 note was convertible at any time into 300,000 common shares of Mid-America; thus, half of it could be converted into 150,000 voting shares. By this time, the note was worth more than twice the value set when it was given to Prudential. They wanted to take some of their profit and also to make certain that we could not lose a proxy fight.

"So, for $3,300,000, Prudential sold half of its notes, con-vertible into 150,000 Mid-America common shares, to Bill Deramus, who bought them for the Kansas City Southern Railway. This was a real shocker to the Louisville men. They knew there was no way of wooing Bill Deramus away from me and that he could always convert his note into enough common shares to beat them in a proxy fight. And so they took their money and ran.

"Barnett and Yarmouth made a secondary of all the MAPCO stock owned in the Katy Railroad. After that stock was sold publicly, Mid-America was able to get a listing on the New York Stock Exchange. Prior to then, we had not had enough stockholders of 100 shares or more to qualify."

The Katy Railroad sold to the public all of its stock in Mid-America to get operating revenue. "I got $19 a share for it," recalled Mr. Merkle, who remained a Director of the Katy Railroad. "I shouldn't have sold it in view of MAPCO's earning record since then, but the railroad needed money so badly at the time, we had to sell."

And so the $3,000,000 "kicker" that the promoters of the Mid-America Pipeline Company had to give Prudential in 1960 to get their $42,000,000 mortgage loan turned out to be a possible lifesaver five years later when the Mid-America management feared that their position was in jeopardy. It was another case of Bob Thomas' and Mid-America's "luck" or something more profound than "luck."

Charlie Russell, Rustic Salesman

15

On May 1, 1967, the National LP Gas Association presented its Distinguished Service Award for that year, along with a Gold Medal and a $1,000 prize, to Charles O. Russell, Senior Vice President of MAPCO's Thermogas Division. These presentations are made annually to one person in the LP Gas field for continued meritorious and unselfish service to the industry. "This tribute to Mr. Russell," commented MAPCO's Annual Report, "was richly deserved by him and reflects most favorably upon MAPCO's status in the LP Gas Industry."

Charlie Russell was chosen for this industry honor because he is one of the genuine pioneers of LP Gas—although at this writing, he doesn't much resemble the accepted image of a pioneer, which is rough and rugged, gaunt and grim. Charlie is somewhat roly-poly these days, with a nice head of carefully tended curly, gray hair, a benign countenance and the general attitude of a jovial Rotarian. And, financially, Charlie Russell has made out considerably better than your average pioneer, including even some of the more fortunate seekers who headed West in the California gold rush of 1849. He and his partner went into business with a joint capital of $350. Thirty-five years later, he sold his business, the Thermogas Company, for $35,000,000. Obviously, thirty-five is a lucky number in Charlie Russell's book. The prosperity and growth that Thermogas enjoyed during those years is indicative of the rise of LP Gas generally in affluence and popular favor.

In 1965, Thermogas became the first of its several acquisitions that changed the Mid-America Pipeline Company from a mere operator of a pipeline into a well-balanced energy merchant and producer, equipped to supply that much needed commodity from several different directions in these energy-hungry times. The acquisition of Thermogas also gave Bob Thomas and his administration a firmer-than-ever control over the publicly owned company that he was most instrumental in founding. Mid-America issued a large block of new stock to acquire Thermogas. And, although for a while Mr. Russell resented giving over his company to another's

145

control, he soon came to appreciate the Thomas managerial genius, and he and his large block of stock became one of the Thomas administration's staunchest bulwarks. Mr. Russell has served on the MAPCO Board of Directors ever since the merger of Thermogas with the now parent company.

Charlie isn't sure—he probably never was—exactly why he got into the LP Gas business in the first place except that "it was a new field and I thought it might go places." He was born and grew up in Mystic, a coal-mining community in southern Iowa. "And so," he likes to say, "I have been around the energy business all my life." After graduating from Mystic High School, he worked for a year, saved his money and went to the University of Iowa, graduating in 1930 with a Bachelor of Science Degree in Commerce. First, he took a sales job on the road, peddling cone-shaped drinking cups over a four-state area. Then for the next three or four years he taught school in the wintertime and sold LP Gas in summer.

In those days propane was little known and not available to Charlie Russell and his partner, who handled instead pentane, made of some of the lighter ends from the old casing head gasoline. It was too volatile for use as motor fuel, but not lively enough to have sufficient pressure to force itself through a gas line, which was one of its weaknesses as a fuel. And so Russell and his partner, Walter Shettlemore, sold mechanical pentane circulating systems as well as the fuel itself, which was easily handled and bought by the barrel. The Delco Division of General Motors also made and sold mechanical pentane systems, but the Delco dealers did not handle pentane itself. Those in the Des Moines area depended on Russell and Shettlemore to furnish the fuel and service for the machines that they sold and installed.

"The LP Gas business in those days," Russell recalls, "was mainly concerned with cooking on gas stoves to keep the heat out of the kitchen during the hot months. The average housewife or farmwife cooked on a coal stove most of the year. But in summer these ladies wanted other fuel—kersosene or gasoline and finally LP Gas. Most of them used only small stoves, often just a two-burner hotplate with no insulation, and only during the summer; then they reverted to their coal stoves for the rest of the year. So we concentrated on selling pentane and pentane systems in summer and that kept food on the table when we weren't drawing our teachers' salaries. In winter I kept books for our gas business while teaching school. We didn't make a lot of money. Even after we went into the LP Gas business full time, I drew a salary of only $50 a month—and only that when we had as much as $50 in the till.

"But $50 went a lot further then," Mr. Russell points out. "There were no withholding taxes or social security; it was all take-home pay. And then, in those days, I seldom had to pay a hotel bill or a restaurant charge. When I delivered gas to a farm around noontime, the folks would say, 'Come in and have dinner with us.'

The midday meal in the country then was 'dinner.' And when I pulled into a farm along about four or five o'clock in the afternoon, they'd say, 'Come in and have supper with us and stay all night.' That old-time hospitality helped to keep expenses down. I guess that sort of thing went along with the pioneering days of any industry.

"We have always operated on the theory that there are two important things in business," Charlie Russell says. "One is profit; the other is romance. And to us, 'romance' meant having fun together and enjoying our work. Those nights I spent with my good farm customer-friends came under the heading of romance."

In 1934, the partners purchased from a Clarinda, Iowa, gas company their first butane, which was a naturally better fuel than pentane because it would vaporize and provide its own pressure in temperatures above 30°F. The butane was kept cool and under pressure in tanks that Russell and Shettlemore buried underground to keep it liquid until time for use. Butane's ability to vaporize on its own eliminated the need for a pentane-like mechanical system, and the butane also produced a more constant flow of BTU's.

"But back in the industry's early stages, the public was afraid of propane," Charlie Russell recalls nowadays. "You must remember that natural gas had come into Iowa and our general area of the Midwest only a few years earlier, and there had been a number of accidents to users of it. Our competition—such as Florence kerosene stoves, Kitchen Cook gasoline stoves and other makers of appliances using fuel other than LP Gas—talked a lot about the hazards of gas. This helped to develop public concern and some reluctance to use our product. One of our policies to overcome this fear was to get a housewife's permission to put in her kitchen a small, two-burner hotplate with a little cylinder of propane attached. After all, such a small amount of gas *couldn't* make a very big explosion. We would let the housewife use this for a few days. Then we would go back and try to sell the family a whole propane system, with the appliances to go with it."

Charlie likes to recall one of his first important sales after he quit teaching and went full time into propane. "I persuaded this farmer down near Clinton to convert his old pentane plant into a new, modern propane plant," he relates. "I sold him a set of new gaslights, a new gas range and put gas under his incubator. While installing these appliances, I happened to hear him complaining about his kerosene-powered refrigerator. So, next day when I was to bring out his new range, I also loaded a brand-new gas refrigerator onto the truck. This was a pretty costly item back then; it took about all the money we had in the bank to buy it. I took the new refrigerator out to this farmer's place and installed it when I put in the range, without any indication from the customer that he would ever buy it. I told him that I wanted him to use the refrigerator for a month, then I would come back and get the appliance so I could sell it to a hot prospect I had. When I went back for it, the man said to me, 'You are never going to take that refrigerator out of here.' This was a good example of the superiority of propane appliances. I really didn't have another prospect for that refrigerator, but I never told this to the farmer. I didn't want to sound pushy.

"Twenty years later, we held a dinner at Clinton, after putting in a new plant there for Thermogas. I had this same man and his wife come to the dinner as my guests and sit at the head table. Good, solid country people like that were the foundation of our success in the LP Gas business."

In 1938, Charlie Russell and a Des Moines attorney, Rufus Scott, bought out Walter Shettlemore, who moved to Minnesota to go into the LP gas business on his own. Three years later, he was drowned and about the same time, Charlie's new partner, Mr. Scott, was killed in an automobile accident. "I buried both of them the same month," Charlie Russell says.

During World War II, Thermogas business was slow. There was no trouble getting the fuel, but it was impossible to obtain new appliances to sell. At this time the Thermogas operation was based on 100-pound and smaller cylinders used still for cooking, water-heating and a few gas refrigerators. From down South, however, came word that propane was being used to heat some homes. After the war, that practice began spreading northward, along with the use of propane for crop-drying, tractor fuel and flame cultivation. This made it necessary to install on users' premises propane containers of up to 500-gallon capacity.

Until the end of World War II, Thermogas had only the one plant in Des Moines. After 1945, however, the company began expanding with new plants—in Ottumwa, Clinton, Shenandoah and Emmetsburg, Iowa; in Galesburg, Illinois; and Madison, Wisconsin. Charlie Russell then began to acquire other existing LP gas operations. And the first one—Rapid Gas Company of Cedar Rapids, Iowa—proved almost too big for Thermogas to digest.

"That merger brought on one of the most traumatic situations we ever had," Charlie Russell recalls. "It was our first big acquisition. Before that, we had grown internally, mainly by putting in our own plants here and there. The Rapid Gas merger with Thermogas was a stock deal. Thermogas had seven plants then and Rapid Gas had four. So they received a sizable amount of our stock. The ownership of Rapid Gas was concentrated in one wealthy family of Cedar Rapids. In 1949, two weeks before our first annual meeting after the merger, we at Thermogas heard that the former owners of Rapid Gas—and now the owners of a large block of Thermogas stock—were soliciting votes with the idea of taking over control of our company. They were going to give me the title of Chairman of the Board, and then get somebody else to run the show. One of our dealers they solicited happened to be a good enough friend of mine to tell me about this a few days ahead of time.

"We then began getting our strength together. We went down the stock list very carefully and counted the number of shares that we could absolutely depend upon. Then we counted the number of shares we knew we didn't have much of a chance for. After that, we concentrated on the ground in between—the holders of shares who might be influenced either way. We rented a suite in a downtown Cedar Rapids hotel as a sort of headquarters and spent the night before the meeting talking to our shareholders. I had a crew out corralling those questionable shareholders, trying to get them to come up to our suite and visit and see if we could get them to commit themselves to our side. The opposition had a much larger and fancier suite than ours. They were wealthier than we were and, of course, they were soliciting votes, too.

"I had practically memorized *Robert's Rules of Order,* since I was to preside and it was obvious that some friction would take place during the meeting. The first issue that came up was not especially important within itself but it did constitute a test, showing which side had how many votes. After the votes were counted, our side wound up with 50½ percent. The other side had 49½ percent. Then they tried all sorts of maneuvers to delay further action, but I was ready for them with *Robert's Rules of Order.* They tried to adopt a motion that the meeting be recessed and reconvened in two weeks. It was obvious that they wanted this time to raise the offering price to shareholders and swing that one percent they needed for control. We defeated that with our 50½ percent majority. And so our management stayed intact, with me in charge.

"One of our renegade Vice Presidents was a man we had taken in from the other family. The man the other side had selected to take my place to run Thermogas was one of my own Vice Presidents who had been with our company for some time. So the next day I fired a couple of vice presidents and we got on with our work. The other side owned about a third of our stock, which we finally bought out. But several of us at Thermogas got ulcer-inclinations after that experience."

That "experience" caused Charlie Russell to become more interested in buying acquisitions with cash instead of stock. Money for this was raised by what he calls "patchwork financing—getting some money here and there from the banks, from insurance companies, from some of our suppliers, Cities Service being the chief one." In 1961, Thermogas went public, selling its stock over the counter, which gave the company more capital for expansion. This also put Thermogas in a position to borrow more money. Acquisitions ranged from a one-man operation, the Kibbee Gas Company of Jewell, Iowa, purchased for $16,000—all the way up to the Zero Gas Company, which served most of the State of Arkansas. Zero, a part of the Warren Petroleum Company's holdings, was purchased for $13,000,000. It became available after Warren had merged with the Gulf Oil Company and the Federal Government ordered Gulf to sell off some of the former Warren LP Gas operations. Besides Zero, former Warren properties Thermogas acquired included the Dri-gas Company of Chicago and a number of other plants scattered throughout Michigan, Ohio, Indiana and Wisconsin. Thermogas also acquired the former West Alabama Butane operations and so entered for the first time the deep Southeast.

Meanwhile in 1954, Thermogas had begun to switch its emphasis from selling propane in the smaller, portable cylinders (or full bottles) to bulk, 500- and 1,000-gallon, permanently installed tanks on the property of customers. The bulk installations meant a shift in emphasis to home heating, and in a year or so the company's sales peak had completely reversed: Thermogas was now selling seven times as much propane in winter as it had sold in summer. After Thermogas began selling propane in bulk, it became more and more apparent to Mr. Russell and his people that railroads were not an efficient means of transporting this product to the distributor. Sometimes a carload of propane would get lost for a week en route when Thermogas was expecting its arrival the next day. At such times Thermogas was apt to run out of fuel to sell. The colder the weather, the more propane was needed and the greater the railroad delays. "If we'd had to depend on rails to haul the volume of LP Gas we handle now, it would be one hopeless mess," Charlie Russell says these days.

And so, in 1961, when the Mid-America Pipeline began operation, Thermogas was one of the pipeline's first and most enthusiastic customers. The distributor found there was "considerable saving" in the cost of transporting LP Gas from the fields to the consuming area along with an "immense improvement" in the efficiency of the service. And so Charles Russell began thinking about a possible unification someday with the pipeline company to better assure his propane supply.

"Beyond that," Mr. Russell says, "money was tight during this period and we were having some trouble getting the financing we needed for our expansion program. We approached the Mid-America Pipeline Company and asked if they would be interested in buying a little stock in Thermogas to help us over the hump. We were one of the larger users of their pipeline service and we thought they might prefer to own part of us rather than have the stock we wanted to sell fall into unfriendly hands who might want to use other means of transportation. Mr. Thomas was most cooperative and bought a sizable portion of stock to assist us in getting our entire issue of stock sold. We were then able to complete our acquisition of Zero Gas and other former Warren properties. "And then, in 1965, we finally worked out an acceptable merger program with the Mid-America Pipeline Company. We joined them in March of the following year."

Robert E. Thomas' version of the Mid-America–Thermogas merger differs somewhat—insofar as Mid-America's real purpose was concerned—from Mr. Russell's account. According to Bob Thomas, Mid-America wanted to help Thermogas get its acquisitions all right—but Mid-America was most interested at the time in eventually acquiring both Thermogas *and* the Thermogas acquisitions. "We wanted a marketing division for LP Gas to give our company a more complete function than we'd had by merely transporting product," he says. "Also, the biggest margin of profit in the LP Gas field is in the retailing end—and Thermogas was principally a retailer. By this time we had learned that our company had to be more than a mere pipeline operation if it was to grow and prosper in a satisfactory way.

"We bought our initial Thermogas stock," Mr. Thomas went on, "after the underwriters, who were trying to sell that big issue of 500,000 shares of Thermogas common, came to us and said the offering was in trouble. They needed a big buyer to get the issue moving. And so we purchased 100,000 shares of Thermogas common at $10 a share. That provided the stimulus for the rest of the issue. We had been looking at Thermogas for some time with a greedy eye. And here came a God-given opportunity to get a toehold. You don't often get a chance like that when the other party is happy that you've got a foot in his door. Under the circumstances, Mid-America was *happy* to help out. Charlie didn't realize at the time that we had such ulterior motives.

"After we had acquired our Thermogas stock," Bob Thomas says, "a young English banker named David Allsopp visited me in Tulsa. He had several accounts in England and Scotland that owned substantial holdings in Thermogas. Allsopp told me that he had been talking with Charlie Russell about merging Thermogas with Petrolane and he wanted our backing as a major stockholder in Thermogas. I told him politely, but firmly, that such a proposal didn't fit in with our plans at all. If Thermogas was going to be merged with anybody, we intended that it become a part of Mid-America Pipeline.

"Actually, David Allsopp hadn't accomplished much in his discussions with Mr. Russell. The banker was a mod type with long hair at a time when long hair styles for men were still confined mainly to England. Charlie didn't like men with long hair and gave Allsopp rather short shrift. I didn't care for long hair too much myself—but I have the ability to overlook such things, especially if I have another motive in mind. I recognized the significance of this English-held block of Thermogas stock—and I wanted it.

"And so, one day late in 1964 when my wife and I were cruising in my boat, the *Seabird,* on Long Island Sound, we put in at a little port in Connecticut. And from a pay telephone on a rickety wooden pier, I called David Allsopp in London. During that call, we made the deal for Mid-America to buy his clients' holdings in Thermogas. With our previous purchase of stock, we were now the largest stockholder, with 23 percent of Thermogas, and we had the muscle to force the merger if necessary."

It seemed at first—especially to the people of Thermogas and most especially to Charles Russell himself—that the notion of the Mid-America Pipeline Company taking over the Thermogas Company was something like the bait swallowing the fish. At the time Thermogas had more than 1,000 employees as compared with Mid-America's possibly 200, and the annual sales of Thermogas exceeded MAPCO's. According to one observer, who had been connected for some years with the Russell Thermogas management, "many of the old Thermogas people at first tended to regard Bob Thomas as a steely-eyed, hard-driving executive type who would cut somebody's head off as a whim." The same observer went on to say that he had noted a "teeth-clenching bitterness toward Tulsa" on the part of Mr. Russell and a number of his executives. This "grinding tension," however, gradually lessened in the months that followed and eventually all executives of Thermogas, including Mr. Russell himself, "did a 180-degree turn in direction," and gave every evidence that they were pleased that the deal had taken place.

"I would be a liar," Charlie Russell says nowadays, "if I claimed that it didn't bother me for somebody else to take over the business that I had built. It hurt—a lot, at first. On the other hand, I had a great deal of respect for Bob Thomas. I knew him to be smart and hard-working, with a background of the sort that qualified him to run a company the way it should be run. I knew he was capable of making wise decisions and that he would keep our staff and allow our people to make their decisions relative to marketing. We knew about marketing. Mid-America had never had any experience in this field. And Bob Thomas did let our executives have free rein to go ahead and do what they knew how to do.

"Aside from a few little ripples," Mr. Russell went on, "there have never been any really serious problems for us in realizing who was the new boss and in getting the full cooperation of the Thermogas staff in our new position. There was never any real letdown in the morale of the Thermogas employees because of the merger. Some of them wondered at first, of course, just what was going to become of them with this changing of leaders—what were they getting into and what would the new leadership expect and demand of them. But everything has all worked out quite well.

"We made the changeover with only one casualty, and that happened over a year after the merger," Charlie Russell said.

(The "casualty" was a top executive of Thermogas, who Thomas felt hadn't given complete loyalty to the new management.)

"I think the smoothness of the changeover was made possible," Charlie Russell says nowadays, "because the Mid-America management recognized that our people were experts in their field and that our operation had been extremely successful, and Mid-America had the wisdom to allow us to continue as we had been doing prior to the merger. And maybe a little bit of credit should go to our people at Thermogas for being able to adjust to the fact that somebody else was the new boss."

Charles O. Russell (right), founder of the Thermogas Company, of Des Moines, Iowa and a pioneer in the liquefied petroleum gas field, spreads the good word during a radio interview in Chicago in 1958. Nine years later, the National LP Gas Association presented Mr. Russell its Distinguished Service Award, given annually to one individual for "continued meritorious and unselfish service to the industry." Thermogas merged with the Mid-America Pipeline Company in 1965.

Maurice C. Maher (center), then Senior Vice-President of the Thermogas Company, was present for the first Thermogas propane truck loading at Mid-America's new terminal at Farmington, Illinois. He is flanked by Robert E. Thomas (left) and Warren Buckner, then a Thermogas regional manager. Three years later, Thermogas was merged with Mid-America, and Maurie Maher eventually became a MAPCO Senior Vice President, in charge of the Thermogas Division.

Forty-five years ago, when Charles O. Russell began pioneering in LP gas merchandising, his average sale amounted to not more than a few gallons of liquid pentane gas, later on a 10-gallon cylinder of liquefied propane. The most popular use of these fuels was for little two-burner hot plates, which kept Midwestern kitchens cooler in summer than the regular big, coal-burning ranges. Nowadays, almost all farm users of LP gas have permanently-installed tanks of not less than 500 gallons—a third have tanks of 1,000-gallon capacity and even larger. These furnish fuel for all sorts of purposes, including central heating and air conditioning of homes, cooking, refrigeration, weed control and crop drying. Above, a Thermogas truck is filling a 1,000-gallon tank that fuels a crop dryer.

The Thermogas Company's first distribution system consisted of one red-painted truck, of modest size, loaded with a barrel of pentane gas and small cylinders of liquefied propane. It was driven by Charlie Russell, the company's founder. In 1975, Thermogas was serving customers in 13 states with a fleet of more than 1,000 vehicles, including several hundred propane tank trucks, such as this 10,000-gallon monster, refueling at a Mid-America terminal.

155

The Irish Cowboy

16

Maurice C. Maher, Senior Vice President of MAPCO, in charge of all Thermogas operations, and his staff of top executives are excellent examples of the policy followed by Robert E. Thomas when MAPCO has absorbed another business concern. All of these men were top officials of Thermogas under the old ownership, headed by Charles O. Russell. They have remained top officials of Thermogas under the new management, headed by Robert E. Thomas.

If a merged property has been doing well when MAPCO takes it over, the Thomas administration's policy is to leave in charge the people responsible for the acquisition's good showing— which had attracted the MAPCO officials' notice in the first place. The old management of the acquired company is allowed wide leeway in making its decisions about matters with which it is expert from long experience, and the MAPCO top managment stands behind and supports—both morally and monetarily—these decisions as long as they prove productive. Bob Thomas' policy is to continue and often add to practices of the management of the acquired property that had been working well. Thus, if the absorbed firm has, say, a profit-sharing or a bonus plan that has stimulated greater employee efforts and made better-satisfied workers, MAPCO will likely increase the benefits under such a plan. The same holds good for hospitalization and other fringe benefits.

Thus, when MAPCO took over Thermogas, there wasn't much question as to who was going to head the operation after Charles O. Russell retired, which he did three years following the merger. Maurice Maher—they call him "Maurie"—had been with Thermogas since 1947 and a Vice President since 1954. For ten years prior to the merger with MAPCO he had been assistant to Charles Russell, who was grooming Maurie to be his successor. Bob Thomas did not disturb these plans. And Mr. Maher was allowed to keep his top management staff of Vice Presidents: Paul Wagoner, in charge of Sales; Dick Stegall, Supervisor of Retail Sales; John Lewis, Farm Sales; and Gene Walden, in charge of Purchasing.

Maurie Maher is a sober and sedate-looking Irishman—but

beneath his stern facade lurks an impish sense of humor and a smidgen of the wild and tempestuous nature of his Celtic forebears. From time to time over the years, Charlie Russell felt it advisable to give Maurie subtle suggestions that he curb some of his outspoken instincts. "Being of Irish descent, I sometime take a rather strong position on things and maybe I am a little too quick to release my feelings and give out with rather resounding statements," Maurie Maher said one day in 1975. "Not long after I started working for Mr. Russell, he sent me a card one day that I still have. It was in the nature of a gentle hint. On the card is a picture of a horse backing up and preparing to run toward a barn door, after obviously having missed the door on several prior attempts, hitting his head on the side of the barn. The caption under the picture reads: 'Not dumb . . . just doesn't give a damn!'"

Mr. Maher has the Irishman's love for horses. He was born and raised on a farm that had lots of horses and, as he says, "I rodeoed a little bit" for years—even after he became a big-business executive. "I kept following those rodeos for some years after I went with Thermogas," he says. "I would take off a week or two each year and go with my horse trailer out through western Nebraska and those parts. I was on the rodeo board and I used to ride those bucking horses. Mr. Russell kept telling me that I ought to quit that damned foolishness or I would get hurt. It didn't seem like foolishness then, though.

"Finally, in 1960, I took off a week or so to ride in a rodeo and I had a fall and broke my ankle. I had to use crutches to walk and I didn't know how in hell I was going to keep Mr. Russell from knowing about it. When I came back to Des Moines, I went to work real early the first morning before anybody else was there, and I hid my crutches under my desk. Pretty soon, though, after our people had gotten in their offices, I had to go to the bathroom and there wasn't any other way to go except on my crutches and I had to walk right past Mr. Russell's office. He saw me and called me in and said, 'I told you this before. But now it's time that you make up your mind: Either give up one or the other—rodeo or the gas business.'

"It didn't take me long to make up my mind. I knew I wasn't the caliber of cowboy who could make a living rodeoing. So I stopped going. I still raise quarter horses, though, and break them myself. And I raise show horses. I still have one show horse left."

Maurie Maher came to work for Thermogas after serving in the United States Army and receiving shrapnel wounds while fighting in the Pacific area in World War II. "I was born and raised in southwestern Iowa," he says, "at Imogene, a small Irish settlement. World conditions were very unsettled at the time I finished school and there was a lot of talk about how every young fellow would have to do a year's mandatory military service. So I thought I would be smart and volunteer for the Army for a year, get my time

157

served and come out, and when they were drafting the others, I would probably be in a better position to take advantage of the military situation. As it turned out, during that year's military service of mine, we got into the war and as a result, I didn't get out of the Army for six years. I served in the Infantry in both theaters of war—Europe and Asia."

He went into the Army as a private making $21 a month, served for a short while in Europe, returned to Officer's Training School in the United States, and later saw a great deal of combat action in the Philippines and Okinawa. He was discharged from the service with the rank of Captain and a number of shrapnel wounds which sent him to the Army General Hospital in Clinton, Iowa, for rehabilitation and convalescence.

"I had no clothes, no belongings at all except what I was issued—pajamas and a robe and some hospital sandals," he says. "The Thermogas Company was building a propane plant at Clinton at the time, right next to the hospital. During the recreation hours I would wander out there and watch the men work. I got acquainted with the manager of the project and, in want of something better to do, I started hammering and sawing and helping with the building. One day Mr. Russell drove up and here I was in my pajamas, robe and sandals hammering away on the building. Mr. Russell asked who I was and then he said to me, 'Anybody who likes to work that well may have a future in our company.'

"And so, after my discharge from the service, I went to work as a trainee with the Thermogas Company in Des Moines. My first assignment was at Shenandoah, Iowa, where for two years I was practically the entire force. That probably gave me an advantage over some of the others—experience that I wouldn't trade for anything in connection with the gas business. At Shenandoah I had to do practically every job, all the way from testing cylinders to valving cylinders, painting cylinders, filling and delivering them, selling appliances, traveling on the road, supervising plants, working in accounting, purchasing, traffic, storage. It is impossible nowadays to expose one guy to that much experience in that length of time because our business has gotten so big and more specialized.

"When Mr. Russell started, he did the early—the really pioneering—work, convincing potential customers that gas was not a dangerous product, and selling some of those early appliances to farm families. I came along on what you might call the second phase of development of LP Gas retailing, helping to consolidate what he had pioneered. We had a network of dealers by then and I would help them with their service calls and special sales of appliances and I helped conduct cooking schools. We would get a group of ladies together—maybe we would rent the local theater in a small town, or get the church basement, or something like that—and we would put on a cooking school and show them how gas worked. We'd generally do this through a dealer and he would work through the theater manager or some type of local promotion or church group and we would come in with our appliances and demonstrate them.

"I remember when clothes dryers first came on the market. They were considered quite an extreme luxury and were not fully understood. But every lady wanted one. We would ask some influential farm housewife to get some ladies together—at least a dozen—and I would bring out the clothes dryer and give a demonstration. Before the ladies got there, we would wash a bundle of clothes—preferably towels and washcloths, because they were hard to dry and they gave a nice effect while drying. The dryer brought out the nap of the material. We wore out a lot of sets of towels and washcloths that way.

"In those days, about 14 pounds was considered an average load for the clothes dryer. It required around 50 to 55 minutes for the clothes to dry and this gave me an opportunity, while the ladies were watching the clothes tumble around, to talk about features of the machine and the advantages of owning one. I would tell them that they could eliminate a lot of diaper rash by using this machine because it had an ozone bulb inside with germ-killing effect.

"Back then," Maurie Maher reminisces, "some people believed a myth about dryers—that to be really clean, clothes had to be hung out in the sunlight and blow in the breeze. But we would point out to them that in wintertime it was too cold for this, and during the summer a lot of times the wind blows dirt into the clothes. And then it is likely to be raining on Monday, which was then considered washday. We showed them that by using a dryer, they could reduce the number of changes of clothing that they needed.

"We had another gimmick called Peanut Day. Our dealer in a town was likely to be a hardware man. The State Hardware Association employed a newscaster named Len Howe, who had a wide reputation throughout the state for his broadcasts. We promoted Peanut Days with him. The idea was that if people visited a certain hardware store on a certain day, they could get all the peanuts there they could eat, and Len Howe would be present to visit with them. The peanuts came in large burlap bags, already roasted. We would have a dryer there, of course, and we would put the peanuts in the dryer and warm them up again. It was quite a gimmick. It attracted people around the dryer and we could then tell them all about it while the peanuts were getting warm. And, of course, nearby we had a second dryer operating on some fabrics. We would not pass up an opportunity like this. The machine was loaded with brightly colored towels and washcloths, which made a fine spectacle tumbling in the light from the blue bulb inside the dryer.

"When we put on cooking schools, we tried to have a new gimmick every year. We would bake big upside-down cakes in large pans, primarily to prove that the oven cooked uniformly and the cake would have the same degree of firmness in the center as it did around the edges. And gas cooked much faster than electricity. We broiled our meats in the stove with the door closed, pointing out that with an electric stove you had to open the door to broil. And we would show how the gas flames burned the smoke. And, regardless of the height of the flame—you could set it on medium, low or high—we still got an even distribution of heat, whereas with an electric stove, if you set it on medium, you got cooking only in the center. We would also put a piece of asbestos, cut to fit on top of the gas burner, and leave it there a while in the flames to show by the marks on the asbestos the evenness of the heat. Then we would use asbestos in the same way on the electric burner to show how that produced hot and cold spots."

Another big item that came out about the time Maurie Maher joined Thermogas was stock-tank heaters. These kept the water for farm animals from freezing during the bitter Iowa winters. Thermogas furnished farmers with charts showing that if an animal had plenty of water, he would eat less food and still gain weight at the same rate. "We tried to pick extremely cold weather to demonstrate these tank heaters," Maurie relates, "because we *did* have a good appliance and it was a money-maker for the farmer. It used about as much fuel during the winter season as a cooking range did, but it eliminated the dreaded task the farmer had of either cutting a hole in the ice once or twice a day and pumping in fresh water for his stock, or trying to put a barrel in there and build a fire out of cobs and wood in the barrel to keep the water from freezing. Sometimes a farmer would use oil heaters in his stock tanks but these would often spill oil into the water and he would have to empty and refill the entire tank before the cattle, horses or hogs would drink the water. Stock-tank heaters have been gradually improved over the years and they still generate quite a lot of winter business for us."

When the Thermogas Company began selling gas furnaces for home heating, it often made the installations free of charge. This served to stimulate sales and to train personnel in selling and installing furnaces. By now, oil was the main competition to LP Gas in home heating, although coal was still used. The costs of LP Gas and oil were comparable, but the Thermogas people pointed out that gas was much cleaner and required less servicing. Coal cost less, but it was emphasized that gas produced no clinkers or ashes to carry out and you didn't need a coal bin in the basement. Families who used hydrocarbons only for cooking, clothes-drying and water-heating were generally served by portable cylinders. When a family went in for home heating with a gas furnace, Thermogas installed a permanent bulk tank and charged the customer less per gallon of gas when sold in bulk.

It was mainly the urging of Maurie Maher, by now promoted from Shenandoah to a larger plant at Ottumwa, that persuaded Charlie Russell finally to get into bulk propane distribution. That was in 1954. Two years later Maurie was transferred into the main office in Des Moines and elected a Vice President.

Since the MAPCO merger, Thermogas has increased its volume of LP Gas sales; it has also entered the liquid fertilizer business to help equalize income over the year. In 1975, the Thermogas Division of MAPCO had 135 retail companies of its own and about 100 dealerships. Some of the latter were associate dealerships in which Thermogas owned part of the equity. The others were wholesalers who owned their own business entirely, and for whom Thermogas was simply a gas supplier. Thermogas operates in a total of thirteen states, ten of which contain active Thermogas outlets: Alabama, Mississippi, Arkansas, Iowa, Illinois, Wisconsin, Indiana, Kentucky, Michigan and Ohio. The company also has customers in three other states—Missouri, Minnesota and Nebraska—supplied by dealers in adjoining states who "lap over" state lines to serve them. In all of the ten states where Thermogas has active distribution points—except in Mississippi, where it has only one outlet—the company enjoys an average of 21 to 22 percent of the total LP Gas business. About 65 percent of the 268,000,000 gallons of LP Gas distributed by Thermogas in 1974 was sold through company-owned outlets.

For that year, Thermogas' total income was around $100,000,000. Of this, something over $85,000,000 came from LP Gas sales. Between $2,000,000 and $3,000,000 derived from sales of parts and fittings, and some $3,000,000 of income was from appliance sales and labor charges. The remaining approximately $8,000,000 came from sales of fertilizer. The latter figure is especially significant.

"In the middle of the summer, when we handled only propane," Maurie Maher says, "our income used to drop down to about 15 or 20 percent of what it was at the peak of the heating season, but during those slow seasons, we did not lay off personnel. It takes trained people to handle our business and they expect security. If we had laid off most of our workers at the start of the slow season, they would have gotten more permanent jobs elsewhere when we tried to hire them back in the fall.

"And so with our fertilizer program we are striving for two objectives: We want to balance our revenues, on a monthly basis, throughout the year and do our best to eliminate those red-ink periods. And we want to keep all of our people and equipment busy throughout the year. Aside from our fertilizer program, we also concentrate during the warm months on selling appliances."

161

Thermogas Vice President Gene Walden, who is in charge of purchasing everything except the gas itself, reported in 1975 that the most popular appliances were outdoor gas grills and gas-operated air conditioners. Their biggest advantage over those operated by electricity is that it costs less than half to operate them with gas.

Gene Walden's purchasing responsibilities range from company vehicles—Thermogas keeps about 1,000 tank trucks, fertilizer spreaders, station wagons and service trucks ready for service at all times—down to the smallest propane containers. These latter are five-gallon "bottles" that hold 20 pounds of propane and are used mainly for camping, gas grills and trailers. One gallon of propane contains 90,000 BTU's, and a water heater may require about 30,-000 BTU's an hour. Thus, a gallon of propane will run a heater about three hours continuously. A five-gallon bottle of propane will last a camper from one to two weeks. Most camping areas have a bottle-refilling facility. The next most popular size is the 100-pound, or 25-gallon, cylinder, used mainly for cooking, water-heating and clothes-drying at home. It is also a portable container.

A great many Midwestern farms that use crop dryers powered by propane have 1,000-gallon tank installations and multiples thereof on their property. Gene Walden figures that about one farm customer out of every three in the Midwest has a tank of at least 1,000-gallon capacity. These tanks, built according to specifications of the American Society of Engineering Codes, are of 3/4-inch-thick steel to contain the highly pressurized liquid, and they last for many years. All Thermogas tanks in the Midwest are painted white, and some in the South are aluminum color. Light exteriors are advisable to reflect the sun and keep the interior cooler. Some customers own their propane tanks while others rent or lease them. Charges run from about $25 a year for a 120- to 150-gallon tank, to some $60 a year for a 1,000-gallon tank. A filled 5-gallon (20-pound) bottle in 1975 cost $24.95, including the bottle. Each refill cost around $2.50.

Most of the Thermogas employees in the field wear the standard uniform of two-tone blue—light blue shirt with dark blue collar and dark blue trousers, with the MAPCO insignia on the shirt. The largest percentage of employees are classed as delivery-men; the other main classifications are servicemen and bookkeepers. "All of our people are expected to work at sales," Maurie Maher says. "We like to refer to all of our employees as salespeople. Our drivers are really 'driver-salesmen.' We don't have any specialists. Our employee groups, at our various plants, are generally quite small in number—five to eight people—and all of them except perhaps the servicemen are qualified to do every job that needs to be done in the plant. This would include delivering bulk gas all winter; then in spring, they start putting out fertilizer. When that season is over, we let them work, maybe, on accounts receivable or they help put in new installations, or paint tanks or do just about any job that has to be done. Everybody pitches in—nobody is a specialist."

The salaries of deliverymen and others are geared to the competitive wage scale in the area where their plant is located. Beyond salary, the Thermogas workers enjoy a liberal profit-sharing plan. It is geared to the individual outlets so that the employees of each installation are paid on the basis of what *their* particular unit was able to do, regardless of the showing of the entire company. The Thermogas Division also provides a first-rate pension plan for all employees who have been with the firm more than a year and who are over twenty-five years old, as well as hospital insurance, including major medical costs up to $100,000. The company pays half the cost of each employee's uniform and also pays him tips, bonuses and commissions for extra effort put forth that results in sales. Each year between forty and fifty of the outstanding "salesmen-employees" are given an extra reward of a trip to some part of the world that they would probably not be financially able to visit otherwise. Some of these junkets in recent years have been to Ireland, Mexico and Hawaii.

In addition to its farm and home consumers, Thermogas serves about 200 industrial accounts ranging from the Briggs and Stratton Motor Company in Milwaukee to malt processors, breweries, steel mills and farm equipment manufacturers. Such concerns use LP Gas to supplement their heating and also as motor fuel for trucks and forklifts. The Division buys about 30 percent of its hydrocarbons from MAPCO's Production Department, one of more than twenty recognized suppliers for Thermogas. Among the other suppliers are Exxon, Mobil, Texaco, Cities Service, Gulf, Pure Oil, and Union Oil. Thermogas deals with MAPCO's Production Department in the same way it does any other supplier, giving no favoritism and expecting none. The Thermogas operation also uses, in addition to the Mid-America Pipeline, any other pipeline carrying LP Gas to areas it serves.

In buying gas supplies or trading gas with other operators, Maurie Maher relies greatly on his Irishman's ability as a shrewd trader. "There are a lot of tricks in this business," he says. "My approach has always been: Never let the other guy know you are anxious to purchase—let *him* keep trying to sell, even though you might need the propane real bad and you are almost out of it. Let *him* keep coming back. He will get a little lower and a little lower.

"I make my profit by getting 'boot.' That is the term I got from horse-trading over the years. If somebody wants your product and you have it, you remain poker-faced and you say, 'Well, I think I can help you—but I'm going to need some differential . . .' I now politely call that profit 'geographical differential,' but in my own mind it is still 'boot.' My Dad always told me never to make a trade 'unless you can get some boot—even if it is nothing more than a dozen eggs.'

"I have kind of followed that theory in trading in hydrocarbons throughout my career. You sort of wave a little carrot out there and you let your prospect know you've got some gas, and you let him come to you. Don't be too anxious—even if you have to pass up a deal once in a while. But once the deal is made, stick to it. Up until recent times, most of our deals were made over the phone or with a handshake. And we have always lived up to our agreements, even if the market changes and we lose by it. It's been only recently that you have got to put all that stuff on paper, because it seems that you just can't trust people any more—they will renege on you if they get the chance."

The most uneasy time in Maurie Maher's career with Thermogas came just after the company had been taken over by MAPCO. This produced great tension for several months. "Mr. Russell was a sort of father figure in running the business, and we always had had a very closely knit organization," Maurie says. "It hurt Mr. Russell to give up his company, and sometimes this showed. But, to Mr. Russell's credit, I can never remember him saying that they (meaning MAPCO) were doing it 'all wrong and it ought to be done this way,' although I knew he was hurting and there were a few tense times between him and Mr. Thomas. I was on the spot as to where my loyalties should lie, but I tried to be honest with both sides. Happily, it all worked out fine.

"Throughout all this time," Maurie recalls, "Mr. Thomas was very understanding. He realized I was on the spot. My only objection to Mr. Thomas now is that sometimes I can't get hold of him on the telephone when I want to talk to him. But when Mr. Thomas wants *me*—even if I'm up on top of the roof—he figures I ought to have a telephone up there so he can talk to me—*immediately!*"

A Friend in the Sky 17

Mather Griffin—"everybody calls me 'Griff' "—is a spritely, slightly built, ageless and energetic man with snapping dark eyes and an engaging manner, who has flown maybe millions of miles looking down at pipelines from up in the air.

He and the four pilots who work for him spend most of their time "flying pipeline patrol" on the lookout for people, animals and acts of God that appear likely to damage pipelines in some way by causing erosion around the pipe, leaks, thefts and perhaps even explosions. Griff and his men work for a number of pipeline companies under contract, including Mid-America. Once a week, Griff or one or more of his men survey from the air the mainline and all of its tributaries from Hobbs, New Mexico, to a point north of Conway, Kansas.

Another airplane pilot, Dave See, of Moberly, Missouri, flies patrol north of Griff's route in northern Kansas, Nebraska, Iowa and Minnesota along the line's West Leg and the entire East Leg through Missouri into Illinois and Wisconsin.

As things turned out, we spent our pipeline air time with Mather Griffin, one of the pioneer pilots in the pipeline patrol business, who is "a real friendly" type. Besides looking for trouble, he and his men—but especially Griff—go out of their way to spread good will, pleasant thoughts, joie de vivre and good public relations generally in behalf of the Mid-America Pipeline along the hundreds of miles they patrol. Griff has been known to glide down out of the sky suddenly into a nearby pasture and compliment the farmer on his fine crop of corn or alfalfa or praise his herd of black Angus cattle.

"I *have* had a little trouble occasionally with some of the people along the pipeline," he says, "but I do my best to keep everything on a friendly basis. A lot of people, especially farmers, have got a deep-seated grudge against pipelines because they didn't want the derned thing laid across their land in the first place. So I try to offset these grudges. I keep candy in the airplane and when I see a bunch of kids down on the ground, I'll drop a little candy to them once in a while—stuff like that. And I do a lot of waving to people.

I want to let them know I'm friendly and that I represent the pipeline company, which is also friendly.

"I try to get the folks who live along the pipeline to understand that the line is owned and operated by good, friendly human beings and not by some flint-hearted automaton off somewhere in a tall building in New York City or some such foreign place. Then maybe the folks living along the pipeline will be less likely to damage the company's property when they get to feeling ornery. The pipeline markers—they are the mileposts that you can read from up in the air—come in for a lot of harsh treatment, for instance. Cows are always rubbing up against these markers and knocking them down. Kids shoot them with their guns. I have seen guys with their horses tied to our markers. And every once in a while a farmer or rancher will get sore about something and he'll just dig one of our markers up and throw it over the fence or into a sinkhole or somewhere. You got a lot of things that give those markers a bad time."

One spring day in 1975, Bud De Masters, Operations Supervisor for Mid-America's Skellytown, Texas, station, and I spent several hours flying the Texas end of the pipeline with Griff in his sharp-looking, beautifuly maintained Cessna 172. During our flight Griff interspersed reminiscences and lore from his years of flying pipeline patrol with comments concerning the immediate pipeline conditions he was observing below as we flew over the beige-colored rangeland, the immense, spreading, irrigated fields of wheat and cotton—and finally above the terribly tortured terrain of the Palo Duro Canyon, which lies about 160 miles north of Hobbs, New Mexico. Griff was wearing that day a blue figured sport shirt with a string tie, slacks and cowboy boots. He *always* wears cowboy boots—says he wouldn't think of trying to fly in anything else. Even when he plays golf, Griff wears cowboy boots, specially built with golf cleats. "I could walk all day in a pair of these cowboy boots," he says "and they won't bother me. But just let me put on a pair of low quarter shoes, and you will have to carry me home."

The pilot walked over to the side of his plane, opened the engine cowling, pulled out the oil stick and pointed to the thin film clinging to it. "Look at how clean that oil is," he said, "you could practically put it on your bread and eat it." And sure enough the oil looked as fine and clear as maple syrup. "I keep my planes in the best possible condition," Griff went on. "Every 100 hours, each plane gets an FAA inspection. We have to fly low down to do a good job inspecting pipelines from the air, and I want my planes able to respond instantly and effectively. The regular Cessna has a 6-cylinder, 145-horsepower engine. But every time I get a new plane, I have the regular engine taken out up at Wichita, and they put in a lighter, 4-cylinder engine that develops 180 horsepower. This gives our planes a lot more power and it also cuts down on the weight, which all adds up pretty good. I like to have extra power to combat the updrafts and downdrafts we may hit when flying low.

166

There's also a lot of headwinds you've got to fight. I have been flying an airplane for 38 years and I never had an accident, or even a close call, and neither have any of the pilots who work for me."

By now, the Cessna had lifted off the runway of the local airport, which Griff owns and operates incidentally, and the little city of Borger was dwindling to our rear. Ahead, the land was a reddish-brown with spots of green. An occasional ranch house with its cluster of outbuildings and a sentinel windmill came out of the horizon now and then, passed us going backwards and sank out of sight. Oil well pumps were nearly always somewhere below, resembling skeletons of strange cowlike animals whose heads were eternally nodding as they pumped away, looking lonely and forlorn.

"One of the things you've got to remember when flying pipeline patrol," Griff was saying, "is: Don't fly too slow. It would seem like the slower you flew, the better you could examine the line down below you—but that is not necessarily so. When I first started working for Mid-America, I had only a small portion of the line. Then one day Ralph Ball came down from Tulsa to see me and he said, 'I've noticed that the part of the line you're patrolling we never get plowed up. How is that? I want to fly with you along the pipeline and see how you do it. The other guys we use have slower airplanes than yours, but you're doing a better job.'

"I said to him, 'Well, I found out long ago that if you have an airplane that will cruise around 120 to 140 miles an hour, you can do a good job patrolling, but if you have an airplane that will go not more than around 80 or 90 miles an hour, you get out here on the line and the ole boy at the controls hits a real strong headwind and he sets there doing only about 60 miles an hour ground speed. At that rate he's got to stop every little bit for fuel. He's going to get fatigued pretty quick and when that happens, he don't do a good job seeing what's under him. I tell all of my pilots that any time they feel fatigued—*land. Right there!* Just land and walk around a little bit. If you are flying along at about 120 to 140 miles an hour, though, you don't get fatigued very much. I like to have enough horsepower that I can maintain a speed like that, even in the face of a headwind.

"There are two big warnings," Griff went on, "that I give my guys when teaching them to fly pipeline: One is: when you cross another pipeline, look carefully in both directions, as you would in a car when you are passing over a busy crossing. Some other guy is likely to be flying patrol along that other pipeline and if you are both coming together while looking at the ground and not watching your surroundings, you might have a bad accident. And there are a lot more pipelines down through this part of the country than anybody realizes. They are so thick underground in some places that they're almost like spaghetti. The other main warning I give my pilots is this: When you see a steel tower ahead of you [and here Griff pointed to what appeared to be a television station mast in the distance] don't worry about the tower—*but watch out for those guy wires.*"

Mather Griffin started flying in 1937 and worked at all sorts of commercial jobs in the air until 1945, when he took over pipeline patrol on a practically permanent basis—first for the Phillips Petroleum Company, then as a subcontractor and finally as his own boss who contracts with various pipeline firms to keep an eye on their property from above. He worked in the oil fields for a while and hired out as an engineer at a pipeline pump station to learn all he could about the pipeline business so that he would know better what to watch for from the air and make his reports more meaningful. When he is training a new pilot to fly pipeline, Griff likes to take the trainee to a pipeline pump station and let him hang around a day or so and learn what is going on. Then he tries to get the new pilot out for a few days with a pipeline crew repairing or building a pipeline.

"What we watch for most," Griff went on, "are crews digging other pipelines, or people leveling the ground for some purpose, and we watch especially for anybody near our pipeline driving some heavy earth-moving equipment. Worst of all are these county road-maintenance crews with their graders. They cut into pipelines more than anybody. The pipeline right-of-way is clearly marked every mile, but some of these fellows don't seem to notice that. When we see heavy equipment approaching our right of way, we circle and drop a note warning the crew that they are near a high-pressure pipeline that is likely to explode if they should puncture it. The message contains the telephone of the nearest MAPCO station, and the fellow on the heavy equipment is asked to telephone the station. If it looks serious enough, we will land and telephone the nearest MAPCO station ourselves and tell them what is going on."

A flight of small, dark-colored birds flashed in front of us; Griff quickly zoomed the nose of the Cessna up, then turned the plane's belly toward them. "You never go *down* to miss a bird," he said. "You see a bird coming at you, you pull up. The bird never goes up to miss *you.* He always folds his wings and dives. You'd be surprised at how many guys with several thousand hours of flying never give that a thought. The most troublesome are those little starlings. They are especially bad in summertime when there is feed around. I usually pull up a little when I see ahead a big field of milo. The birds are gonna be pretty thick in there. We don't have any trouble with duck or geese; it's mainly those *little* birds. Crows are pretty good at dodging you, but watch out for those hawks. They are mean birds and will attack an airplane sometimes. A hawk will come nearer doing damage to your plane than almost any other bird in these parts. But whatever kind of bird is coming at you, you've always got to pull up to miss him. I tell all my pilots, 'Go up, and turn your belly toward those birds.' "

When we flew over a dry creek bed, Griff circled the Cessna back over the sandy wash and carefully studied both banks where the pipeline went under the sometimes stream. "We have to watch creek crossings especially carefully to see that the water has not washed out around the pipe and exposed it," he said. "There are badgers in these parts. They dig a pretty good size hole. Badgers will dig down close to the pipeline because it is warm down there and keeps them cozy in wintertime. Often they'll dig close to a creek crossing and that starts the bank washing."

An LP Gas line is under a greater strain from pressure than most. Since propane boils at 44 degrees below zero F, it is necessary to keep the liquid under at least 200 pounds pressure per square inch to prevent the substance from becoming gaseous. When a propane line is broken, the escaping propane will freeze the ground, sometimes to a depth of 20 feet. Griff and his kind detect propane and other LP Gas leaks by watching for big patches of frost on the ground. He says leaks in ammonia pipelines are easy to detect because you can smell ammonia even way up in the air, and it turns the ground a gray-white color.

Griff reports he has never observed thieves stealing product from a Mid-America line, but one time while flying patrol on a Phillips gasoline line, he detected an unusual thieving scheme that employed a haystack. "This ole boy had built a big haystack right alongside that pipeline," he relates, "and when I telephoned in and told the station man at Phillips about the haystack, he said, 'Well, when are you going to start counting the cows and chickens along your route?' He kept laughing at me about reporting that haystack. I said, 'Well, I thought you might like to know it's there.' He said, 'Yes, I do. It's of real big interest to us.' He was sort of razzing me about that haystack, like it didn't matter whether it was alongside the pipeline or not.

"Well, I kept watching that haystack for about six months. And then one day as I was flying over, I thought I saw a bale of hay move. So, I flew across the area and circled and came back and I still didn't see anything for sure. I thought, 'Well, I'll make like I'm going on down the line.' And so I flew on a little ways and then I whipped back real quick and came over that haystack and here was a truck coming right out of the middle of all that hay, loaded with barrels. They had tapped the line. I landed and called in to the station and asked for the same guy I'd told about the haystack the first time. I said, 'Hey, remember that haystack I saw about six months ago?' He said, 'Yeah.' I said, 'Well, a truck just came out of it loaded with gasoline barrels.' So, the Phillips people rushed down there and they caught him."

The most impressive spectacle from the air along the southern end of the Mid-America Pipeline is the Palo Duro Canyon, an immense and unexpected, deep and tortuous wound in the otherwise flat terrain of west Texas. Nobody is certain just how the Palo

Duro Canyon came to be there. Some dry creek beds crisscross the bottom of the canyon, but none of them appears to have been powerful enough to have wrought such a tremendous gash in the Texas High Plains. The canyon is probably 40 miles long by 10 miles wide and half a mile deep, with red clay and red rock sides, trimmed in green mesquite bushes. Flying over the Palo Duro Canyon gives one a rather overwhelming and frightening impression of stark and arid grandeur. But to Mather Griffin the canyon is mainly a place where pipeline hazards are unusually harsh.

As we flew along the Palo Duro's northern rim, Griff peered down intently at the area where the pipeline comes down the canyon's side and is buried along the floor. He found no exposed pipe and paid some compliments to the builders, Williams Brothers of Tulsa, for their care in construction along this especially difficult terrain. Griff turned the airplane on its side and flew along looking out the side window, which meant straight down. "This is the way I usually do it when I want to take a *good* look at where the pipeline enters the canyon," he said. "You want to look carefully at that steep side . . . the line is holding pretty good, I'd say. . . . It takes a real good installation job to hold in ground like this. Take a look at how steep that side is. You see along where the pipeline is buried, they have terraced it with rocks. That is one reason why it is holding so well."

On the way back to Borger, Griff got to talking about flying pipelines in general. "It's real interesting work," he said. "I've always liked pipeline patrol. I've done all kinds of flying—you name it—from test pilot on up or down. But I like pipeline flying, because—well, I just *like* it. I am interested in pipelines, and flying patrol on one like this is a lot safer than driving a jeep over it. And you can see a lot more from the air than from ground level. The air sometimes gets pretty rough at this height during the warm weather, but you get used to rough air. You need a little exercise, anyway.

"One of the advantages of pipeline flying is all the nice things you can see. You know, you can fly around the country way up high for years and years and never realize the beauty of what's under you, the way you do when you fly real low to the ground. The country is always changing. The yucca is in bloom down here now, and on out there in New Mexico you get other kinds of blossoms coming in—different kinds of things—changes in scenery. I don't find that it gets boring at all, even though I am flying over the same route day after day at 300 to 600 feet.

"And there are always people you can see down there when you are flying low. They are always busy, always active. They look up when they hear me, and quite often they wave at me. Fortunately, most of the people I see are not up to any mischief with the pipeline. With the kind of planes we fly I can land almost anywhere in any of these fields through here, but I don't often have to do that. Once in a while, though, you know, if something looks real suspicious down there, I may feel I ought to go down and investigate. Then I will land and go and talk to the folks—just sort of make friends with them. I want them to be friendly with me—and with the pipeline.

"As I've said, a lot of farmers are annoyed at pipeline companies for disturbing their land. Some people are nice and don't seem to mind, but others don't like it at all. So I try to make as many friends for the pipeline among them as I can. And *I do* have friends all along the pipeline and they wave when they see me coming. They are glad to see me. I try to fly along the same areas the same day of the week and at about the same time of the day so they can be on the lookout for me.

"And, of course, there are some who don't like anything about pipelines, and I don't guess there is anything we can ever do to change their minds. One time I was flying down the line and here was an ole boy down there digging up one of our markers. Even though he had taken the pipeline's money for its right-of-way, he still resented that air marker. So I circled around. He stopped and looked up at me and he shook his fist at me. I quit circling and went on off, and after I'd landed, of course, I reported it. They told me that this ole guy had been known to take shots at pipeline pilots with his gun. You never know what that man down there is thinking and how mad he might be at the pipeline.

"But I wave at the people in the fields and try not to fly too close to their houses and make too much noise that might irritate them. And I think most of them feel real friendly toward me—but, of course, you can't make friends with *everybody*."

Progress Protects   18
the Past

"The high mesas, wind-swept plains and river valleys of New Mexico have been continually occupied by people for over 12,000 years. The evidence of their existence is scattered around the State in the form of wind-blown campsites, grass-covered pueblo ruins and crumbling early Spanish and Anglo towns. These remains constitute the records in which today we can read the story of man's efforts to adapt to the ever-changing conditions of life in this varied land. Every bit of evidence that survives is testimony to this story and every fragment has its tale to tell to those who care to decipher it. For over a hundred years archeologists have come from all over the world to study this rich heritage of archeological and historical resources.

"In an area in which so many significant sites exist, any kind of construction project must be carefully planned or it will destroy these records of now vanished times and peoples. The Mid-America Pipeline system, a Division of MAPCO, Inc., of Tulsa, Oklahoma, recently completed an 8-inch petroleum products pipeline from Bloomfield [New Mexico] to their pumping station near Hobbs. In crossing the State from northwest to southeast, this 400-mile-long line traverses many areas with archeological and historical remains. MAPCO employed this writer as an Archeological Consultant to assist them in protecting the sites along this route. A reconnaissance of the route located seventy-seven sites, most of which were previously unknown . . ."

Thus wrote Curtis Schaafsma, a professional archeologist who lives amid the arid splendor of the New Mexico mountains at Arroyo Hondo, about one of the most fascinating and unusual of all of MAPCO's endeavors. The most significant of several unique features involved in laying the pipeline through New Mexico was MAPCO's introduction of what Mr. Schaafsma calls "preventive archeology." He explains it this way:

"The Southwest is rich in historical sites—the remains of past civilizations—one-time villages and towns where people lived as long ago as 10,000 years before Christ. In recent years, public and governmental agencies have become increasingly aware of the importance of these sites and the desirability of preserving them.

172

But, until the MAPCO Pipeline project came along, no explicit plan had ever been adopted *ahead of time* for a construction project to traverse this country in a way that would *avoid* disturbing these historical remains.

"Until recent years, builders of pipelines, roads, power lines simply ignored the archeological sites, plowing them up, largely destroying them and forgetting all about them. More recently, increasing public concern with preserving such sites has brought about stricter enforcement of antiquities and historic preservation laws. And so, when land-disturbing projects have blundered into the obvious remains of ancient villages and towns, the builders have had archeological teams come to the site to dig and sift through the remains before they are all destroyed in the name of progress."

The trouble is that these "wham-bam" excavations, whether funded by government sources or private enterprise, are done under such a press of time that much of the information is lost to hurry. The artifacts are usually gathered up and removed in bulk. Unless the archeologists are able to map and measure everything on the site, they are not able to make an effective analysis of the tribal customs, manner of living, social mores and economy of these departed peoples. And that is the principal purpose of archeology. As Mr. Schaafsma points out, the real object of archeology is not merely to find artifacts and treasure them. "When we dig," he says, "it is mainly for information. These artifacts are the things we use to reconstruct cultural patterns of the past. Once we are through with artifacts, we pass them on to museums or stick them back in the ground.

"The long-time significance of MAPCO's policy regarding archeological sites," Curtis Schaafsma went on, "is shown in what has happened since that pipeline was built. There have been numerous 'clearance surveys,' as we have come to call them, of archeological sites prior to the building of other pipelines, roads and such projects that have been undertaken since the MAPCO pipeline was completed. We believe that this enlightened attitude was influenced by MAPCO's policy. That experience really brought to archeological awareness the fact that private industry and archeology could cooperate in a useful way to protect the nation's cultural heritage. And rather than everybody sitting around blindly sort of regarding other people (mainly archeologists and ecologists vs. industrial enterprise) as uncooperative and impossible to be dealt with, we demonstrated that we could get together and work out our differences in a mutually agreeable manner. And that has served as a lead for any number of interaction projects between archeologists and private industry and archeology and federal agencies—MAPCO sort of broke the ice. This kind of thing had never been done before, at least in such a definite and effective way."

Mr. Schaafsma says that "current archeological thinking" in this area is expressed in editorial comment found in the *Newsletter* of August 1974, published by the American Society for Conservation Archeology, which reviewed MAPCO's policy and Curtis Schaafsma's work in building the pipeline across New Mexico:

"Schaafsma's main point is that intensive advanced archeological surveys of rights-of-way for proposed pipelines, power lines, roads, etc., can help companies plan to avoid archeological sites. It is usually cheaper to plan *around* sites before trenching or grading begins than to salvage sites which lie within the rights-of-way. In theory, one knows all this, but, in fact, many past pipelines and other projects have destroyed much more than has been preserved. Clearly, any strategy such as that employed by Schaafsma and MAPCO to *conserve* archeological resources by *avoiding* them is an advanced and a welcomed one."

As a direct result of MAPCO's showing the way, according to Curtis Schaafsma, the Bureau of Land Management's San Juan District in northwest New Mexico, followed by the Albuquerque and Roswell districts, and now practically the entire state of New Mexico, is requiring archeological clearance surveys before any land-disturbing projects are approved. He feels that similar restrictions will soon be adopted by other states.

In 1971—a year before the pipeline was begun—MAPCO officials learned of the ecologists' concern for preserving archeological sites. After Eugene G. Bell, MAPCO's Secretary and General Counsel, conferred with the New Mexico Corporation Commission, the Bureau of Land Management, the Bureau of Indian Affairs, and other state and federal agencies, the company hired Curtis Schaafsma as its Archeological Consultant, on the recommendation of the National Park Service. Mr. Schaafsma worked for MAPCO off and on for the better part of a year through 1972 and into 1973. It was his suggestion that MAPCO spy out the land ahead of time, to locate the archeological sites and build the pipeline around them whenever possible. The survey revealed seventy-seven archeological sites within the 50-foot-wide, more than 400-mile-long right-of-way across the state, and MAPCO's engineers were able to avoid disturbing all but two of them. It was impractical to build around one of the sites. The pipeline crew stumbled into the second accidentally because of an error in direction by one of the grader operators. It was necessary to make fifty-eight line changes in the original route of the pipeline in order to miss the remaining seventy-five sites. An interesting example of a major site on private land bypassed by the pipeline is an 18th-century Spanish village near Placitas. The right-of-way, as originally surveyed, would have gone right through the middle of this site for nearly a quarter of a mile. It was missed entirely by rerouting the line over a high hill. This site had been little known, but after the MAPCO survey it was placed on the New Mexico Historic Sites Register and, in 1975, was nominated for the National Historical Sites Register.

174

Although in dress, habits and appearance, Schaafsma reminds some citybound observers of a sort of youngish "Desert Rat," he is an engaging, erudite man, wiry from tramping hundreds of miles across the desert in his archeological researches. Of Norwegian descent, he is bearded, blue-eyed and rugged-looking, and likes to avoid modern-day civilization as much as possible. The MAPCO people had to argue with Schaafsma at length before persuading him to have a telephone installed in his home, deep in the desert, so that they could communicate with him when necessary. A native of California, Curtis came to New Mexico when he was fifteen years old, worked for a while as a hotel bellhop, became interested in antiquities and has since devoted his life to archeology. At the time he was employed by MAPCO he had a Master's Degree in Anthropology from the University of New Mexico and was working on his Doctoral thesis.

The survey began when Curtis Schaafsma and J. H. "Hank" Lieber, Senior Pipeline Engineer for MAPCO, studied the entire 400-mile-odd route from a low-flying helicopter to locate the more obvious sites, such as ruined pueblos. (A pueblo is a Southwestern Indian village, a sort of an apartmentlike complex of anywhere from three or four up to 100 or more rooms and built of adobe mixed with a few stones.) The ancient ones, which are collapsed into piles of rocks and old mud, can be spotted more easily from 15 or 20 feet in the air than at ground level. Mr. Lieber was able to make a number of pipeline relocations from what he saw from the air. Schaafsma completed some 300 miles of the survey from helicopter height and didn't have to return to those areas again. The helicopter, however, passed over more than 100 miles of "suspicious terrain"—thickets, wooded areas, creek bottoms, where the ground could not be seen clearly enough to ascertain whether archeological sites were located there. Schaafsma made notes and later walked those areas, charting the sites he found. All of the sites were numbered on a map and labeled MAPCO 1, MAPCO 2, etc.

"A culture as a whole can be viewed as an energy transformation system which takes in energy, usually in the form of plant and animal products, transforms it into the activities of the culture, and then discards the waste," Curtis Schaafsma explains. "In archeology we are left with only the residue, such as worn-out houses, discarded vessels, lost and discarded tools, burial sites and the like. Their nature and the spatio-temporal distribution provides us with a fossil record of the former system in which we attempt to read the nature of the original structures—the ritual cycles of these people, warfare patterns, settlement changes, energy intake derived from gathering wild forest products, domestic herding and other such activities. The sites that we located in the MAPCO survey cover a wide variety of sociocultural systems that existed in this area we now call New Mexico. People have lived here since the latter days

175

of the last Ice Age, and the physical records of their activities are widely dispersed."

According to the archeological evidence so far discovered, the earliest human inhabitants of New Mexico depended on hunting large animals near the lakes and ponds formed during that last Ice Age more than 12,000 years ago. These people were predators, following the herds of mammoths, camels, bison and such, roaming through the wet, wooded savannas around the lakes. The earliest hunters are called Clovis, after the currently named areas where their artifacts have been found. Later human systems have been given names like Folsom and Eden. None of the archeological sites dating from this earliest era were found within the MAPCO right-of-way, although several were spotted nearby on the former beaches around the Pleistocene Lake which once filled the Estancia Valley near Moriarty.

The next cultural stage of human beings in the Southwest, according to Curtis Schaafsma, is known as "the desert culture, or the Western archaic." It was well developed by 5000 B.C. and lasted until replaced by the agriculturists in New Mexico around 600 A.D. "When this way of life was coming into being in New Mexico," Mr. Schaafsma has written, "Egypt was just a string of independent, dusty farming villages along the Nile. When it was terminating, Rome was being sacked and the Middle Ages were beginning. The economic phase of the desert culture . . . was based on intensive gathering and preparing of wild plants (Indian rice grass, amaranth, pinyon nuts, juniper berries, choke berries, yuccas) and the hunting of small game such as rabbits, rock squirrels, woodrats, birds and medium-size animals such as deer and mountain sheep. The economy is reflected in the many grinding stones, small projectile points, knives and scrapers that they left scattered over the country and particularly where they made their camps. Occasional cave sites have preserved their perishable tools, and these reveal a wealth of nets, snares, baskets, ropes, hafted knives, seed gatherers and other tools not found in the open sites. Their tool inventory was fairly complex and adequate to the demands of their hunting and gathering mode of life."

The one area it was necessary to excavate, because there was no way for the pipeline to bypass it, was a campsite once occupied by these desert hunters and gatherers. MAPCO paid for this archeological excavation, which was done by a group of students from the University of New Mexico under Mr. Schaafsma's direction. They came in pickup trucks loaded with wheelbarrows, trowels, shovels, string, tape and plane table mapping equipment. The archeologists carefully removed layer after layer of topsoil and on the second day the tip of a stone began to appear. Although everyone was curious about this, they left it in place and removed additional layers of soil from around it, carefully brushing the dirt away. Other stones began to appear in a rough semicircle, finally revealing themselves to constitute part of an ancient hearth, blackened, cracked and quite brittle from the many fires that had burned there thousands of years ago. By using the carbon dating method, with C-14, the archeologists established that one of the hearths had been used about 800 years before Christ, the other some 250 years B.C. Also found in this site were more than 1,000 artifacts, including grinding stones, flake knives, scrapers, chopper tools, hammer stones and other small objects used by these primitive peoples in their daily lives. The survey reveals numerous sites where desert culture people lived along 300 of the 400-odd-mile MAPCO route—eleven of which lie between Bloomfield and the Pecos River and five along a 5-mile stretch on the south slope of Kutz Canyon. In the clay hills and sand dunes south of the Jamaz River, desert culture sites were found in abundance. After the operator of the grader misread his directions and plowed into one of them east of Santa Ana, the archeological crew from the university was hastily summoned and went to work. While their excavations did not result in as many artifacts as the first exploration, this one was still regarded as important, and the site dated from 500 A.D.

In the hills east of the Rio Grande, the MAPCO reconnaissance revealed a ridge thick with stone tools. These included an unusually fine example of an ancient grain-grinding device—a *mano,* a rounded stone that the grain grinder held in her hand and worked against the grain, which was held in a *metate.* The latter is a rounded, bowl-shaped stone that rested on the ground. The MAPCO people found the *mano* sitting in the *metate,* just the way some primitive woman probably left it when she walked away from her grinding task 3,000 years ago.

Perhaps a couple of centuries after Christ, the desert culture peoples, depending upon wild food resources, began to change into tribes that cultivated foods such as corn and squash. Wandering bands were replaced by semi-permanent villages where people lived in one place at least during the growing season to be near their rainfall-dependent crops. Pottery, permanent houses and larger social units began to appear. Mr. Schaafsma believes that one site uncovered by the MAPCO survey, near Bernalillo, represents this period of change from wild food to the beginning of horticulture.

Remnants of this early agricultural system were found at ten sites along a 4-mile stretch of the MAPCO pipeline route near the modern Zia Pueblo. These sites are characterized by pithouses dug into the ground five or six feet deep. The depressions remain but the coverings of the houses, a type of thatch, have long since disappeared. Artifacts found in these sites included black-on-white pottery, plain cooking pottery, an abundance of grinding tools, knives, scrapers and pointed projectiles, indicating a degree of reliance upon hunting small game. Carbon dating showed that the ten sites date from around 700 A.D. to about 950 A.D.

After 1200 A.D., according to Curtis Schaafsma, the natives of this region gradually changed their way of life to form the base for the Pueblo culture that continues to exist today. "The most obvious change we see in the archeological records," he says, "was the complete abandonment, in the area under consideration, of pithouses as domiciles, and the appearance of aboveground houses—occasionally with more than 100 rooms. The pithouses were converted into ceremonial rooms, called *kivas,* and are so used today in many conservative Pueblo villages. Another significant change after 1200 A.D. was a settlement shift away from small sites in the higher elevations to larger villages in lower stream valleys. The pottery found in these villages is called Santa Fe black-on-white. In the Las Huertas Valley, we found two sites along the MAPCO right-of-way that represented this era. The move out of the higher elevations and the development of some fairly large villages near permanent streams all hint that the system that produced Sante Fe black-on-white pottery was beginning to rely upon minor amounts of irrigation."

During the next century, full-scale irrigation developed along the Rio Grande and its permanent tributaries. A striking example of a village that came into being during this period is on the west bank of the Rio Grande near the MAPCO pipe crossing. In 1300 A.D., according to Schaafsma, there were virtually no villages along the hot, sandy banks of the river. But by 1350, this was an established village and by 1400 it was a thriving place with more than 1,000 population, a priesthood and an elaborate religious iconography that has been miraculously preserved in murals on the walls of the *kivas.*

Around 1340 A.D., a new form of pottery called "glaze" began to appear—a black lead glaze paint on a colored background of red, yellow, orange or white. The MAPCO pipeline passes quite near several sites where the glaze pottery is in evidence. Mr. Schaafsma's theory is that these sites were seasonal farmhouses where people grew irrigated crops during the summer only, then stored their produce in larger villages of the area where they spent the winter months. A sufficient number of sites were located during the survey in the Las Huertas Valley, the archeologist reports, to demonstrate that by 1450 A.D., these people were living in sturdy masonry houses of from one to six rooms, built on terraces above the stream. Some of the houses had flagstone floors.

The Spanish settlers who followed Francisco Vásquez de Coronado's army into the area built homes, established farms and ranches and lived at peace with the Indians until 1680. Then the Indians rebelled, killed some of the Spanish settlers and drove the rest out of the country. Twelve years later, the Spanish forced their way back, whereupon many of the Pueblo Indians took to the hills to join the Apaches, who had moved down from Canada about 150 years earlier to occupy the high plains.

The Navajos, who migrated south from Canada around 1500 A.D. to inhabit the northern areas of New Mexico and Arizona, are now the largest single Indian tribal group in North America. Mr. Schaafsma says, "Between 1700 and 1775, the Navajos adopted a cultural and economic system resulting from a hybrid combination of the Apache-Pueblo and also the Spanish way of life. Thus, the Navajos gradually took up the Athabascan language, the forked-stick hogans and the conical-bottomed pottery from the Apaches—a religious and social order that was heavily Pueblo—and an economy based upon Spanish sheepherding, Pueblo agriculture, Spanish fruit trees and the Apache knowledge of hunting and gathering. The MAPCO survey in the area of Lybrook, New Mexico, located a number of Navajo villages, some recently, some long abandoned. These locations included Navajo sweat lodges used in religious ceremonies, also sheep camps and corrals that dot the sage-covered landscape all the way to the Puerco River.

"The most interesting of these places to me," Curtis Schaafsma says, "was a village site uncovered by the MAPCO survey that apparently predates the 1680 revolution. Pottery found here indicates that the site may have been occupied by the 'Apaches del Navahu' before the Apaches were joined by the refugee Pueblos. This site promises to shed light on the Apache before 1700 A.D., about which we know so little.

"In the period between 1600 and 1850, Spanish and Indians came to be closely interrelated," according to Archeologist Schaafsma. "They frequently shared many items of material culture, built similar houses, farmed fields of corn, beans, wheat, peas, squash and other crops. They maintained orchards of apples, peaches and apricots, and kept the same types of domesticated animals. The ecological adaptations in both cases were very similar, and the Spanish more or less moved into and shared the same environment with the Pueblo Indians.

"A good example of this condition is MAPCO 2, near Placitas in north central New Mexico. This is primarily a Spanish village from the 18th and early 19th centuries. It is situated near a permanent spring on a wide terrace in the Las Huertas Valley that had been favored as a place for farming by the Indians since at least 1150 A.D. Pottery on the site shows that there had been an Indian village there before the Spanish arrived."

Prior to the MAPCO survey, there had been few archeological finds to shed light upon this period. And this is why MAPCO 2 was being considered in 1975 for listing on the National Historical Sites Register as of unusual historic significance.

"After the Civil War, Anglos and Spanish gradually spread out from the Rio Grande to many new areas of New Mexico," according to Curtis Schaafsma. "Prior to that time, the Navajos had kept the farmers and ranchers out of the plateau, and the Apaches and other tribes had kept them off the high plains, except for well-protected wagon trains. This period of expansion has left a few sites scattered about which we discovered on the MAPCO survey and which we were able to avoid with the pipeline. MAPCO 21, for example, is a trading post or a ranch house from the 19th or early 20th century in rough country west of San Ysidro. MAPCO 77 is a ranch complex or other settlement from about the turn of the century, near San Pedro Creek, that today consists of some weathered stone foundations and scattered tin cans."

And that is how MAPCO has become archeologically and ecologically oriented. This is part of the extending horizons and the arrival of unexpected responsibilities that come in the course of a commercial enterprise's growing up. Certainly, when Robert E. Thomas and his associates were putting together the Mid-America Pipeline Company only a few years earlier, they never envisioned a time when their enterprise would help historians to unravel the archeological background of the Great Southwest, from the distant age of crude stone implements to the era of canned sardines and Campbell's soup.

Before building its 400-mile, eight-inch LP gas pipeline across New Mexico, MAPCO pioneered in preserving historic sites from industrial molestation by exploring ahead of time the proposed route of the pipeline and, by making 58 changes in its proposed course, avoided almost all areas regarded as important by historians and anthropologists. Of the 77 historic sites discovered along the route—generally ruins of settlements of ancient peoples—it was possible to avoid all but two. These were carefully "dug" and their artifacts analyzed and catalogued by archeological task forces from the University of New Mexico, with their tapelines and brushes.

180

In the hills west of the Rio Grande River, MAPCO's reconaissance of the proposed pipeline route revealed a ridge strewn with stone tools of a long-vanished race. Among these was an unusually fine specimen of a primitive grain-grinding device—a rounded stone, called a "mano," that was held in the grinder's hand and worked against grain contained in a bowl-shaped piece of stone, called a "metate."

The ruins of an adobe house is part of a long-abandoned 18th Century Spanish village, near Placitas, in North Central New Mexico. Situated near a permanent spring, this site had been favored as a farming area by Indians for 500 years before the Spanish arrived. MAPCO's pipeline leaves the abandoned village undisturbed, after being re-routed over a nearby hill.

It's Better Than Manure 19

Ever since the Mid-America Pipeline carrying liquefied petroleum gas began operation in 1960, Robert E. Thomas and his associates have been striving to offset the effects of seasonal fluctuations in the use of these fuels, ranging from heavy sales during the cold months to heavy red ink in warm weather.

Their most dramatic move toward spreading pipeline operations more evenly over the year occurred in October, 1968, when MAPCO began operating the first anhydrous ammonia pipeline in the United States and the first truly long-distance pipeline in the world to carry this potent liquid plant food. Anhydrous ammonia, which is 82 percent nitrogen and is derived principally from natural gas, is a relatively recent development in agriculture, and is used extensively to fertilize corn and wheat.

The MAPCO ammonia line begins at the Camex Chemical Plant at Borger in the Texas Panhandle, which until 1974 had been the line's only supplier. The ammonia pipeline follows generally the right-of-way of the Mid-America LP Gas pipeline for some 720 miles into the consuming areas of Kansas, eastern Nebraska and northwestern Iowa. It is capable of carrying about 4,000 tons of anhydrous ammonia per day, but for the first six years of operation, it "loafed along" carrying only 1,000 to 1,300 tons a day —the full production of the Camex Plant. Then, in 1975, Farmland Industries opened an ammonia-producing plant at Enid, Oklahoma, which tied into the MAPCO line and doubled its throughput. Two more producing plants were scheduled to tie in during 1976–1977 and thus increase the pipeline's throughput to full capacity.

The reader can better appreciate the significance and importance of Mid-America's anhydrous ammonia pipeline by taking a brief look backward into the history and development of plant foods in general and of anhydrous ammonia in particular.

The name ammonia is said to have derived in the Libyan Desert, where nomadic farmers in ancient times used for fertilizer the white deposits left from their burned-out campfires of camel dung. These deposits actually were ammonia salts, and they were called ammonia because this practice was followed near a holy place called the Temple of Ammon.

182

Since prehistoric times, men have used decaying organic matters to help grow better agricultural crops. The first fertilizer techniques probably developed after primitive peoples observed that grasses grew more luxuriantly where plant and animal residue had decayed. Until comparatively recent times, animal manure had constituted the principal fertilizing elements, and is still widely used for gardening of flowers and vegetables and small crops. Centuries ago, the Egyptians spread silt deposits from the overflow of the Nile on poor land to make it rich. Since prehistoric times Chinese have saved their "night soil" and applied it to rice paddies. The American Indians, at the time the first European arrived, fertilized each hill of maize by putting a dead fish in it. The interesting point is that all of these substances are heavily laden with nitrogen, which is the principal component of ammonia.

About 135 years ago, agricultural fertilization began to pass out of the realm of handed-down folk techniques and into the era of science, when Justus von Liebig, a German chemist, concluded during the 1840's that plants grow because they absorb certain chemical substances from the soil and air. An English contemporary, John Bennett Lawes, conducted experiments on his estate at Rothamstead, England, which showed that the principal elements needed for fertilizer are nitrogen, phosphorus and potassium. These findings are still accepted by agriculturists everywhere, and Rothamstead continues as one of the world's most renowned agricultural experiment stations.

The first nitrogen commercially marketed as fertilizer came from saltpeter deposits in India and the famous fields of nitrate of soda in Chile. Although these deposits were extensive, it was soon recognized that a method should be devised to obtain usable nitrogen compounds from the air, since nitrogen makes up about 78 percent of the earth's atmosphere by volume, or 75.5 percent by weight, and serves to dilute the oxygen we breathe. It is a colorless, odorless, tasteless gas that will not support combustion. There are about 12 pounds of nitrogen above every square inch, which means 20,000,000 tons over every square mile of earth. But this uncombined nitrogen cannot be used directly by plants.

In 1898, Sir William Crooks, a famous English physicist, delivered a remarkable address in which he predicted that the food salvation for the growing populations of the world lay in taking nitrogen from the atmosphere by chemical processes. It was only seven years later, in Norway, that the first plant was constructed to manufacture nitrogen materials from the air. About the same time, a process was developed to make ammonium sulfate from coke ovens. These two processes, along with the supply of nitrate from Chile, provided the main nitrogen fertilizer until after World War I.

In 1908, a German chemist, Fritz Haber, developed a laboratory process for synthesizing ammonia directly from hydrogen and air nitrogen. His co-worker, Karl Bosch, adapted this to commercial production. Using high temperature, pressure, and iron as a catalyst, the Haber-Bosch process became the foundation of the huge ammonia industry that originates 90 percent of the world's commercial nitrogen compounds. The Haber-Bosch process supplied Germany with its ammonia needs—principally for making explosives—throughout World War I, when that country's access to other ammonia raw materials was cut off. The German achievement brought the Haber-Bosch process into great prominence, and by 1920 plants were being constructed throughout the world, including several in the United States.

In this country, no great attention had been given to developing fertilizer because of the abundance of land and the underpopulation. Migration continued toward virgin lands in the West while the older fields in the East were kept productive with animal manure, and growing of legume crops or alfalfa to replace nitrogen in the soil after a corn crop. Nitrate was also extracted from bat guano deposits in the great caves in Kentucky and used as fertilizer.

Until about 45 years ago, in fact, agricultural authorities had not thought in terms of injecting ammonia directly into the soil as fertilizer. The increasing production of ammonia was primarily for military and industrial purposes. Then in 1930, J. O. Smith, of the Delta Branch agricultural experiment station in Mississippi, applied ammonia directly into the soil from a small cylinder attached to a walking plow, pulled by a mule. The ammonia went into the soil as a gas, but once in the ground, the moisture content of the soil united with the ammonia and held it there until needed to nourish a plant. It wasn't until fifteen years after the Smith experiments, however, that pure ammonia was adopted as fertilizer on a widespread commercial basis. This began in 1932 when the Shell Development Company's laboratory at Anaheim, California, started field experiments by applying ammonia to irrigation water.

The man who did most to promote ammonia as fertilizer was W. B. Andrews of Mississippi State College. He realized that ammonia could provide an efficient, economical source of nitrogen to replenish the impoverished fields of the South. With several associates, Mr. Andrews did extensive research work on direct injection of anhydrous ammonia into the soil. The findings were favorable and were published in a comprehensive Mississippi State College bulletin in 1947. After that, the use of anhydrous ammonia as a soil fertilizer swept through the South and then the rest of the country. Annual consumption for agricultural purposes was only 20,000 tons in 1947. This increased to 800,000 tons in a few years. The United States Government had built a number of large ammonia plants during World War II to supply explosives for the war effort. After the war, these were sold or leased to private enterprise, and their production was devoted to agricultural uses. The greatest concentration of plants was along the Texas and Louisiana Gulf coasts because of the many gas wells in that area. It had been learned that ammonia could be most efficiently and cheaply produced by using natural gas. The widespread use of anhydrous ammonia as fertilizer throughout the rich farming areas of the Middle West is a major reason for the immense production from United States agriculture in the post-World War II years. And yet, until MAPCO constructed its anhydrous ammonia pipeline, this vital product was transported rather inefficiently by barge, railroad tank car and tank truck. Again, there was a need for a swift, efficient, large-scale new method of transportation, such as Mid-America had supplied to the liquefied petroleum gas industry.

Gilbert Rohleder recalls that Mid-America was first approached on the matter of transporting anhydrous ammonia via pipeline by the Occidental Petroleum Company, which was considering building a large-scale ammonia plant in west Texas. "That plant never developed," Mr. Rohleder reports, "but while it was still under consideration, we decided to do some research on the feasibility of transporting anhydrous ammonia in pipelines. We financed a University of Tulsa research project aimed at learning all there was to know about anhydrous ammonia's characteristics —how it is used, where they put it, where the market is, the problem in transporting it in pipelines. When the research was finished, we built a pilot pipeline at Conway, Kansas, to learn by experimentation whether we could batch anhydrous ammonia with propane and other LP gases through our existing pipeline. We soon learned that batching anhydrous ammonia when put in an LP Gas pipeline presented far too many problems. Ammonia would contaminate and corrode the copper fittings in our valving and pumps in the propane-butane distribution system. So, after all this research, we decided it would be much easier and cheaper to build a line dedicated to transporting anhydrous ammonia only. But then the deal with Occidental fell through and the whole thing sort of died off for a while."

The deal that eventually resulted in the nation's first anhydrous ammonia pipeline was brought to MAPCO's Mid-America Pipeline Division by a young chemical engineer named Robert Poston. But, according to David A. Roach, Senior Vice President in charge of the pipeline system, the moving force behind the proposed project was John Hill, a promoter from Dallas, Texas, and one of the most colorful and spectacular of the many memorable characters to cross MAPCO's path during its first fifteen years in the flamboyant fields of oil, gas and pipelining. "John Hill," Mr. Roach recalls, "is a great promoter. He gets things done; he built the biggest ammonia plant in the world at the time, which supplies our pipeline. And he built it with no capital of his own—it was all other people's money."

The concept of the project originated with Bob Poston, then employed by the Sinclair Oil and Gas Company in Tulsa, and his friend Frank Armstrong, a young lawyer with a gas transmission line headquartered at Houston. Their idea was to build an immense (for the time) ammonia-producing plant in Texas that would use as raw materials natural gas from the Amarillo Basin. Poston and Armstrong also favored moving the finished product from their proposed plant to the consuming areas via pipeline. After failing to get financial backing from several Texas money-men, Poston and Armstrong approached John Hill, who was low on funds but strong on salesmanship.

John Vance, currently Vice President of Agrico Chemical Company, a division of the Williams Companies, was in charge of Marketing for the Hill Enterprise at the time the ammonia plant was being promoted and built at Borger, Texas. He has some interesting insights into the personality of John Hill and how the big ammonia plant and the Mid-America anhydrous pipeline came into being:

"John Hill is one of those wild Texans," Vance says, "the special breed that dig holes in the ground—an entrepreneur extraordinaire. I guess you would call him a 'typical Texan,' at least from a New Yorker's point of view. In those days at least, he was very colorful; he dressed and acted the part. John is the guy who got me started wearing sports clothes. I never saw him wear a hat. He is just the stereo type of a flamboyant Texan. If he had a cigar, it had to be the biggest one available. If he had a drink, it had to be the best; I don't think he ever drank Scotch that wasn't Chivas Regal. If he had a brandy, it had to be Courvoisier. If he bought a suit of clothes, it had to be first class all the way.

"At the time Poston and Armstrong came along with their idea, John Hill badly needed a project, and he bought it. Then Hill, Bob Poston and Frank Armstrong took their idea to MAPCO, which agreed to become a partner in the project. At about this time I quit my job with Sinclair Petro Chemicals and joined John Hill's enterprise. We made several trips to New York City and I had meetings with a number of investment bankers and with Metropolitan Life Insurance Company. We finally worked out some long-term financing through Metropolitan—a $20,000,000 loan to Hill Chemicals. MAPCO was handling its own financing."

As it turned out, MAPCO did not participate in building the Hill Chemical Plant and never owned any part of it. At a meeting in Chicago, the MAPCO Board of Directors did not give approval to the company's becoming an equity partner in the Hill Plant, although the Directors *did* look favorably upon Mid-America building an anhydrous ammonia pipeline to transport the plant's products. "Actually, as things turned out, I think it was probably better for all concerned that MAPCO did not become an equity partner in the chemical plant," Mr. Vance said in 1975—and MAPCO officials agree. "Bob Thomas and his people ran into an awful lot of opposition while trying to lay their pipeline through

Iowa and maybe some other places. If Mid-America had owned part of the Hill Chemical Plant—and since that was the only one feeding the pipeline—the pipeline management might have had difficulty defending its position as a common carrier.

"But when MAPCO's Board decided not to participate in building the Hill Chemical Plant, that left us in the Hill organization standing out there high and dry with no money. There were probably five of us on the payroll at the time. One of our principal prospective customers was Cominco American—the U.S. branch of a large Canadian concern that operated a plant at Beatrice, Nebraska, making ammonium nitrate. Cominco had expressed a strong interest in connecting with our proposed pipeline to get its raw materials. Figuring they were pretty well on the hook now as a customer, John Hill and I went up to see Fred Burnet, President of Cominco American, at the company's U.S. headquarters at Spokane, Washington. We said to him in effect, 'Besides taking a supply of anhydrous ammonia from us, wouldn't your company like to take an equity in the plant?' Burnet expressed strong interest.

"John and I left Spokane on a high note of enthusiasm because of Burnet's favorable response. And this will give you an insight into John Hill's modus operandi: On the way back to Dallas, we stopped over at Las Vegas, where John was known as a kind of high roller. We walked into the Sands Hotel and asked the desk clerk for two single rooms. He said he was sorry but the hotel was sold out and there was no way to get any rooms. John then asked, 'Is Bunky Harris on the floor?' The clerk said, 'I think so.' I'm following John; I had never been to Vegas before. We went back into the room with the crap tables and Bunky Harris, who was the pit boss, welcomed John like a long-lost brother. John told him our problem. Bunky said, 'Just a minute.' He went to the telephone and apparently talked with the desk clerk. Then he said to us, 'Go to the desk clerk now and he will take care of you.' We went back there and in a few minutes, John Hill and I had separate suites in the Tower, with fruit in both suites and the hotel picked up the tab.

"That night, John shot crap and won somewhere between $5,200 and $5,300. He walked away from Vegas a winner in that amount and that is how he got the money to meet the next payroll of the Hill Chemical Company.

"Well, anyway Cominco put $7,300,000 of equity capital into the project and, with the $20,000,000 loan from Metropolitan Life, we were off and running," John Vance reports. "We hired an expert named Hayes Mayo, who had been with the Kellogg Corporation and was one of the two men instrumental in designing what is now the standard of the industry—the Kellogg Ammonia Plant, capable of producing 1,000 to 1,200 tons of ammonia a day. We got some short-term loans from banks to start construction until we got our money from Metropolitan Life. And that is the way we glued the plant together, and it worked, and we started pumping through the MAPCO pipeline in 1968."

According to John Vance, John Hill was such a good negotiator that the Hill Chemical Company ended up with half of the equity in the ammonia plant at Borger, although Hill and his people had not put a penny into it. "But," Vance says, "John Hill is like so many entrepreneurs. He is a great promoter, but not worth a damn when it comes to running something. John got the idea that this was *his* company. This attitude, plus some expensive trips to Europe, South America and elsewhere, which the company paid for, completely disenchanted the Cominco people. They got rid of him." Eventually, Cominco bought full ownership and changed the name from Hill Chemical to Camex.

This internal dissension did not hinder ammonia production at the plant, which has steadily supplied the Mid-America Pipeline with 1,000 to 1,200 tons of ammonia each day since 1968. The anhydrous ammonia pipeline was financed with an $11,000,000 loan from the Prudential Insurance Company of America. When it opened, the only other anhydrous ammonia pipeline anywhere was a 6⅝-inch line running 150 miles from Minatitlan to Salina Cruz in Mexico, which had opened only a few months before the MAPCO line did.

The only other anhydrous ammonia pipeline in the United States is the Gulf Central Pipeline, owned by the Santa Fe Railroad, which opened in 1970, two years after the MAPCO project. Gulf Central is about twice as long as the MAPCO line—1,880 miles from the Louisiana Gulf Coast into the corn-belt states of the Midwest. Gulf Central, however, has always been a heavy loser on its operation, while the MAPCO line has always made a profit, although not an "acceptable" one because, until 1974, it was operating at only one-fourth capacity.

The ammonia pipeline is constructed and operated pretty much like the LP Gas transmission system, except that steel trim instead of copper is used for the valves and pump fittings in the ammonia line. Storage facilities at the various terminals are great steel tanks, situated both above and below-ground, and owned by customers of the pipeline and by Camex. A typical large storage installation is the Camex-owned steel tanks at Early, Iowa. Each tank is 125 feet in diameter, 75 feet high and surrounded by an 8-inch thickness of insulation which helps the refrigeration keep temperatures down to 30 degrees below zero so that the ammonia remains liquid.

Anhydrous ammonia is stored for about 200 days a year and marketed the rest of the time. It costs around $12 to $15 a ton per year for storage, which is more than Mid-America charges for transporting the product. About 80 percent of deliveries are made during two relatively short periods of application known as "preplant" time (late March and early April) and "side dressing" (late May and early June.) Terminals with truck-loading facilities are situated at Conway, Kansas; Greenwood, Nebraska; and Whiting, Early, Garner, Ogden and Sanborn, Iowa. The line also supplies the Cominco ammonium nitrate manufacturing plant at Beatrice, Nebraska. Each terminal has the ability to load from 100 to 110 truck transports a day.

"Our main difficulties in building the anhydrous ammonia pipeline," Gilbert Rohleder says, "were not physical or technical—they were legal in acquiring rights-of-way and getting construction permits in various states. We had far more trouble getting these for the ammonia line than for the LP Gas Project. A lot of people thought ammonia was more dangerous than LP Gas. The railroads were losing one of their last heavy-volume liquid items of traffic, and they were making an unusually hard effort to block our line. And we were undertaking the building of our line at a rather unfortunate time from a public relations viewpoint. Not long before, there had been a big railroad wreck at Crete, Nebraska, when anhydrous ammonia being carried in the tank car engulfed the town and they lost a lot of people there. Several other railroad accidents involving ammonia tank cars had occurred around that time, releasing vapors into various populated sections, injuring or killing people."

After the Iowa Commerce Commission had granted permission for construction of MAPCO's anhydrous ammonia pipeline into fifteen Iowa counties, the Des Moines *Register* reported that in so doing the Commission had overridden the objections of six railroads which now shipped liquid fertilizer by tank cars. According to the newspaper, the railroads contended they would lose 50 to 80 percent of their anhydrous ammonia hauling business if any pipeline was constructed into Iowa. The newspaper made the editorial comment that allowing the MAPCO line into the state would probably hurt "new job opportunities, since much of the recent industrial investment in the state had been associated with new fertilizer plant construction." The *Register* the following day quoted the President of Terre Chemicals, who forecast "there will be no more ammonia plants built in Iowa or adjoining states . . . if the Iowa Commerce Commission deliberately had set out to deal the state a severe economic blow, it couldn't have been done better than it did in granting permission for construction . . . of this pipeline . . ."

The Iowa Commerce Commission's ruling stood, however, and, according to Mr. Rohleder, "we won all of our legal cases, but we still have [in mid-1975] to settle in some cases the exact value of damages and right-of-way awards. Most of these cases center on construction damage made when we went through somebody's property, and the question is how much is the right-of-way across that property worth considering the damages."

Since the line began operation in 1968, there had been, up until the middle of 1975, only two serious accidents and no fatalities. The worst accident, according to Mr. Rohleder, "was a break in the line in Conway in 1973. Nobody was hurt. The pipeline staff isolated the leak promptly, and the Highway Patrol, local police and fire departments helped us block the roads, isolate the affected areas and keep people out. Two truck drivers did drive into the vapor clouds and inhaled some ammonia, but they were not seriously affected and were quickly released from a hospital. I believe we shut it off within 30 to 40 minutes, isolated the area within an hour, and had the line back in operation in 18 hours. The rupture was caused by another pipeline that had been laid across ours. They put a scar mark on top of our pipeline, unknown to us. The pressure got a little higher than normal at Conway, and broke through this piece of pipe.

"Our other notable accident was down near Hutchinson, Kansas, six months later, when our dispatcher closed the valve at Conway and kept restarting the pumps at Borger. This built up the pressure until it broke the line. I would call this a human mistake. Nobody was hurt in this one, although we had to evacuate the little community of Willowbrook and we did cause a fish kill in the Arkansas River near Hutchinson. There was some damage of shrubbery, but all that has been regrown. We had the line back in service 16 hours after the accident."

J. Kennedy Kincaid, Jr. (left) and his partner, Loren E. "Butter" Hopwood, are busy checking the growth of their Indian Point Farm Supply Company, now MAPCO's Indian Point Division. Mr. Kincaid, now a Senior Vice President of MAPCO, and Mr. Hopwood, a Vice President, were young farmers living across the road from each other who started a sort of "home town" enterprise back in 1954 to supply neighborhood farmers with liquid fertilizer. Their business grew amazingly, and finally merged with MAPCO in 1968. Between then and 1975, its sales quadrupled to a gross of some $25 million annually, with more than 200 outlets in Illinois, Iowa, Indiana, Wisconsin, Alabama, Missouri, Georgia and Michigan.

A major reason that middle western United States has become the world's "bread basket" has been the comparatively recent widespread use of liquid plant foods, especially to fertilize crops of corn, wheat and soy beans. Here, one of MAPCO's spreader trucks is spraying Hopcaid liquid fertilizer on a Midwestern field.

Back in 1954, when Kennedy Kincaid and "Butter" Hopwood started in business near the little town of Athens (pronounced *A-thens*), Illinois, their little enterprise was so small it was difficult to find out there among the tall corn. Now the headquarters plant has grown until it requires a staff of more than 30 people, and the physical layout (above) has increased until it is quite easy to find nowadays, even though the corn keeps growing taller.

Chemistry in the Cornfield

MAPCO's Indian Point Division, which manufactures and distributes liquid plant foods, reflects the most bucolic and "down on the farm" atmosphere of any of the company's operations. The headquarters plant sits out in the country, several miles from Athens (pronounced locally A–thens, population 1,035) in central Illinois, about 25 miles north of Springfield. In summer it is surrounded by fields of corn that grow so tall you can hardly find the place. The enterprise developed from the experiments of two young farmers trying to learn how to fertilize more effectively the lands they had inherited from their fathers. And, although by 1975, the Division was grossing perhaps $25,000,000 a year, it was still exuding a definite "down home" personality.

Indian Point's two founders—Kennedy Kinkaid, Jr., and Loren E. Hopwood, were still running the operation in 1975, in line with MAPCO's policy of continuing in charge the people who had been managing successfully any enterprise it acquires. Mr. Kincaid, with the title of Senior Vice President of MAPCO, was chosen to be directly responsible to Robert E. Thomas because he had been handling the company's financing and bookkeeping at the time of the merger. His partner, Loren Hopwood, was—and is—in charge of Production and Distribution.

After seven years as a part of MAPCO, the Indian Point Division had some 200 outlets in Illinois, Iowa, Indiana, southern Wisconsin, Alabama, Missouri, Georgia and Michigan—about double its distribution points when the merger took place in 1968. There are some thirty employees at the Indian Point Headquarters—a couple of buildings painted in MAPCO white-and-blue and adorned with the MAPCO "Big M" symbol, situated about a mile off the main highway across a winding country road from a stone quarry. Everybody goes home for the midday meal or else brings his food in a lunch box. The only restaurant operating in the area is a little store nearby that dispenses sandwiches wrapped in oil paper and cold soft drinks.

The two founders and their families live nearby on the farms their forebears settled back at the time the community got its name of Indian Point, nearly 150 years ago. At that time, two Indians, named Shick Shack and Chambalee, were still residing in a growth of timber that formed a point like an arrowhead in the local prairie lands. Kennedy Kincaid's family moved into the area in 1832, and he still lives in the big, old, white-painted frame house, surrounded by a white fence, that has been the family home for several generations. Loren Hopwood has built a new residence, but still lives on the farm from which his great-grandfather marched off to fight in the War between the States and to which he returned after Appomattox. Everybody in the area knows Mr. Hopwood as "Butter," which is about as country as you can get. That nickname derived back when he was a small boy and couldn't speak plainly. The family horse was named "Buster," but young Loren pronounced it "Butter." The hired man began calling Loren "Butter," and the name has stuck.

After graduating from the University of Illinois, where they majored in Agriculture, Kincaid and Hopwood, who are third cousins, came home to run the family farms, across the road from each other. Like every other farming operation in the area, they specialized in corn and soybeans. Kennedy Kincaid also operated a dairy and raised hogs, and Loren Hopwood had a dairy. Neither of them, however, was entirely satisfied with the per acre production of the rich prairie lands. They felt that their farms—and all the others in the area for that matter—could profit from a more intelligently conceived program of fertilization than was then being employed in central Illinois.

"The farmers in these parts usually just purchased the sort of fertilizer their neighbors had bought the year before," Mr. Kincaid explains. "We felt that there really should be more testing of the soil and that we should buy fertilizer on the basis of the needs of the soil. This was around 1952 and, of course, soil-testing programs were in effect in other parts of the country—the Southeast, for instance, where the fields had become depleted long before the inherently fertile soil of the corn belt."

When Kincaid and Hopwood began farming, the fertilizer used in the area was mainly a 3–12–12 mix or a 4–16–16 mix. These figures refer, in order, to the number of parts in the mix of nitrogen, phosphate and potash—the three major ingredients in any fertilizer. The two young farmers believed that these formulas were chosen arbitrarily, and were usually not the best proportion for any given piece of land. Their idea was, first, to test the land on their own farms and fertilize that more intelligently. Then, if any of their neighbors were interested, they proposed to sell their testing service and a scientifically proportioned fertilizer mix to them.

"We really started this business in the Fall of 1953, when we took some soil samples to Swift and Company and got them tested," Kincaid reports. "After testing a customer's soil, we would order the formula the tests showed his land needed from St. Louis, where they had mixing facilities. The fertilizer was dry powder in bags, which was shipped out to us in a semitrailer in 20-ton lots that we would distribute to the farms or store in our barn until it was sold. We bought a couple of dry fertilizer spreaders and let the farmers use them, after telling them what sort of mix to put in their ground.

"In 1954, after Loren and I had been in business a little over a year, we happened to read in a magazine about *liquid* fertilizer. It seemed to us that liquid fertilizer would be easier to handle and we might get a better crop response. So we went back to Swift and Company to see if they would sell us liquid nitrogen. They told us there wasn't much future in that, and we ought to forget about it. We then wrote directly to Allied Chemical Company, the major manufacturer of this solution. They set us up as a dealer in liquid nitrogen solutions, and in November, 1954, we got our first tankful of this product. Actually, Illinois was ahead of the other states going into liquid fertilizer, but, at that, we were only the fourth plant in the State to do so. We stored liquid fertilizer in a 22,000-gallon aluminum tank which we bought for that purpose, and then we began to spray the local farmers' crops with fertilizer. We had a tractor and a sprayer and a nurse tank, and we would sell the mixes to anybody we could persuade to use liquid plant food. There were a lot of skeptics through these parts at the time because the product looked like water and the farmers thought they weren't getting enough fertilizer. But, little by little, it gained acceptance. Our first customer was my father-in-law, the late John W. Graham, who owned a farm eight miles east of here. He had faith in me, so he bought some of our liquid fertilizer."

The liquid fertilizer increased yields even more—perhaps 20 percent more—than the dry fertilizer had done. When Kincaid and Hopwood began their project, corn yields in the area averaged around 80 bushels to the acre. Nowadays, the average yield runs between 125 and 150 bushels an acre. The liquid fertilizer and improvement in hybrid corn have been responsible for this nearly 100 percent, in some cases, increase in production.

For the first few years, Indian Point Farm Supply was an extremely informal operation. When they went into business, the two cousins drew straws to see who was going to be president, and Hopwood won. They hired their first employee about two years after going into business—a former schoolteacher who became their bookkeeper. Up to this point, the two young farmers were really not getting a profitable return for all the time they put into the fertilizing business, but they were having "a lot of fun at it." So they continued to farm in order to augment the relatively low monetary return from their fertilizing endeavors. Then, in 1954, Kincaid and Hopwood decided to build their own soil-testing laboratory—a building 12 by 20 feet that is now one room in the sprawling plant that houses the Indian Point facility. In the Fall of 1955, the partners built a liquid mix plant that allowed them to add phosphate to their liquid nitrogen by pouring in phosphoric acid, and to give the mix the third desired component by adding soluble potash. They were now able to *manufacture* a complete mix—a liquid fertilizer that could be sprayed. The plant began operating in September, 1955, and 20 years later this original equipment is still in use in the Indian Point facility.

"We then began selling wholesale to other dealers in the area," Mr. Hopwood recalls. "All they needed was a truck applicator. They came here, bought the mix, resold it to farmers and applied it to their fields." After putting in their mixing plant, the partners decided to incorporate. Until then they had been a partnership. The business was given the name of Indian Point Farm Supply at the time of the incorporation in February, 1955. And they named their liquid fertilizer products "Hopcaid," taking the first and last syllables respectively, from the names Hopwood and Kincaid. The two partners owned all the common stock in the company, but in the following years when they needed money, they sold preferred stock with no voting rights at $100 a share, drawing a 7 percent dividend. All of this was retired at the time the company merged with MAPCO.

"After building our own mixing plant," Kennedy Kincaid says, "we thought it would be a good idea to get into construction of plants and sell these to dealers. By now we had a pretty good idea of what was required, and we thought it was an opportunity for other people to do the same thing we were doing. The plants we manufactured for sale consisted of a 1,200-gallon reactor tank mounted on scales. A pipe was built into it with little holes through which ammonia was sprayed into the solution. A mixer inside the tank did the stirring, and there were smaller storage tanks all around the mixer to hold the various ingredients.

"In the wintertime when we couldn't sell fertilizer and we had the time, we built these plants," Mr. Kincaid went on. "We sold them at about $10,000 each. The early ones were just pieces of equipment in a bag that we sold along with some drawings that told the person how to screw them together. After selling four or five of these, I happened to get a customer from Missouri, who lived near the Missouri River. This man said, 'Now you realize we can't put this thing in a hole in the ground. The water level is so high where we are situated that if we go down a couple of feet we have a well.' Up to that point, we had advised our customers to dig a pit and install the equipment in that. I told this customer to go ahead and buy the plant—which he did—and 'Don't worry about it; we will figure out some way.'

"So Butter and I came home and we worked with an equipment company in Springfield and designed a skid-frame, which would let us put this plant together all mounted on the frame. Now, instead of shipping the plant piece by piece, we could as-

196

semble it and sell it so there was very little work for a customer to do when the plant arrived on his premises. Our skid-frame is just a steel framework welded together with tank, scales, electrical panel and all the valves. Skids on the bottom of the frame allow us to slide it onto a truck. When the truck reaches the point of destination, the plant can be slid off with a minimum of effort and set up as a permanent installation in concrete. We are still using this type of mixing plant, and we have sold probably 300 or more skid-frame plants over the years. Nobody else was making anything like them when we started, and there was a good demand for them.

"First, we just sold the equipment to get the money to keep our business going. Then, after we had accumulated a little capital, we got the idea that it would be better for us to own these plants and to lease rather than sell them. So we changed the direction of our program and said to customers, 'Let us come out and put in a plant for you. You buy your ingredients from us at competitive prices and you pay us so many dollars a ton, based on how much equipment you have of ours.' This, of course, was a franchise deal and we leased our first equipment to a man in Virginia, Illinois. We had made five or six outright sales before starting the leasing, and we continued to sell because we needed to sell three or four plants in order to have enough money to lease one."

The first step in the merger with MAPCO resulted from a trip that Kennedy Kincaid and Richard Nelson, the Indian Point Marketing Manager, made in the Fall of 1967 to Des Moines, Iowa, headquarters of MAPCO's Thermogas Division. At that time, Thermogas was selling Hopcaid liquid plant food through only two of its outlets, and the men from Indian Point hoped to interest the Thermogas management in selling Hopcaid throughout its system in connection with its LP Gas marketing. "After Richard and I made our presentations," Mr. Kincaid recalls, "Charlie Russell introduced us to Robert E. Thomas, who was in the audience. Mr. Thomas and I got to talking, and I happened to have my analysis book with me on our little company. We sat down and went over the projections that I had, and Bob told me he felt we had a real good idea. But, he added, he was not about to help us build *our* company. He wanted to know if I had ever thought of a merger, and I told him that I had. At the time, in fact, I was working seriously with Union Oil and Collier Carbon in California on a merger plan.

"During the Des Moines meeting, we set a date when Butter and I would go to Tulsa a little later on and discuss the possibilities of a merger. Originally, we had thought of selling only a half interest in our company, but Bob said that would not be satisfactory. So Butter and I had to do a lot of head-scratching. You have a sentimental tie with a business that you created and have worked with for fifteen years. On the other hand, our business had grown to where we were selling $6,000,000 or $7,000,000 worth of fertilizer a year. If something happened to either of us, that business would have been quite a responsibility to leave on our families, and we weren't sure, either, how good the profits were going to be in the future in fertilizer. It had been very good to us, but we felt if we could get a little bit of stability, our whole organization would probably be a lot happier.

"After mulling over MAPCO's interest in acquiring us, we finally said that we were interested, too. They gave us a definite proposal, which we brought back, and then we made a couple of trips to Tulsa and finally agreed on the number of shares that they would give each of us. There is a certain amount of nostalgia, of course, attached to something you built up and it was going to be gone now. But after making the deal, we've never looked back, never had a sad moment. I'm just tickled to death at the whole thing. Butter and I had put in $5,000 each when we started the business; we invested in all $40,000 each over the years that followed until the time of the merger. Today that $40,000 I put into our business is worth $8,000,000. We each received 200,000 shares (adjusted for stock splits) of MAPCO stock from the merger. Butter has given away and sold some of his, but I still have all of mine."

Mr. Kincaid's attitude typifies that of the owners of all the companies which have become a part of MAPCO. They all say that they have been treated more than fairly and that MAPCO's aggressive management and broader financial base have allowed their former businesses to progress far more than would have been possible if the original owners had continued operating them. "As far as Butter and I are concerned," Kennedy Kincaid says, "the merger with MAPCO has let us continue doing the same thing that we were doing, which is what we like to do. Our marketing is the same and we continue to work through franchise outlets. We're strong on training, soil-testing and the research aspect. We are still building fertilizer-mixing plants. Butter and I had some objectives that we had hoped to pursue, and MAPCO let us do that on a larger scale than we would have been able to do otherwise.

"In exchanging our stock for MAPCO stock, we got immediate diversification through the other divisions. At the time of the merger, my thought was that in a few years I would take at least a third of my MAPCO stock and invest it in some other company. But I have never found a company that I thought equaled MAPCO since then, and consequently I still have all of my MAPCO stock."

In 1956, a dozen years before the merger, Indian Point Farm Supply branched into another type of operation by franchising "associate producers" of so-called Hot Mix, which is a suspension, meaning that the liquid contains more than 32 units of total plant food. This liquid fertilizer contains five parts nitrogen, 15 parts phosphate and 30 parts potash. Such a high concentration of potash is achieved by neutralizing phosphoric acid with anhydrous ammonia. Heat is produced during the reaction of these two components, hence: "Hot Mix." This product is used as a chemical base to blend with various other combinations and give each individual piece of land the formula it requires. Each one of Indian Point's twenty-eight associate producers is equipped with mixing and storage facilities to produce Hot Mix and operates in a retail area of perhaps 10 miles in diameter with an average of about 200 potential retail customers. In addition to these customers, the associate producers ship Hot Mix to satellite fertilizer dealers who serve their own group of retail customers. The Indian Point associate producers setup became a part of MAPCO in connection with the merger.

Later merged into MAPCO were two other corporations that the busy owners of Indian Point had put together. One, called AnAmo Company, is a cooperative group of fertilizer dealers that bought anhydrous ammonia in large quantities and sold it back to dealer members at cheaper prices than they could otherwise enjoy. Some member-dealers were equipped with an aqua-converter used in mixing water with anhydrous ammonia to produce a diluted ammonia product that is a base for many liquid fertilizer formulas. Also merged into MAPCO was a corporation called Poly P, organized by Kincaid and Hopwood. This consisted of a group of dealers who built three plants to produce another liquid fertilizer base consisting of 10 parts nitrogen, 34 parts posphate and no potash. Many different formulas for treating specific soil conditions can be formulated from this base.

Since its merger with MAPCO, a sizable proportion of Indian Point production, representing probably $8,000,000 worth of its $25,000,000 sales in 1975, was distributed through MAPCO's Thermogas outlets. In that year, 69 of Thermogas' 126 retail districts were handling Hopcaid liquid fertilizer. According to Thermogas Vice President Dick Stegall, "Everyone of our district managers who handles liquid fertilizer has gone through a rigorous training by our Indian Point Division or by John Lewis (another Thermogas Vice President) of our staff here in Des Moines. They also take part in field days given by various state university agriculture departments, such as those at Purdue, Iowa State and Illinois. Because of this training, our men have become quite expert in the application of insecticides, herbicides and fertilizer. Many of our liquid fertilizer customers are farmers who previously were customers only for our propane or butane. When one of our districts begins to handle liquid fertilizer, we make some mailings to farmers in that area and invite them to a dinner where we generally have a representative from some chemical company to assist us. These are usually quite successful in convincing potential customers of the value of liquid fertilizer. After that, it is only a matter of individual counseling, visitation and recommendations to the farmer as to the formulas he should use."

The formula for each individual piece of land is mixed at the Thermogas plant that serves that particular area with liquid fertilizer, and the product is hauled to the fields in 5-ton trucks. Application begins in early April and continues until mid-June, when about 80 percent of the liquid fertilizer is put into the ground. The remainder is spread during October and November after the corn crop has been harvested. On a busy day, one truck can haul about eight loads. The fertilizer is sprayed from a spreader with booms that allow coverage of a 40-foot-wide swath on each trip. From 500 to 1,000 pounds of fertilizer is put on each acre, the amount dictated by a chart based on the results of the soil testing. The average cost is about $41.50 an acre, including the application charge of $1.50 an acre. The farmer who is making full use of liquid fertilizer on, say, 600 acres will spend anywhere from $10,000 to $20,000 a year for the fertilizer—but the bountiful crops he harvests makes the big fertilizer expenditure profitable.

"The Indian Point Farm Supply merger has been a very good situation for MAPCO, totally," Kennedy Kincaid says, "although right after the merger, the fertilizer business went into a terrible slump. In 1968, the industry lost $70,000,000, and when an industry loses that much money, nobody in the distribution end is going to make very much. As a division, we did not make as much money for MAPCO as we had hoped and told Bob Thomas that we would—that is, for the first two or three years. But what we *were* able to do during this time was bring fertilizer to a lot of the Thermogas outlets so that they could become more efficient operations. Thermogas, of course, has some of the same problems we do in the fertilizer business. Both are seasonal operations. When a gas company like Thermogas takes on fertilizer sales, this gives them three more productive months out of the year, and so Thermogas, because of fertilizer, has become a more profitable operation for MAPCO."

As far as the Indian Point Division's total sales are concerned, they went from 124,952 tons in 1968 to a high of 191,283 tons in 1973. "Our whole immediate future is pretty much tied to the prices of agricultural commodities," Kennedy Kincaid says. "Commodity prices have the greatest effect on whether we are going to have a bang-up fertilizer year or not. If farm commodity prices remain good, and we have a good agricultural economy for the farmer, the farmer will continue to buy a lot more fertilizer."

"The Lucky Dot"   21

As early as 1966, Robert E. Thomas had become convinced that coal was going to be one of the future mainstays of this country's energy resources—and that MAPCO should begin studies immediately aimed at entering coal production. In 1966, the energy shortage was still half a dozen years away, and it seemed to be the popular assumption that abundant supplies of cheap oil and gas would continue in the U.S. forever. Coal was still regarded as a sort of backward stepchild in the energy family. It was selling at between $3 and $3.50 per ton as industrial fuel, and nobody in his wildest dreams—including Robert E. Thomas—could imagine the price of coal increasing to $30 per ton by 1974.

Based upon his experiences as a producer and merchandiser of liquefied petroleum gases and of oil, however, MAPCO's Chairman and President was convinced that the price of coal had to increase significantly within a few years. "As early as the middle 1960's, I knew that an 'energy crunch' was coming," he recalled nearly ten years later. "I knew that the BTU's from coal were going to become extremely important in the years ahead, and that the then very low price of coal was going to move upward. Of course, it moved up beyond my fondest dreams and expectations. I was also convinced that the time was coming when we would have to liquefy coal, gasify coal and maybe make chemicals from coal. When you added up all these things, it clearly showed that MAPCO ought to get into coal production.

"And so, in either 1966 or 1967, I really began to look seriously for a good coal company for MAPCO to acquire as a means of getting us into the business and securing the people and the expertise we needed. We examined a number of coal mines and came near buying a quite large one, but the five families who owned it could not agree on terms of sale, and we were never able to make the deal. We kept on looking, though, and finally, in the early part of 1970, White, Weld and Company brought me a prospective deal for a coal mine near the little town of Clay in Webster County, western Kentucky, and we were able to acquire that."

The company bought this first mine, with the unusual name

"Dotiki," on February 24, 1971, in exchange for 500,000 shares of MAPCO common stock. This seemed an extremely high price, in the opinion of numerous financial authorities, including some members of MAPCO's Board of Directors, for a rather obscure mine that, during 1970, had produced about 1,100,000 tons of Number Nine Seam bituminous coal. On the other hand, according to Bob Thomas, "Dotiki was a good operation—a safe operation and non-union. It had excellent productivity and an unusually high type of employees with first-rate work habits. The mine was making a profit of about $1,000,000 a year, unusually high for that amount of production, and it was physically situated so that we could expand production significantly without prohibitive expense. In other words, Dotiki was—and is—one of the best coal mines in the country, and for such a quality property, you have to pay a higher price. Of course, subsequent events have proven that we didn't pay too much."

Its success with Dotiki has encouraged the MAPCO management to expand rapidly its coal holdings and production. In 1975, only three years after entering the coal business, MAPCO had almost tripled its 1971 coal production—to 3,208,000 tons. This was accomplished through improving and enlarging Dotiki's facilities, increasing the miners' benefits, and putting into production two more mines—Retiki near Dotiki in western Kentucky, and Martiki, a big strip-mining property in eastern Kentucky, which began production in 1974. A fourth mine, Pontiki, an underground operation in eastern Kentucky, was expected to begin production by late 1976. A fifth mine, Mettiki, an underground holding in western Maryland, was scheduled to go into production late in 1977. MAPCO's Coal Division was also making plans for developing a total of 220,000 acres of coal properties it had leased elsewhere in Montana, Wyoming and Colorado. Through 1975, however, the Dotiki Mine remained MAPCO's largest producer—about 55 percent of the total tonnage—and was chiefly responsible for the fact that coal production in 1975 had become the Energy Merchant's largest single source of income.

Meanwhile, the former owners of Dotiki had not been doing too badly themselves. The 500,000 shares of MAPCO common they received for the mine were worth about $12,000,000 at the time of the deal. Since then, MAPCO's stock has split twice. The price of coal has multiplied, and MAPCO's accelerated earnings combined to increase the value of its securities until the $12,000,000 worth of common stock in 1971 had skyrocketed in value, by late 1975, to about $75,000,000.

The principal former owner of Dotiki, Joe C. Davis, a tennis-playing bachelor of Nashville, Tennessee, and his family now own more than 1,250,000 shares of MAPCO, worth in 1975 about $50,000,000. This has made Mr. Davis probably wealthier than any of Nashville's country-singing superstars who like to wear $500 suits, drive around in gold-plated Cadillacs and dwell in palatial estates, which are gaped at every weekend by thousands of tourists who swarm into that once-sedate Southern city to attend the Grand Ole Opry and observe how the stars live. No tourists, however, show the slightest interest in viewing the home of Joe Davis, who continues to live in the modest, two-story house where he and his mother had resided for a dozen years before Joe became a rich man. Mrs. Davis, who was eighty-one in 1975, continues to do most of the housework, helped one or two days a week by a cook–cleaning woman who comes in. A yard man works once or twice a week on the Davis lawn.

The Dotiki has been a "lucky" mine for all concerned. Perhaps its name has had something to do with that. Joe Davis said he gave the mine the first syllable of its name after a lady friend with whom he was keeping company at the time he built the mine. Her name was Dorothy, "Dot" for short. "The 'Tiki' is a Polynesian term for luck," Joe Davis says. "I figured when we opened the mine we were going to need a lot of luck, so I joined the 'Tiki' part to Dot."

MAPCO has continued to use the suffix "Tiki," for good luck, in naming the mines it has subsequently acquired. Retiki, its second mine, gets its name because "Re" is the next note up from "Do" in the musical scale and because the first three letters are also the initials of Robert E. Thomas. The Martiki Mine is so named because it is located in Martin County, Kentucky. The Pontiki gets its name because the Pond Creek Seam of coal will be mined from it. The Mettiki Mine in western Maryland gets its name because it contains metallurgical coal, which can be made into coke for producing steel, and which sells for $18 to $20 more a ton than regular steam coal.

MAPCO's first coal property, the Dotiki Mine, had enjoyed a tradition of hard work, big per-man production, no nonsense and high employee benefits ever since it was opened in 1966 by Joe Davis, who created the mine with savings he had been carefully gathering all his life. Back in the 1930's, Joe Davis, of a respected but depression-poor middle Tennessee family, received a tennis scholarship to Vanderbilt University, where he won three Southeastern Conference Singles Championships. He made money on the side by selling suits of clothing to affluent students, heading sales of football programs and in his senior year managing the college annual. Mr. Davis, who is notoriously close with a dollar, made $1,100 from the latter project, and, he says, "I saved every dollar of it." Thus, his profits from the Vanderbilt annual became the nest egg of his savings that went into building the Dotiki Mine a quarter of a century later.

After his graduation in 1941, Joe became a coal salesman for the Nashville Coal Company, owned by the late Justin Potter, a prominent Southern coal operator and friend of the Davis family.

A year later, young Davis joined the Navy and served three and a half years during World War II, then returned to the Nashville Coal Company. Over the years that followed, he invested his salary and savings successfully in various mining and other projects of Justin Potter's so that his holdings amounted to between $350,000 and $400,000 at the time the Nashville Coal Company was sold, in the middle 1950's, because of Mr. Potter's ill health.

Joe Davis set up his own coal jobbing and sales company in Nashville, and a dozen years later, with two partners, he obtained mining rights to about 12,000 acres of Webster County land that the Nashville Coal Company had optioned, then dropped, back in the late 1940's. Mr. Davis had access to the findings of the prospecting and borings, which indicated a seam 4½ feet thick of Number Nine West Kentucky bituminous coal of unusually low moisture content that produced 12,200 BTU's per pound. This is 700 to 800 BTU's better than average per pound for that type of coal. About 90 percent of the leased property was underlain by coal that would produce some 4,500 tons per acre, or about 45,000,000 tons in all. The borings also showed that mining conditions were good, with no serious faults, shears, or upthrusts, which means broken veins. The low moisture content indicated that the mine would have a dry bottom, and that is always highly desirable.

Before starting to dig the mine, Joe Davis secured a contract to supply 700,000 tons of coal a year to the Tennessee Valley Authority, about two percent of the coal that agency required for running its electric-generating plants. Then he put $300,000 of his money into the project. His partners invested $200,000, and they got a $350,000 line of credit from a bank. Mr. Davis hired twenty local workers to dig the mine's slope through 916 tough feet of limestone and sandstone. It was all hand work. The men used hand drills and shovels and hauled out the rubble in little hand-propelled cars. It cost about $150 a foot to dig the slope, about $50 a foot cheaper than a regular contractor would have charged. The work began on November 1, 1966, and the mine produced its first lump of coal on March 16, 1967.

Joe Davis bought for his mine the best, most modern equipment available, under the most liberal time payment terms he could negotiate—as little as 10 percent down in most cases and the remainder over a 3- or 4-year period. But, he admits, "Above ground we were not very pretty." The mine offices were housed in a rickety little former farmhouse where field mice and flights of bumblebees and dirt dobbers kept the office workers company. The water system consisted of a dug well with a bucket and windlass. Sanitary facilities were an outdoor privy. The first woman office employee at Dotiki had to confine her labors to a 4½-hour day at the longest, because there were no toilet facilities for women. Sometimes, she now recalls, she had to go home after only two hours on the job.

Tom Patterson, now a Divisional Vice President of MAPCO

who has been General Manager of the Dotiki Mine since it opened, recalls, "When I first came to work at Dotiki, our bathhouse was so small that two men couldn't stand side by side in it. When they did, the men were practically washing each other's backs. [An adequate bathhouse is extremely important to a coal miner, who comes out of the ground after working each day looking like part of a black-face act.] Our bathhouse was only about 20 feet long, but we kept building on to it by adding tin sheeting. Aboveground, we weren't a bit fancy."

Nevertheless, both the spirit of the workers and their production was high from the first. "We started out using as miners the same men who had dug the mine slope," Joe Davis recalls, "and we gradually added people and equipment until we had about eighty working there. There were union mines all around us, but we went nonunion and have stayed nonunion ever since. I told our people that they didn't need to have anyone to represent them; we would treat them right. We paid an incentive bonus from the first and instituted a profit-sharing plan. The unions don't have either. We had hospitalization equal to that provided in any union contract. Coal had always been regarded as a tough business—hard to make a profit," Joe Davis says. "Traditionally there was always more production than demand. But the Dotiki Mine made a profit from the first month. I operated the mine from 1967 until we sold to MAPCO in 1971. By that time we had increased production to about 1,000,000 tons a year. We were completely out of debt and had $1,000,000 in the bank."

In 1970, Mr. Davis was seriously ill for several months from an aneurysm, which was largely responsible for his decision to sell Dotiki. "I controlled the mine with 75 percent of the ownership," he says. "My two partners, Nashville brothers named Akers, had 10 percent each, and a man who had worked with me in acquiring the land owned five percent. When we set up the company, it was provided that, in the event of my death, my partners could acquire control of the mine for its book value (about $2,500,000 in late 1970.) I could not afford to run the risk of dying and letting them acquire control for peanuts, and the best way out, I figured, was to sell it in exchange for marketable securities."

According to Mr. Davis, "A fellow here in Nashville, who is a sort of investment banker, got in touch with White, Weld and Company in New York City and told them that Dotiki was for sale. Not long after that, Jim Needham, of White, Weld, telephoned me and asked if I wanted to talk to a fellow named Thomas about buying our mine. I said, 'Yeah.' Thomas came down a few days later and said, 'I'd like to buy your company.' I said, 'Well, we might be interested in selling it. We are interested in selling it to somebody.' He stayed around until after supper and we took him to the airport and he said, 'We will be back in touch.' I said, 'If you're serious we will be interested in talking further. Otherwise it has been a nice afternoon.' He said, 'How about a week from to-day?' He said he would be back with a representative of White, Weld and I said I would bring my brother (the late Rascoe Davis) and a couple of other people. We met in the Third National Bank Building here in Nashville and made an informal agreement the day he came. A few days later they drew up a formal document, an agreement to agree. That was in January, and the deal was closed February 24, 1971."

The 500,000 common shares that MAPCO gave for the Webster County Coal Company made Joe Davis a sizable MAPCO stockholder, and he was elected to the Board of Directors. It was also agreed, as part of the deal, that his coal jobbing firms, Davis Coals, Inc., and Davis Fuels Ltd. of Nashville, would continue as sales agents for all coal produced by the Webster County Coal Company (the Dotiki Mine and later the nearby Retiki after MAPCO had acquired that).

Mr. Davis was a MAPCO Director for more than 4½ years, until mid-October, 1975. He resigned at that time when MAPCO announced termination of its coal-selling agreements with the two Davis-owned companies, effective August 27, 1976. The reason, according to the MAPCO announcement, was that the Davis sales commissions had grown to be "noncompetitive."

The MAPCO Board of Directors terminated the Davis sales contract on the insistence of Robert E. Thomas, who contended that the sales commissions to Mr. Davis' companies were out of line. He said that the commissions had risen from considerably less than $500,000 a year in 1971 to more than $2,500,000 annually by 1975. This growth had resulted, Bob Thomas maintained, because of increased production of the mines under MAPCO management and because of the accelerating price of coal since 1971—and not as the result of any especially increased efforts by the two Davis-owned firms. Mr. Thomas said that the action was taken under provisions of a clause in the sales contract with Davis Coals, Inc., and Davis Fuels Ltd. which specified that the agreement could be canceled if the sales commission became "noncompetitive." He added that before canceling the contract, the company had already received bids from other would-be agents who proposed commissions considerably more favorable to MAPCO than those being paid the Davis companies.

The Davis sales commissions—and MAPCO's profits from its coal operations—resulted from three principal factors: MAPCO has more than doubled production of its two Webster County mines since 1971. The price of coal had more than tripled in those years, and at the worst of the "energy crunch" in 1974, it had quadrupled the 1971 price. The third factor was another example of MAPCO "luck"—its habit of getting into the act at the right time.

The final reason in MAPCO's decision to buy Dotiki may

have been the mine's sales contract with Tennessee Valley Authority. "We had gotten that contract by competitive bidding back before we started building the Dotiki Mine," Joe Davis reports. "It specified that we would furnish the TVA 700,000 tons of coal a year for a dozen years for use as fuel in that agency's steam-powered electrical generating plants. Our 700,000 tons represented a fairly good chunk of the coal needed by TVA, which burns about 35,000,-000 tons each year. The price was $3.45 a ton, which was considered pretty good back then. I figured we ought to make a dollar a ton at that price—and we did.

"Then the federal mine safety laws were passed and that increased our costs. In view of this, the wording of our contract with TVA was changed so that, in case the general price of coal went up more than 24 cents a ton, we could renegotiate the contract. When that happened, we renegotiated our price up from $3.45 to about $6.50 a ton. This new contract contained a clause stating that in case the national wholesale commodity index increased as much as 50 percent from what it was from the date our contract was signed, this contract with the TVA could be canceled or renegotiated.

"I guess that clause was sort of put in by mutual agreement," Joe Davis recalled in 1975. "But I am inclined to believe that it was more TVA's idea than ours. TVA was always trying to out-trade you. They figured, I guess, that the wholesale price index was not going to go up much more, or might even go down. But, instead, inflation set in and the price index went up dramatically. I'm sure that the TVA people thought our price of $6.50 a ton was going to be the high mark for coal for a long time to come. Then when the index went down, that would have given TVA the right to renegotiate the contract, and we would have had to reduce our price again. It was a double-barreled agreement. If the wholesale commodity price index had gone down, TVA could have said, 'We're going to cancel your contract—unless you want to sell us coal considerably cheaper.' Under that $6.50 contract, we were making a profit of between $1.50 and $2.00 a ton, and we felt that we were making all the money in the world."

"That new contract made the Dotiki Mine attractive enough for MAPCO to purchase it," Bruce Wilson says, "because it had put the mine on a real money-making basis. We continued to supply TVA with 700,000 tons of coal a year until 1973, when Dotiki's contract to supply coal to the Wisconsin Electric Company expired. We were having trouble placing that coal, so we went to the TVA and asked them to take, under the same contract, the amount of coal we had been supplying to Wisconsin Electric. The price of coal had gone up a year or so earlier, and at the time we made this request our contract with TVA had been escalated from $6.50 to about $7.25 a ton. But the price of coal had now gone down a little, so the TVA people said to us, 'Well, we will take it, but we are going to require a concession in price.' So they made us swallow a 25-cents-a-ton reduction in price before they would take the additional 700,000 tons of coal a year. But this made the TVA more dependent on our mine than it had been, because we were now supplying them with a bigger proportion of their total coal than before—about 1,450,000 tons a year, instead of the old 700,000 tons."

And then, in 1974, a series of developments combined to skyrocket the price of coal. For one thing, it was time to renegotiate a new three-year contract between the United Mine Workers Union and managements of all union-operated mines in the country. Whenever this time rolls around, it is customary for all utility companies to try to build up their stockpiles of coal before the contract expires so that, in case of a strike, they will not run short on fuel. This increased demand always puts a three-year high on the price for coal. Beyond that, however, a series of other unforeseen developments had taken place. Congress had passed some new mine-safety laws that had decreased coal productivity generally. Then the Arab oil boycott developed; the price of oil went up, and this increased dramatically the demand for coal. The railroads did not have the locomotive power or enough hoppers to haul coal in sufficient quantities to meet the new demands. And the coal industry itself was not able to gear up fast enough to accommodate the market. A combination of all these factors created the most severe coal shortage in modern times and the highest prices in history.

This was only a temporary crunch, but it happened at exactly the right time for MAPCO. What had been unthinkable a few years earlier now occurred: The wholesale consumer price index reached 51 percent above what it had been at the time Joe Davis and the TVA had negotiated their contract. Under its terms MAPCO immediately canceled and told the TVA management that any coal it bought in the future was going to cost $29 a ton. (This was based on a market survey the company had made, which showed that coal was then selling at around $30 a ton.) "Of course, TVA could have just said, 'We won't pay that,' and we would have sold our coal to somebody else," Bruce Wilson says. "But TVA was in real bad trouble as far as fuel supplies were concerned at the time. They were burning a lot more coal than they were able to buy. If they lost our coal also, TVA would be in a lot worse shape.

"The TVA officials screamed and hollered," Bruce Wilson went on. "Actually, we were not too anxious to continue the contract with them, which had several more years to run. TVA is considered a very bad customer by most coal producers. Coal people have always felt that TVA beat them down to the last penny and tried to keep them from making any money. There are a lot of companies that just won't sell coal to TVA. No doubt we will also refuse to sell any coal to TVA, once this contract has ended."

"I was really trying to avoid making another extended contract with TVA," Bob Thomas reports. "I looked on the termination of this contract as a means of getting rid of them. I didn't want them as customers. We'd had our belly full. We were actually talking to other prospective buyers who were very ready to purchase our coal. And then we received by registered mail a notice from TVA contending that, in their opinion, we were not negotiating with them in good faith as we were bound to do under the contract. After discussing this with legal counsel, I concluded that we had to go on and negotiate seriously. So we dropped our price 50 cents a ton.

"And then one day I went over there to TVA and settled the matter with them. I just made it extremely clear to them that $28.50 per ton was our bottom price. And they agreed to take it under the contract that extends into 1979." This is just about the highest price that TVA pays any producer for coal. The agency in 1975 was still paying around $7 or $8 a ton to some suppliers under old contracts. Bob Thomas says, " 'Red' Wagner, Chairman of the TVA, got into the newspapers and on television and whatnot at the time by accusing us of being price gougers and profiteers and all that sort of thing. And then, just as a crowning blow, he ended up by saying that TVA had no choice but to pay the $28.50 a ton, because MAPCO could have turned around and sold the coal for $30 a ton. To me, this meant that he was trying to get me in dutch with my own stockholders.

"But the important thing as far as our company is concerned is that in one single day—while taking tremendous verbal abuse from the TVA people—I added $17,000,000 a year to our after-tax earnings. I thought it was a very nice day's work."

Thirty-five Tons   **22**
and What Do You Get?

> "I dug sixteen tons of Number Nine Coal,
> And the foreman said, 'Well bless my soul.'
> ********
> "Sixteen tons and what do you get?
> Another day older and deeper in debt.
> St. Peter don't call me 'cause I can't go,
> I owe my soul to the company store." *

Thus does Tennessee Ernie Ford, in one of his most popular numbers, sing of the physical prowess and economic slavery of the Kentucky coal miner.

Loretta Lynn, in her country-music hit, "I'm Proud to Be a Coal Miner's Daughter," tells of the struggle for a decent existence of a coal-mining family at Butcher Hollow, a mining village in eastern Kentucky, where this "Queen of the Blue Collar Blues" was one of eight children born in a one-room cabin, papered with pages from movie magazines—and raised there until she married at age thirteen.

But those times when the coal miner led a life of back-breaking drudgery and legal slavery are long gone nowadays—especially among the miners working for the Dotiki Mine in Webster County, Kentucky, that first coal mine acquired by MAPCO, in 1971. Instead of "owing their souls to the company store," at least some of the Dotiki miners owe their dues to the country club.

The approximately 200 miners who work at Dotiki, in fact, are probably the richest workingmen in west Kentucky. Some of them own power- or sailboats, in which they disport on the nearby lakes each weekend in good weather. Some participate in golf tournaments now and then. At least one of the men drives to work in a Lincoln Continental. A few of these miners make—in salary, overtime, bonuses and profit-sharing—as high as $30,000 a year. And now and then one of them will take his family on a weekend trip down to Nashville, Tennessee, to see the sights and attend the Grand Ole Opry, where they are likely to hear the likes of Loretta Lynn singing those long-gone coal miners' blues.

The economic and social situation of all coal miners has improved vastly in recent times, because of rising wages and fringe benefits—due in part to pressure by the United Mine Workers, and in part to various safety and other regulations made into law by Congress and the State legislatures. Almost any young coal miner in Kentucky these days will tell you that he got into the business because the pay is higher than any other salaried job available in those parts. The average west Kentucky coal miner nowadays probably makes half again as much as a clerk in a local store or a bookkeeper or a truck driver. But the income and general working conditions of MAPCO's miners—especially at the Dotiki Mine —are far ahead of average. MAPCO has outdone itself to give its mine employees better financial status and more favorable working conditions than are provided by union mines. All of MAPCO's mines—the Dotiki and Retiki, underground enterprises in west Kentucky, and the big Martiki strip-mining operation that was just beginning in eastern Kentucky in 1975—are nonunion, and to date MAPCO has never had any labor problems with any of them.

A principal reason for the greatly accelerated coal miner's wages is that the 16 tons Tennessee Ernie sings about is not considered much of a day's production in these times—at Dotiki, anyway. According to Tom Patterson, a MAPCO divisional Vice President and General Manager of the Webster County Coal Company, the national production average per man in the coal industry was about 11 tons a day in 1975. The per man average at Dotiki Mine was 33 tons per day. "At the Retiki Mine," he says, "we are averaging 28 tons per man, and we have miners in Retiki who had never seen the inside of a mine before they started to work there. We opened Retiki Mine with thirteen miners and now have about eighty there. We fed in some people from Dotiki and carefully hired others. I have one crew in Retiki with a section foreman who is only twenty-five years old, and he is the oldest of the eleven men in the crew. And so we have a bunch of young, dedicated people who, when they're on the job, don't think of much of anything but working. An honest day's work has been the principal element in the success story of the Dotiki and Retiki Mines. I'd say that our people are the primary reason for our good record at these mines—along with good planning, the right selection of equipment and, of course, we had a good vein of coal, especially at Dotiki, to start with."

John Claby Garrett, Director of Personnel and Public Relations for the Dotiki and Retiki mines, believes that the "competitive spirit" of the miners there may be the most significant reason for their exceptional records of production. "In union-run mines," he says, "a lot of workers drift into a pattern where they are trying to get all they can out of the company all the time. If they find some piece of equipment even slightly out of order—some little thing they can point to that needs fixing—they will quickly do this, so they can sit around for three or four hours while it is being repaired. Our miners—unless it's some major malfunction they can't handle—will pitch in and fix a piece of equipment right then and there and get back to work as quickly as they can.

"I'll tell you a good example of what I mean by our miners' 'competitive spirit,' " Mr. Garrett says. "Late one afternoon, the mine engineer and I went down into the Dotiki to move the belt sections up to a point where we would begin a survey for extending the mine. To avoid stopping production, we waited until the day shift got off work. Well, at quitting time the men left and started on the trip that would take them aboveground. The mine engineer and I had no more than gotten our transit set up when here came a shuttle car with another load of coal. We had to move the transit and get it out of the way. When we asked the shuttle-car operator what the hell was going on—it was after quitting time —he said: 'Well, I've hauled ninety-eight carloads today, and the other shuttle-car operator has hauled a hundred. The loading operator is waiting for me, and I'm gonna get this load and then one more and then I will have my hundred cars for the day.'

"In a union situation," Garrett continued, "the miners would probably all have been sitting on their fannies, waiting to leave at quitting time. I'm certain that nobody would have been concerned about hauling another load or two of coal just for the sake of 'competition.' "

"In union mines, a lot of the men are constantly looking for an excuse to strike," says Bruce Wilson, Senior MAPCO Vice President in charge of the Coal Division, who was an executive in union mines before coming with MAPCO. "It may be opening day of fishing season, or the first day of deer-hunting season or maybe just a nice day when they'd like to do some drinking. The least little excuse will set them off. Our workers probably make nearly double what an average union miner will, and a main reason is that our people work five days a week, sometimes six, whereas the average union man will have high absenteeism, plus a number of wildcat strikes. Our men work probably an average of 240 days a year, compared with an average union man working maybe 200 or as low as 190 days a year. We try to hire people who want to work, and if a man is off he has to have an excuse. If he comes in without one, he must go to the superintendent's office and get permission to go back to work, and generally the superintendent will make him wish he had an excuse.

"Many problems with union mines relate to high absenteeism—15 to 20 percent every day. This means that management has to shift its personnel around constantly. A man may get to work at his regular job only two days a week. The other days he's on strange jobs he doesn't want to do or doesn't know how to do well. When you tell him to do this strange job the third day in a row, he often gets mad and balks and doesn't want to do it. And then there is usually some other guy beside him who says, 'Hell, they can't make you do that; tell them you ain't gonna do it.' So you have a confrontation that many times leads to a strike.

"Our absenteeism is less than five percent, and we do very little shifting around of jobs. But when our management *does* tell a man to do something, the miner doesn't have to worry whether they *can* tell him to do that or not. He knows he *has* to do what management tells him, so it takes the pressure off the worker. In a union mine, if a man does what the boss tells him, he sometimes gets in trouble with the union. We don't have that kind of divided loyalties."

Bruce Wilson believes it is unusual for miners to have morale as high as those employed by MAPCO at this point in U.S. industrial development. "In times past, coal miners were very proud of their jobs and the work they were doing and proud of themselves," he says. "But I think unions tend to destroy that by convincing the men that the only reason they have jobs is because the union is keeping the jobs for them. And that just destroys a man, in my opinion. If I were in the union and they were telling me basically, 'You are no good. The only reason you have a job is because we are saving your job for you . . . ' why, man, that would destroy *me*. But our people know they wouldn't have a job if they were no good because we would fire them. So they know they are worthwhile and pulling their own weight. They also know they have a piece of the action—not only with the production bonus but also our profit-sharing program. If the company gets more money for its coal, the employees are going to get more money. This gives us a feeling of unity, whereas in many union mines it is the company on one side and the union on the other.

"Our company's strong financial position makes possible the benefits it is able to give our miners. When MAPCO took over its first mine, Dotiki, Joe Davis had already set up a profit-sharing plan and a production bonus of 20 cents a ton. MAPCO has increased the bonus in steps to 55 cents a ton. The bonus plan works like this:

"The company multiplies by 55 cents the number of tons produced by each mine each month and divides into that total the number of hours worked by each employee that month. Miners who work regular five days are credited with 40 hours each week. If they work a Saturday they are credited with 12 hours extra. Supervisors are credited with 44 hours a week, no matter how many hours each one works. Clerks, secretaries, all aboveground employees participate, and there is no production limit. If the Dotiki mine should produce only one ton of coal in a month, the production bonus would be 55 cents divided by over 200 people. If it produced 100,000 tons, the bonus would be $55,000 divided among over 200 people. Under the profit-sharing plan, the greater the profit, the larger each employee's share, up to 15 percent of his salary, the limit imposed by the Federal Government. For the last two years, employees of both Dotiki and Retiki, the only ones in full production in 1975, have received the limit."

Employees receive nondeductible medical coverage, including full hospitalization, drugs, doctors' visits and major medical up to $100,000. If an employee is injured on the job, he receives full base pay for six months, after which he benefits from a long-term disability coverage, providing half pay for an indefinite period. An employee injured off the job or sick receives $150 a week after he has been away from work for one week.

"Our pension plan is especially good," Bruce Wilson says. "It is wholly paid by the company and amounts to about $30 a month for each year of service. A man with 15 years' service gets $450 a month upon retirement. An employee with 20 years' service gets $600 a month. The pension fund in union mines is about one-third ours in benefits, around $10 a year for each year of service. And the union pensions are not funded, as ours are. If they did not receive money from the coal companies for two or three months, the pension fund would go broke. Ours is fully funded, so that if we went out of the coal business tomorrow, whatever benefits each man had built up would still be there for him. Our base pay is about the same as the union, but, since union mines have neither a production bonus nor a profit-sharing plan, it is possible for our people to average close to double what the union miners make."

Next in the chain of command under General Manager Tom Patterson is Ben J. Quinn, the Mine Superintendent, directly responsible for safety and production. Mr. Quinn is a remarkably able and likeable individual and probably the most popular man at the Dotiki. Tall, slender and soft-spoken, the Superintendent is known as "Ben J." by everybody—management and miners alike—and most of them will tell you that, in their opinion, he is undoubtedly the best mine superintendent in the United States of America. Bruce Wilson says of him: "A lot of mine superintendents base their authority on bluster and bluff. Ben J. is a very quiet, yet authoritative, guy who goes down into the mine and *never* finds everything perfect. There's always something wrong. But he tells the men about this in such a way that they seem glad to pitch in and correct the situation. Ben J. is quite articulate, very communicative and he will take great pains to explain the situation to his people, especially new men. He takes a lot of time with new men, explaining safety rules to them and how to get the job done right and he never seems to make anybody mad at him."

"Thirty years ago when I was growing up in this part of the country," Ben J. says, "there was a lot of coal-mining going on and they say the miners were pretty well downtrodden—that they were worked like slaves. I'm inclined to think some of these tales are exaggerated, but I do know at the coal-mining town in west Kentucky where I grew up, one big mining company had its offices there. And as late as the 1930's, most of the people in town worked for the coal company and were pretty much controlled—lock, stock and barrel—by its management. The same situation existed in a good many other coal-mining towns. The mining companies paid off in scrip, which was honored only in the stores in town that the coal-mining company owned—the grocery stores, drugstores, just about any other commercial enterprise in the community. Back then, most of the coal was sold for heating homes. In summertime when coal sales were low, the people who worked for the coal companies would get coal delivered to their homes—whether they ordered it or not—and it would be charged to their account with the company.

"I've been told of occasions when a truck from one of the coal company's stores would pull up to an employee's residence and unload a new refrigerator. This would be charged to that employee's account, whether he had ordered it or not, and he would have to pay for it through deductions from his salary. I was too small to have witnessed these things and I'm sure that such conditions have been exaggerated. But to quite a degree, there was an effort by coal companies to keep the coal miners pretty much under their thumb.

"When we interview potential employees," Ben J. went on, "we are looking mainly to hire the type of individual who is concerned about his family and wants a better life for them. If he has no desires like that, it is not likely he will be a success here. We want a man interested in building a new home, or giving his family a home just a little better than the fellow next door or down the street has, a man who has some hobbies to take part in for his relaxation. We question these people closely when they apply—we become pretty nosy. We want to get into a man's personal life a a little bit and find out what type of fellow he is, how well he gets along with his neighbors, friends and co-workers. We have several part-time preachers among our employees and a large percentage of our people are affiliated with some church. I don't know of any outlaws in the bunch. We feel we've got a good track record in our hiring, and part of the reason is because we are so nosy.

"Some people just don't believe our production figures of around 30 to 35 tons per day per man. Our average miner probably makes in the neighborhood of $15,000 annually, although some of them have made twice that much or more through working overtime and for double time. No other industrial job in our area pays that much. Sixty percent of our miners make more money than the best-educated people in this area. The Superintendent of the Webster County School System, who must have a Master's Degree in Education, doesn't make as much as our average miner. At our Retiki Mine, we hired the Music Director of the Union County High School, who had been making $10,800 a year. He's doing a lot better than that with us and has made an outstanding miner. We also have a chiropractor who closed up shop and came to work for us. And we have some veterinarians, a number of college-degree people and a lot of folks with college credits, although you don't have to go to college to work in a coal mine."

Ben J. wants nobody to get the impression that coal miners —especially *his* miners—don't work hard for the big money they make in these times. "You hear tales across restaurant tables and in coffee shops about how coal miners do little or nothing to earn their living these days," he says. "I guarantee you that *our* coal miners do a whole lot to earn their living. They are making a lot of money now, but they do a lot of work. True, it's not the drudgery it was years ago, but it still involves a lot of physical effort.

"We pay a lot of attention to a man's physical condition when we interview an applicant for a job. Here's a young fellow maybe twenty-one, -two or -three years old and he tells you about all the places he has worked, oh, for the past three or four years of his work experience. You see by his application that he has had some time working in a factory and then you shake hands with him and it is like shaking hands with a dishrag. You know from the start this man hasn't done any physical work to speak of; he probably hasn't even done work on his lawn. He hasn't kept his body in good physical condition. And a man who is not in good physical condition has got no business in a coal mine.

"When we have visitors to the mine, including officials of MAPCO even, it just about kills them to get around in a coal mine. There is a lot of physical conditioning connected with working in a coal mine. Most of these miners are a physically hard bunch of characters—they *have* to be tough. After all, we are working in a vein of coal only 55 inches high (four feet seven inches), and our men spend an eight hour day bent over to do their work. Their bodies must get accustomed to this uncomfortable position, and I guarantee you if you go in a mine with me for three hours, you will have some trouble rolling out of bed next morning."

"I must admit that many of us were apprehensive when we heard that the company was being taken over by MAPCO," Claby Garrett recalls. "Our mine had been quite successful under Mr.

Davis. None of us had ever heard of MAPCO. We had fears that maybe some union company was buying us out, and we were not sure what was going to happen to us. Then a few days after the takeover, we met with Mr. Thomas and some of his people. He assured us that, since MAPCO was pipeline- and oil-oriented and had little knowledge of coal—up to that point at least—there would be no changes in our personnel or operating procedures. And there have not been. The MAPCO management has let us continue to operate the mine the way we did before they took over, although MAPCO has spent a great deal of money improving the mine physically. Now ours is just as modern and good-looking as anybody's coal mine. Our money and fringe benefits are *better* than anybody's coal mine."

Tom Patterson had worked in coal and other types of mines since 1936 in his native Ohio, in West Virginia, New Mexico and Wyoming before coming to Kentucky as General Manager of the Dotiki Mine when it opened in 1967. "One reason I came with Dotiki," he says, "was that here was an opportunity for me to set up a mine the way I'd always wanted. It is seldom a mine manager gets such an opportunity—to go in right from the start and do it right—lay out the mine, select the right people, upgrade the equipment continually. Dotiki has been good to me because it allowed me to see something I'd always wanted to do actually come to life.

"And then, after five years, we were told that the company was being sold to MAPCO—an outfit we knew nothing about. My own personal feelings were: 'Why the hell did I leave my job in Wyoming and come back to Kentucky to have the job here sold out from under me.' What happens in most mergers—and I have been through mergers—is that the new owners of the coal company have their own people and no use for the old management. But that was not the case here. Mr. Thomas explained from the first that MAPCO operated nonunion all over and intended to continue that policy with us. He told us that he would make no personnel changes—and then everybody began feeling better.

"MAPCO has been good for us in several ways," Mr. Patterson went on. "When we started out, Joe Davis had to watch his money, and we did without a lot of things we should have had. At the time MAPCO took over we were in dire need of an airshaft, because our coal mine was getting so far underground. We needed new facilities, replacements for worn equipment and better quarters for our aboveground staff. MAPCO spent close to $3,500,000 on the complex then. Last year we asked almost $1,000,000 more in capital expenditures, and we had no problem at all getting it. And that is the big difference between working for an individual who doesn't have a great deal of capital and for a big company that does have money and is not afraid to spend it. MAPCO has the finances also to purchase other mining properties, and that provides greater opportunities for our people than they ever could have had under the Davis ownership. All of our key people at Retiki, for instance, were promoted from the jobs they had held in the Dotiki Mine."

The Retiki was the former Goldsberry Mine, which MAPCO purchased from the Davis family and renamed about ten months after buying the Dotiki Mine. "We had bought the Goldsberry Mine in the summer of 1970 at a fire sale, because we could get it cheap—at about $50,000," Joe Davis says. "The Goldsberry property was a sort of junk mine, with no modern equipment. Workers were lowered into it and brought out in a kind of big metal bucket on a windlass, like an old-fashioned well bucket. The shaft went straight down, as opposed to the present method of entering and leaving a mine in cars on rails that follow a slope. We thought we would fiddle with the mine for a while, but it soon became apparent that a sizable investment would be required to make it a paying proposition. At the time I just didn't want to put the money in it, so we sold the mine to MAPCO."

"The Goldsberry Mine was a loser all right," Bruce Wilson says. "It was antiquated—not modern at all—with no long-term contracts, and it was losing perhaps as much as $150,000 a year. But it did have a fairly good reserve of coal. We bought it on a cash deal, for about $700,000, with two or three hundred thousand down and the rest to be paid from earnings."

MAPCO put a great lot of new equipment into the Retiki Mine, dug a slope, installed bathhouses and coal-handling facilities, modernized the mine, increased the work force from about a dozen to eighty miners and turned the Retiki into a money-maker. It produced 1,000,000 tons of coal during 1975 and, although MAPCO doesn't make public such figures, it may have shown $1,000,000 profit after taxes.

"MAPCO has been good for all of our miners," Tom Patterson says. "Benefits for all of us have been greatly increased, and everybody has respect for Mr. Thomas. We see him once a year when he comes down to our profit-sharing dinner. That has gotten to be so big we have had to take it to the Executive Inn at Evansville, Indiana, the only dining room in this part of the country large enough to handle a dinner of that size. Everybody eligible for the profit-sharing plan comes and brings his wife.

"And MAPCO and the Webster County Coal Company have been good for people in management, such as Ben J., Claby and me—all of our people. I never got too many fringe benefits or too much retirement from my associations with other coal companies. But now I won't have any trouble in being pretty well off financially when I get ready to retire. And I have to thank MAPCO for that. It would not have happened under the Davis administration. Joe Davis is my good friend, but he would not have had the financing to do all the things that MAPCO has done for our men and for me."

218

Monsters in Martin County

23

"If this nation follows a rational course, coal is going to be our most vital natural resource—probably for the next century, anyhow. All coal deposits are pretty well mapped by now, and the United States has about 48 percent of the entire world supply. We have twice as much energy in our coal still in the ground as the Arabs have in their oil under the deserts of the Middle East."

Thus does Bruce Wilson, Senior Vice President in charge of MAPCO's Coal Division, express his own—and the company's—feelings about the importance to America of coal in the coming decades. It was this thinking that caused Robert E. Thomas to decide, back in the late 1960's, before the "energy crunch" had become obvious, to take MAPCO into coal production. Ever since MAPCO acquired its first coal mine in Kentucky, Dotiki, early in 1971, the company has so concentrated on opening new mines, securing new coal-producing properties and increasing production in its operating mines that, in 1975, the Coal Division became MAPCO's greatest revenue producer, replacing in that position the Pipeline Division, which had always been its leading generator of income.

"If we develop our coal resources wisely and eliminate—or at least reduce—our dependency on foreign oil, coal can be our energy solution throughout the foreseeable future," Mr. Wilson went on. "Nuclear power cannot come along fast enough to fill the gap that depleting oil supplies and increasing oil prices have created. Coal is an extremely versatile resource. The Germans made fuel for their tanks from coal during World War II. The South Africans have a liquefaction plant, where they are making liquid and gas fuels out of coal, and in the United States there are several experimental plants producing different kinds of liquid fuels from coal. You can make ammonia out of coal. You can make methanol —diesel fuel—there are a lot of things you can make out of coal to produce energy. You can use coal to make gas like methane for heating homes.

"For environmental reasons, we will have to change much of the coal in the future into forms that burn without pollution.

There are several processes for changing coal into a kind of liquid and into a pelletized fuel without ash and sulfurs. And outside the energy field, coal can be used to manufacture fabrics—nylon, rayon, automobile tires and I think, probably not far in the future, synthetic foods. At the present rate of consumption, we've probably got a 1,500-year supply of coal in the United States. At projected increased rates of consumption, we probably have a 300- to 400-year supply. From the standpoint of ourselves and our children, the coal supply in this country is inexhaustible.

"We certainly have enough coal to last us until we learn to use solar energy effectively," Bruce Wilson says. "Solar energy is not that far in the future, and it is going to be a major source of energy. But for the next several decades, coal is our answer. It was not economical to think about changing coal into oil when crude oil was selling at $2 a barrel. But now, crude is selling at $13 dollars a barrel, and that has changed the whole picture. Long before crude reached its present price, I understood that coal could compete economically with crude in making gasoline, if all the taxes were removed from the coal-made gasoline."

Bruce Wilson, tall, slender, quiet-spoken and knowledgeable, was only twenty-eight years old when he joined MAPCO in 1971, the year the company entered the coal business. He is the youngest member of MAPCO's top management, but Bruce has packed an impressive store of experience into his career already. Born and raised on an Ohio farm, he went to Ohio State University with the idea of being an agricultural engineer because that seemed "down to earth and practical." Young Wilson abandoned that career after making a field trip to one of the Peabody Coal Company's strip-mine operations in southeastern Ohio. "I was just fascinated," he says, "by all that big equipment and how dynamic this industry was and how down to earth—you can't get much more down to earth—it's real, tangible; you're not dealing with theory. So I switched to mining engineering and went on from there."

After graduating in 1965, Bruce went to work for the Island Creek Coal Company, the country's third largest, in its Western Kentucky Division. In college, he had set his professional goal at becoming a mining chief engineer, but Bruce attained this with Island Creek at age twenty-five. So, as he says, "I had to reassess my goals. I discovered that being a chief engineer is somewhat of a dead end. The real money and responsibilities are in operations, so I decided I'd like to be the head of a large coal company." When he was twenty-six, Bruce left Island Creek and went with Barnes and Tucker, a smaller mining operation in central Pennsylvania, mainly to get diversified experience. Within a year, he had become manager of two of Barnes and Tucker's four mines. By May, 1971, he was in charge of a large exploration and development project in Canada, but by this time he was already talking with Bob Thomas about joining MAPCO. Bruce had been recommended to the MAPCO President by Sam Cassidy, the coal consultant who had steered MAPCO in buying the highly profitable Dotiki Mine.

"I have been very happy at MAPCO, in spite of my fears at first that I was taking quite a chance," Bruce Wilson says. "My background had been strictly in union mining. I didn't really know what I was getting into in joining a nonunion operation. But I was much impressed by Bob Thomas. He seemed a most aggressive, straightforward type of fellow. And I quickly came to appreciate the advantages of MAPCO's type of nonunion operations, which enable management to concentrate on managing without having to deal with a lot of union problems. In a union mine, such as Barnes and Tucker, we spent 90 percent of our time dealing with union matters and 10 percent thinking about better methods for mining coal. At MAPCO it is just the reverse. Because of our profit-sharing and various incentive programs, MAPCO's miners are looking for production and profitability, and they are on the side of management."

During 1973, MAPCO leased from the Pocahontas Land Corporation, a subsidiary of the Norfolk and Western Railroad, nearly 20,000 acres of coal lands in mountainous Martin County in eastern Kentucky, now the Martiki Coal Mine. Martiki has proven coal reserves of more than 67,000,000 tons, in addition to a probable 5,000,000 tons more and a possible 2,000,000 beyond that. During 1975, the company was spending about $38,000,000 developing the Martiki into the most modern strip-mining coal operation in Kentucky and that general region of the Appalachians. Although construction was not completed, the mine was producing about 60,000 tons of coal a month in late 1975, and total production was expected to reach capacity of 3,000,000 tons a year in 1977.

MAPCO's Coal Division during 1975 was also digging the slope of an underground mine, near the Martiki in Martin County, which the company had acquired earlier in the year. And it has 30,000,000 tons of proven and 14,000,000 more tons of probable reserve of low-sulfur Pond Creek and Upper Elkhorn Number One Coal. This is high-quality steam coal meeting all environmental requirements under present laws and thus commanding higher prices. The mine, named Pontiki, is expected to reach its full annual capacity production of 1,450,000 tons late in 1978.

The company expects to begin production in 1977 or early 1978 on still another mine, lying under some 6,000 acres in Garrett County, Maryland, with over 40,000,000 proven reserves of low volatile metallurgical coal. In addition to these properties, MAPCO has under lease about 170,000 acres of coal lands in Montana, Wyoming and Colorado, with more than 275,000,000 tons of strippable coal. Development of these resources was being delayed, however, because, in the words of the 1974 Annual Report: "It borders on the inconceivable, but the timing of possible commercial development is highly uncertain at this time in view of the continued threat of Congress to make difficult and possibly impossible, the mining of the country's tremendous Western coal reserves."

In mid-1975, the most ambitious and exciting of MAPCO's coal operations, actually in production, was the big Martiki strip mine in Martin County, in eastern Kentucky. "When we went in there in 1973," Bruce Wilson says, "there was nothing but hillsides and trees and rocks and rattlesnakes." By mid-1975 they were actually "moving mountains" to get at the Martiki coal. And, in the process, the MAPCO miners were throwing the mountaintops into the valleys. All this is being accomplished with immense machines, the wonder of the countryside—shovels, draglines and trucks—that rumble through the eastern Kentucky mountains the way the dinosaurs of millions of years ago once disported.

The coal deposits in this area of Martin County had long been left undisturbed because it is classed as "dirty coal," meaning that the fuel contains about one-fourth rock when it is scooped up with the great shovels in the strip-mining process. The coal has to be "washed" to rid it of impurities, and the washing process is expensive. So the "clean" coal in other areas was mined first. Until recently, there was no railroad close to these deposits; any coal mined had to be trucked at least 15 miles over the narrow, twisting roads to the nearest railway, and that was not economical. In 1971, the Norfolk and Western Railroad Company, which owned most of the coal-bearing properties in the area, completed construction of 22 miles of track at a cost of $24,000,000, especially built to serve these undeveloped coal resources. When Bruce Wilson heard about the new fields opening in eastern Kentucky, the big Island Creek Coal Company and A. T. Massey and Company had already leased part of the lands and were putting in mines, but 18,000 acres of coal-producing lands were left. MAPCO put in a bid, as did Island Creek, Massey, and a number of other coal companies, but MAPCO was the high bidder and got the option.

To reach Martiki, you go to Huntington, West Virginia, then proceed by automobile into the heart of Appalachia along the tortuous blacktops, crossing old, narrow bridges of rusting iron, through the little town of Louisa, Kentucky, then into wilder country where the land always seems to be rising straight up from the roadside. Little mountain homes and cabins cling to the stingy stretches of almost level land at the base of the hills, surrounded by old rusty automobiles and log outbuildings. Four miles past the town of Inez, the Martin County seat, you turn off the main road onto a rough, still narrower blacktop that seems to struggle through the woods to no purpose. Finally, after 10 miles or so, you come to the Martiki Mine. Here the whole side of a mountain has been blasted away into a great perpendicular face of rugged stone. Construction was still under way in mid-1975, and about one-third of the way up the rock face was anchored what looked like the steel framework of a square-built office building of some five or six stories. This is the "preparation" or "processing" or "washing" plant—a "tipple," in coal miners' language. This plant, which alone cost more than $9,000,000 to build, is designed to remove the rock and debris from the coal and dry out its moisture, making the product ready for consumption.

The other most striking objects are four immense concrete silos, which, against the rugged background, resemble the towers of a colossal castle of medieval times. The two smaller silos —60 feet in diameter and 90 feet high—will hold 5,000 tons each of unwashed coal, waiting for processing. The two larger silos—70 feet in diameter and 170 feet high—together will hold 26,000 tons of clean coal that has been processed and is ready for shipment. That is 2½ train loads. A coal train usually has 100 hopper cars, each holding 100 tons. It takes about 4 hours to load a train—2.4 minutes per car—as the hoppers move steadily under the coal chute, which is shut off the few seconds required for each gap as the cars pass.

Yates Storts, the Martiki's General Superintendent, had been working in coal mines and mine management for more than 30 years when he came into the MAPCO organization. He was born and raised in a coal-mining town in Ohio, and had a job with a coal mine while he was still in high school. Yates figures it will take about 25 years to finish mining out the coal in the Martiki property.

"When we get all of our equipment," he says, "we will have a dozen 170-ton trucks. [Anybody who hasn't seen one just can't appreciate how immense a 170-ton truck is. It looks like a ship rumbling around the mountain.] We will also have three 100-ton trucks," Mr. Storts went on, "four 50-ton trucks and four C-90 trucks. All of these are for removing overburden, the dirt and rock that covers each seam of coal. And we have three 130-ton Goodberry trucks, which are strictly coal haulers. It's necessary to remove an average of 20 cubic yards of overburden to get one ton of clean coal. In some places we have to remove up to 40 yards of overburden for a ton of coal; in others we remove only two tons of overburden for a ton of coal. It averages out about nine to one."

The mountains in the Martiki vicinity range from about 800 to 1,250 feet high. The veins of coal run through the hills like the layers of filling in a three- to four-layer cake, except that the mountains are shaped more like flat-bottomed ice cream cones sitting upside down. The lowest seam is about 910 feet elevation. The mountains under 1,200 feet have three layers of coal and those above 1,200 have four.

"The top seam of coal is about 40 feet under the dirt and rock that form the top of the mountain," Yates Storts says. "It runs 60 inches in thickness and is a real good seam of coal. Then you've got to go down about 35 feet and you have another seam of coal about 40 inches thick. That's a good seam, too, although it has some impurities in it. After that, you've got to go down 125 feet to come to what is called the 'Stockton Elevation,' and that one is about 66 inches thick. It is our best seam. It is clean with high BTU content, low sulfur, low ash and low moisture. And then anywhere from 70 to 90 feet under that we get to the bottom seam, known as the 'Coalburg.' That runs 15 to 17 feet in thickness, but actually only about 80 inches of this is coal, the rest shale and other impurities."

The first step in strip-mining a Martiki mountain is to select the usable timber from the top, cut that and log it off. Then the top of the mountain is pulverized by blasting. The miners drill holes about eight inches in diameter straight down to the seam of coal 40 feet below. The holes are spaced 25 feet apart and one shooting project may cover several hundred square feet. Each hole is filled to the top with explosives, which are timed so that each blast goes off separately, a second or two before the next explosion. If all these explosions were to let go all at once, it might wreck that end of the county. At that, the detonations can be felt for several miles. After that area of the mountain has been decimated, the great machines creep up to what is left of the top, using roads recently built for that purpose. The big mechanical shovels scoop up the piles of crumbled rock and dirt in 20-yard bites and deposit these in the immense trucks, which carry their loads to the brink and dump what was a mountaintop into the valley. When the miners reach the seam of coal, they load it into coal trucks, which haul it into the processing area and dump their load into the raw coal silos to await processing. The same procedure is followed in reaching and harvesting each seam of coal, working from the top down, moving the mountain as they go.

"But," as Bruce Wilson points out, "this process allows us to have the most comprehensive plan for environmental protection in Kentucky, if not the entire country. By taking the tops off these mountains and putting them into the valleys a layer at a time and then removing the coal, we will end up 20 years from now with approximately 10,000 acres or more of level land, made by filling those valleys after shaving off the mountains. And, of course, this is an area where there is practically no level land, so we are producing a very desirable quantity of a commodity terribly scarce in eastern Kentucky.

"This method of ecological control contrasts with contour stripping, which shaves off the sides of mountains and produces situations where it is extremely difficult to control erosion and siltation. So our method is very desirable, and the State Government of Kentucky has recommended it to other areas. This concept was begun only five or six years ago, but I don't think anyone has attempted it before on such a large scale as we are doing and with such large equipment. The approximately 10,000 acres of flat or rolling land that result 20 years from now will gradually become fertile as the shale converts into topsoil. You add fertilizer and the next thing you know, it will grow vegetation. The flat lands we are creating can be used for grazing and for perhaps industrial and residential sites."

Donald G. "Buddy" Reid, Preparations Superintendent, is in charge of the big washing and processing plant at Martiki, which will wash, crush, size and dry the coal and make it ready for the market. As the coal enters the plant, he says, smaller pieces are separated from larger ones of six inches in diameter and larger, which then go through a rotary crusher. All of the coal follows a complex and confusing path through sprays, belts, screens and passages. But, basically, what happens is that the coal and accompanying rock eventually go through a liquid bath that floats the lighter coal and allows the heavier rock to sink to the bottom. The rock is taken out and returned to the valley as part of the fill. The preparation plant can process about 12,000 tons of clean coal a day from 17,400 tons of raw coal, which includes 5,400 tons of rock and other useless debris.

"We hire as many local people as we can," Yates Storts says, "but we do a lot of research on every employee before hiring him. We check into his background, his work record, who his parents are, and we have built up quite a fine working force. A number of the leaders in the county have complimented us on the type of people we have working here. Right now we've got about 100 miners, 55 percent of whom are local people and 97 percent Kentuckians. One of the greatest troubles in hiring help is the absence of housing in the area. Some of our miners have to drive 40 and 50 miles a day to get to work, and we have had to try to provide some housing for those living farther away. That has not been too satisfactory. Several men who have come here with the idea of working have turned around and left because of poor housing conditions.

"As a result, we are now planning a project that will allow our employees to buy desirable building sites at a reasonable price and construct their homes there. We have already bought 280 acres for this purpose and are negotiating to buy another 24 acres. MAPCO intends to develop this acreage into a subdivision. Before homes are built there, we will put in blacktop roads, sanitary sewers, water mains, gas and power lines, storm sewers and such. We will sell lots to our employees at cost and, if necessary, do what we can to help a man finance his new home. Our idea is to get a contractor to put together 25 or 30 different designs of homes, all of which will fit into the setting and provide comfortable, attractive living quarters. I would say that these homes will range in price from the $25,000 to $45,000 class. We will be quite restrictive on the type of houses that go up. We're not going to let some guy build a $5,000 or $8,000 house beside one that costs $25,000 to $45,-000. If a miner builds a house on this land and then decides to leave, we will have the first option to buy his house, and our present plans are to restrict the houses to fairly large ones with at least three bedrooms and one and a half to two baths, and all will be modern design. Our employees will be able to afford nice houses because the average Martiki miner is making around $20,000 a year."

Incomes of $20,000 a year and $45,000 residences are still regarded as almost dream stuff by the citizens of Martin County, one of the poorest in the United States. Only a few years ago, the per capita income was a mere $300 a year, and unemployment stood at 70 percent. Back in the middle 1960's, President Lyndon B. Johnson flew there to the county seat, Inez, to open his "War on Poverty Program" for the nation, choosing Martin County because it was so poor. There wasn't a traffic light in the entire county. Martin County had only one physician, two lawyers, no dentists, no druggists, no industry, no theaters and no recreation facilities except for four poolrooms. About the only thing the county had to be proud of was the fact that the Inez High School basketball team had won two State Championships in years gone by.

And then, in the early 1970's, MAPCO and the other coal companies began arriving. By 1974, unemployment had gone down to only 12 percent. The number of families supported solely by welfare had decreased from nearly 600 ten years earlier to 159 in 1974, and the per capita income rose from $300 a year to an estimated $8,000. Before the coal companies came, the county's tax revenues were about $50,000 a year. By 1974 they had gone up to $500,000 a year. And land values in only two years increased 200 percent and in some areas as much as 1,000 percent. MAPCO was greatly responsible for the increase in land values, having paid about $3,600,000 to Martin County people for surface deeds to the land of the Martiki Mine. Lee Mueller wrote in the *New York Times Magazine* about a mountain woman who several years earlier had traded three acres of hillside property for a used washing machine. At the time it was considered a fair bargain. MAPCO paid exactly $7,000 for the same land.

And so, prosperity at last is arriving in Martin County, Kentucky. But at this writing, the greatest source of wonder among local citizens is the great behemoth-like machines that devour the mountains for Martiki. The mountain people turn out on holidays and Sunday afternoons to come through the woods and along the narrow roads to admire and gape at the great machines. They are especially overwhelmed by the giant 170-ton trucks—anybody would be. They are about 20 feet high and cost $400,000 each. The wheels stand 11 feet high, and one tire costs $14,000. The trucks are powered by immense electric motors, round in shape, built into each wheel and produce enough power to propel a small ship.

As Buddy Reid says: "We've got people coming through here on Sundays in a regular parade. They just look in wonder. We have to sit down and try to explain to them what draglines are and how these trucks operate. It's hard for them even to imagine these things while they are looking at them. They just can't believe anything mechanical can be this big. These trucks have a tremendous attraction. I have been in coal-mining for 25 years and this is the first time I've seen anything like these trucks. There just aren't any others in this part of the country to compare with them. Why, just to come and look at them is better than going to a circus."

Bruce C. Wilson (standing), Senior Vice President in charge of MAPCO's Coal Division, checks over equipment in the Hoist House of Dotiki mine with William T. (Tom) Patterson, Vice President of the Webster County Coal Corporation that operates MAPCO's Dotiki and Retiki mines in Western Kentucky. Back of them is the massive electric motor and power winch that takes more than 200 miners, equipment and supplies in and out and along the seven miles of underground passages of the mine and which moves in and out the trains of little coal cars. Dotiki may be the highest producing per capita underground coal mine in the U.S.A.

Accompanied by great crunchings and groanings and clouds of rock dust, a giant shovel picks up "overburden"—masses of shattered rock that have been blasted away from the seam of coal—and loads it into an immense 170-ton truck at MAPCO's Martiki Mine in Martin County, in the mountainous northeastern tip of Kentucky.

On Sunday afternoons in good weather, residents of Martin County, Kentucky travel the mountain roads to ogle the great machines that work MAPCO's Martiki Mine. Coal mining has been the area's principal industry for a century, but never before have natives of these hills seen such behemoth machines. "It's sort of like the circus," one MAPCO employee says. Chief source of wonder are the great 170-ton overburden-hauling trucks that cost $400,000 each, stand 20 feet tall.

Black gold from the Martiki Mine flows into a 100-car coal train—each hopper holds about 100 tons—from a "tipple" that serves as a temporary coal-loading facility pending completion of the mine's immense concrete loading "silos." The greening bank in the background results from MAPCO's policy of re-seeding scars in the earth left from the strip mining operations. Such ecological precautions are designed to leave the mined country better looking than it had been made by nature.

A group of Indonesian workers with overseer pause in their constant battle with the Irian Jaya jungle and smile for the camera. Nearly 4,000 Indonesian Nationals at a time have been employed by Trend Exploration, Ltd. to clear the lush tropical vegetation for drilling sites, helicopter pads, living and working areas and paths through the jungle.

Photo, Courtesy Petromer Trend Corporation.

A tanker waiting to take on its cargo of Indonesian oil lies in the Sele Strait off the Irian Jaya shore, where Trend Exploration is building a permanent camp. Six storage tanks, each of 300,000-barrel capacity, are the most prominent installations in the cleared area that was recently jungle. At the extreme lower right are box-like, metal houses, living quarters for some of the over 400 expatriate Americans, Europeans, Canadians and Australians who handle the more complicated jobs.

Photo, Courtesy Petromer Trend Corporation.

The Indonesian jungle surrounding the Trend Exploration oil wells, in which MAPCO owns an interest, is so thick and impenetrable that all personnel, supplies and equipment—from small tools to immense oil drilling rigs, broken down into some 3,000 parts—must be flown through the air to each drilling site. Trend has a number of Bell 205 helicopters for this work. Each can carry 3,500 to 4,000 pounds, including crew.

Photo, Courtesy Petromer Trend Corporation.

Until the early 1970's this area was thick jungle, where giant pythons coiled around the branches of the great teak, ironwood and mahogany trees that rise up to 200 feet. Now progress has arrived with its chain saws, bulldozers, miles of gleaming pipe, great tanks and metal houses. Population of the nearby Indonesian town, Sŏrong, has jumped from 3,500 to 75,000 since Trend Exploration, Ltd. struck oil in large quantities in the area.

Photo, Courtesy Petromer Trend Corporation.

How to Succeed in a Swamp

24

Almost anybody in the know in Wall Street circles will tell you that the remarkable success enjoyed by MAPCO, Inc., over its brief history has resulted mainly from brilliant managerial acumen, in great part the policies and decisions of Robert E. Thomas, founder, President, Chairman and Grand Panjandrum of that energetic young energy company. "Bob Thomas is just as smart as hell," is the usual comment.

And yet, being human, Bob Thomas has committed his share of boo-boos. One of the most notable was what he and his associates now term the "Bob Thomas Thirty Million Dollar Speech," delivered before the New York Society of Security Analysts on December 13 (a significant date), 1969. The event is so called because it resulted in the value of MAPCO stock dropping $7 a share in three days and another $7 per share during the weeks that followed. In all, those unfortunate remarks on that December 13 shot down the value of MAPCO's stock by something over $30,-000,000 in the first three days.

"All I did," Mr. Thomas now reminisces, "was to explain that we at MAPCO obviously were in the oil and gas business. Anybody could tell that who looked at our figures because we produced oil, we produced gas and we produced gas liquids. And now that we had arrived at a time when we were paying substantial taxes and could do so with 50-cent dollars, we were commencing to explore for oil. Our policy would be to look for elephants, but we would limit our dry-hole expenses to about five percent of pretax net, which at that time figured out to about $500,000 a year.

"Well, sir, I had no sooner gotten this out of my mouth than I lost my audience. Those people just couldn't get out of that room fast enough to begin selling MAPCO stock and advising their clients to do likewise. The value of our stock dropped in three days from $28 down to $21 a share. And that started a whole psychological landslide of MAPCO stock. That's the way Wall Street is; it's more emotional than logical.

"Take the behavior of one block of 150,000 MAPCO shares as an example. After our stock began to slide, Edward A. Merkle bought a block of 150,000 shares for the Madison Fund, which he heads and with which I was once associated. I'm not sure what he paid for it, but it was probably around $21 a share. In a few weeks Ed decided to dump it, probably at around $18 or $19 a share. I don't know exactly the price but it was still going down. The block was bought by a mutual fund, whose people then asked me to come and see them and talk to them about the future of MAPCO. I did and they seemed quite happy. The next thing I knew, *that* company was selling its MAPCO stock at a loss. The reason: They had gotten a new man in charge who had never heard of us, so he just dumped our stock. By now, MAPCO was down to $15 or $16 dollars a share. Then another mutual fund bought the block, and *they* dumped it at the bottom of the debacle, in May, 1970, at about $13 dollars a share. Their reason: MAPCO was not a household word in America, and this company had decided to get rid of all the shares it held in companies that were not household words.

"Supervised Investors of Chicago, with which one of our directors, John Hawkinson, is affiliated, bought this 150,000-share block," Mr. Thomas went on. "MAPCO stock soon began to climb, and it has been increasing in value ever since—except for a brief time in 1974, when we had a very bad market, when money rates were high. Stocks of all types were going down and we went along with them, but it was nothing like the slide in 1969. We quickly recovered and our stock has been coming on stronger than ever since then. And the crazy part of it all during that horrible slide was that our company was doing fine. Absolutely wonderful. We were making money and enlarging our operations all the while. The whole thing was just absolutely nuts, as far as I'm concerned. Wall Street is a funny place."

Donald B. Ross, MAPCO's Financial Vice President, who is able to view the 1969–70 slide less emotionally than Bob Thomas can, analyzes the reasons for the panic selling as follows: "At the time Bob made that speech, oil and gas stocks were the kiss of death on Wall Street. These securities had fallen out of favor in the financial community—and I think rightly so. The financial experts were figuring that the major oil companies were incrementalling themselves to death. They were adding incremental surplus service stations, and their marketing policies were lousy at the time. These companies were not getting a fair return for what they were doing, and the competition among themselves was resulting in perpetual price wars. Then, to compound the problem, the large oil companies had jumped off into merchandising fertilizer among other things and, again, these same lousy marketing policies characterized their operations. So Wall Street was just fed up at the time with the performance of the oil companies as a group.

"And so, here Bob Thomas gets up and bravely tells the assembled analysts that MAPCO was going to commence drilling for oil because MAPCO at last had valid tax reasons for doing so.

He explained carefully in his speech how we were doing this and what our approach would be. His speech and our program were logical and sensible. But it was one of those times apparently when nobody listened. These analysts just said quickly, 'Oh my God, they're getting into oil and gas drilling—GET OUT OF MAPCO!' I guess Bob can laugh at his "Thirty Million Dollar Speech" now, but it wasn't so damn funny for us at the time."

Since its great slide in 1969, MAPCO common had increased —counting splits—about fifteen times over, from about $13 to almost $200 a share by mid-year 1975. The reason has been the company's phenomenal growth—from about $74,000,000 in sales and revenues in 1969 to around $340,000,000 in 1975. This has meant an increase in net income from $7,500,000 to some $49,000,000, while earnings per share increased from around 38 cents to $2.64 per share in the same seven-year period, and, rather than impoverishing itself from dry holes, MAPCO has found its oil explorations quite profitable. Production had risen from an average of 1,690 barrels a day in 1969 to 7,834 barrels in 1975. This, of course, does not put MAPCO in the class of major producers, but in its 15th year the enterprise was producing quite a respectable volume and its oil program faced a promising future.

The company's greatest production in 1975 was coming out of Indonesia, where MAPCO has a 10 percent interest in a syndicate that discovered oil in the jungles and swamps in the far southwest extremity of Irian Jaya, formerly New Guinea, where oil in commercial quantities had never been found before. By mid-1975, these fields were producing 60,000 barrels of crude oil per day. When larger storage facilities were completed, production was expected to increase to 120,000 barrels per day in 1976. MAPCO's Indonesian oil comes from the company's participation in a project of Trend Exploration Limited, of Denver, Colorado—an enterprise that provides a good illustration of the imagination, audacity, technical know-how, financial backing and—yes—luck, that are necessary to find oil in new places in these energy-hungry times.

Indonesia, the world's largest archipelago, lies along the equator, southeast of Asia and northwest of Australia. It consists of some 3,000 islands with a total land area about six times that of New Mexico. The largest of the islands are Java, Sumatra, Kalimantan (most of Borneo), Sulawesi (Celebes) and Irian Jaya. The Indonesian population is estimated at around 125,000,000 and is made up of many races native to the South Pacific. Indonesia is one of the richest of all countries in natural resources, principally tin, oil and coal. The archipelago was owned by the Netherlands for about 300 years until World War II, when many of the islands were occupied by Japanese forces. At the end of the war Dr. Achmed Sukarno proclaimed a republic, and after four years of intermittent warfare with the Netherlands, the latter country gave up ownership of all the islands except New Guinea, which was later turned over to the Indonesian government by the United Nations.

Dr. Sukarno was elected President and headed the government for twenty-one years until March, 1966, when he was forced out of office by anti-Communist forces. During the last seven years of his administration, Dr. Sukarno was a virtual dictator with pronounced Communist leanings and close ties with the Soviet Union and Red China. His government discouraged all commerce and connection with Western countries, especially the United States. The overthrow of the Sukarno regime was accomplished by forces led by General Suharto. On August 11, 1966, Indonesia rejoined the United Nations, which it had left under the Sukarno policy, and the United States resumed economic aid. General Suharto made it known that Indonesia would now welcome Western capital and technology for exploiting the country's natural resources under production-sharing agreements, whereby the Indonesian government and Western companies which found and developed oil and other production would share the profit. General Ibnu Sutowo, a medical doctor, a military man and an excellent administrator who had been instrumental in the anti-Communist counterrevolution, was placed in charge of Indonesian oil operations, now known as Pertamina.

There followed a great rush by oil companies, large and small, from Western industrial nations to get production-sharing contracts to explore for hydrocarbons in Indonesia. Among these was Trend Exploration Limited, which had been organized by a young lawyer, geologist and economist of Denver named Tom Jordan. He had gotten into the oil well-drilling business in North Dakota in 1954 and had spent his entire professional career as an independent oil man. Jordan's idea was to attract bright, energetic young people from the oil industry by offering them significant participation in his company. Trend secured financing from a French and a Swiss bank and from a Canadian oil company that felt Trend had a workable concept and a group of better than average technical people, but these finances were so limited, according to Tom Jordan, that "we had to live more by our wits than by our bank account."

"In 1969," Jordan says, "our technical staff became extremely interested in two areas in Indonesia. One was on the island of Java; the other, which was of greatest interest to us, was on the west tip of Irian Jaya. This latter was an area where oil had never been discovered in commercial quantities, although the Shell Oil Company had prospected for oil there, dug a great many wells and spent a whole lot of money from the early 1930's until Shell finally discontinued operations in 1958. All of Shell's drillings resulted in dry holes except for one, which discovered a small field that produced oil in small quantities that were not considered commercially profitable.

"We were especially interested in the coral reefs that lie off-shore of the Irian Jaya tip. This was because there are three conditions for finding an oil field: First, you must find a reservoir. Second, you've got to find a trap for the oil. And third, there must be a source for oil in the area. We felt that the reef itself fulfilled the first two conditions—and seismic tests later backed up our theory. And the fact that Shell had found at least a little oil there indicated a source of oil existed in the area. Shell apparently had just not drilled in the right places."

Trend Exploration now ran into trouble attracting the favorable attention of Indonesian authorities. In fact, the infant company got no notice at all. Indonesian oil had become a very hot subject and oil companies throughout the world—including practically all of the giants—were trying to get into Indonesia with production-sharing contracts. Trend was hardly a household word over there—nobody in Indonesia had ever heard of the little Denver outfit. "We got no encouragement whatever—no answers to our letters and cables that we had been sending to Indonesia authorities asking for appointments," Tom Jordan says. "But at this point luck—or fate—entered the picture. During the revolution and counterrevolution between the Communists and anti-Communists, all of the underwater telephone cables had been cut leading from Jakarta, the capital, so that it was impossible to make or receive overseas calls. To get a telephone message to Jakarta, a person had to call Singapore and get someone to fly the message from there to Jakarta. It was an awkward, lengthy and intricate arrangement.

"And then one day in January, 1970," Tom Jordan reports, "one of our associates, Keith Marks, read in a newspaper that direct telephone service between the United States and Jakarta by way of satellite was about to go into effect. Early the day that service began, our Keith Marks picked up the telephone and put in a call direct to General Sutowo, head of the Indonesian National Oil Authority. It happened that Mr. Marks' call was the very first to arrive in Jakarta from overseas via the new satellite connection. This was such a novelty that General Sutowo took the call himself, even though he had never heard of Mr. Marks or Trend. Having accepted the call, the General was practically duty-bound to give us an appointment, which he did for the following month.

"Well, we went to Indonesia and called on General Sutowo at the appointed hour. As I say, every big oil company and his uncle were running into Indonesia at the time, trying to make deals, and here we were from Trend Exploration, an unknown. It is fair to say that our reception was less than enthusiastic. The General was courteous but not exactly warm. But at this point, again, luck or fate—depending on your viewpoint—played an important role.

"Just a few months earlier," Mr. Jordan went on, "General

Sutowo had been in the United States on a business trip. While in California, he asked the U.S. State Department if they would arrange a trip for him to see Disneyland, so that he could go home and tell his children about it. It just so happened at that time that my wife, Sally, was doing some special work in California for the State Department, which asked her to show the General through Disneyland. She, General Sutowo, and our eight-year-old daughter, Judy, spent most of a day there. And so, during our interview in Jakarta, I reminded the General of this outing and showed him a photograph of himself and our little girl in Disneyland. General Sutowo is known to be extremely fond of children and has quite a number of his own.

"After he took a look at the picture, General Sutowo broke into a big smile and recalled fondly that day at Disneyland. Then he ordered coffee sent in and the atmosphere changed perceptibly. Things went very well for us from that point on. It is hard to attribute anything substantive to all this, but the General's recollections of his day with my wife and little girl seemed to improve the atmosphere for further discussion."

Late in 1970, Trend Exploration began making seismic tests of the area by drilling deep holes and exploding heavy charges of dynamite down there. Sensors situated at regular intervals for several hundred yards on all sides measured the force of these blasts as reflected by the various formations of rock far below earth's surface. These first tests were made by shooting in the shallow rivers from a boat and were relatively inexpensive. Encouraged by results of the shallow-water surveys, the Trend crews took their seismic operations inland to extremely difficult terrain, mostly a swamp where men often worked waist-deep in water. To carry on operations there it was necessary to have a crew of 2,000 people, mostly natives with machetes who hacked paths through the jungle. The exploration party also contained a technical corps of expatriates, a French seismic crew, representatives from Trend, and some professional geophysicists.

This work was so expensive that it was soon necessary for the young company to seek additional financing. Trend now went through a long and difficult ordeal of trying to put together a syndicate of oil companies to join in the project and help share the expense. The exploration company got sixty turndowns from prospects before it was able to persuade seven oil companies to join it in the Irian Jaya project. The last prospect approached was MAPCO, which joined in the project with greater alacrity and enthusiasm than any of the others, according to Tom Jordan.

"We presented our ideas," Jordan says, "to Lee Wright (Senior Vice President in charge of MAPCO's Production Division), to Guy Irvin (Exploration Manager) and to John Botkin, their geophysical consultant. They immediately grasped the significance of our analysis of the area, and it was apparent that the

MAPCO people were progressive thinkers who could see the merit in what we were trying to do. They very quickly accepted our offer to join the group. These three gentlemen are very capable explorationists and, when shown the information and data we had, they recognized it for what it was—an exceptional opportunity."

The on-site operations in Indonesia were under the general direction of Jim Wilson, who became President of Trend Exploration Limited after Tom Jordan left the company in 1974 to form another exploration enterprise, Filon Exploration Corporation, of Denver. The geological work was under the direction of Dr. Richard Vincelette, an original employee of Trend. The seismic surveys were developed by Shelby Dark, now with Filon Exploration.

"While preparing to begin drilling," Jim Wilson says, "We decided to take a group of drilling contractors out to the area and determine what sort of rig we needed—whether it should be a land operation or a helicopter-based project. So we invited six drilling contractors, two from the U.S., two from Canada, one from Australia and a French contractor who was already operating in Indonesia. We also invited a construction contractor to go along. All of these gentlemen were officers of their companies and probably in their fifty- to sixty-year-old range. None of them was in the best of physical shape for heavy jungle travel. And we encountered some very difficult conditions, to say the least.

"When we got to the little town of Sōrong, in the contract area," Jim Wilson went on, "we could find only one boat available for the trip of several days to take us along the south coast and look at the proposed drilling sites. Well, after visiting two locations, I lost most of my guests, who found conditions too rough for walking. They had to wade in swamps up to their waists, and pretty soon all of them were utterly exhausted. We were all living on a 40-foot boat with six to eight people in each room. It rained a lot and there were a lot of bugs and mosquitoes and it got awfully warm down below so that our people generally slept up on deck to keep as cool as possible. They were attacked viciously by mosquitoes. There were also a lot of leeches that got to you as you walked through those swamps.

"I became quite worried about some of my charges who just weren't physically up to the ordeal," Jim Wilson says. "None of us had proper clothing, and we were not adequately equipped for all that wading through swamp waters. We used little dugout canoes to get from our main boat up the rivers to the coastline. One day, we had gotten about 100 yards along one of our seismic lines, wading waist-deep, and I could see there was no point in going further because we were losing everybody. I happened to look back and see a contractor with the Westburne Drilling Company, a Canadian firm, named Paul Callahan, in trouble. He is a large man, in the age range I mentioned and he was getting very, very tired. With the help of a couple of natives he finally got back to the dugout, where we sat side by side and then all of a sudden he started gagging. I immediately thought he was having a heart attack and became terribly alarmed.

"As it turned out he wasn't having a heart attack at all. Another big man in the party, Guy Abramson, who weighed about 300 pounds, was having a horrible time getting through the swamp. Two natives, one on each side, were trying to help him and they looked like midgets beside his great bulk. Abramson would get set and take a great stride forward, and each time one side of his body went up as he lifted a leg, he pulled the native on that arm completely out of the water then dropped him back as he set his foot down. Then when he got set and took another big stride with the other leg, the native on that side flew out of the water and then dropped back. Watching this show, Paul Callahan got to laughing so hard he swallowed a wad of chewing tobacco and started turning purple. That's when all of us in the boat thought he was having a cardiac attack."

Mr. Callahan finally got his chewing tobacco out of his windpipe, and later his firm submitted the successful bid to drill for oil in the jungle area. This operation is entirely supported by helicopters. Instead of building roads to the various drilling sites, the contractor brings in everything aboard several Bell 205 helicopters capable of carrying about 3,500 to 4,000 pounds each, including the crew. This means that the immense drilling rigs must be broken down into pieces weighing not more than 3,500 pounds. It sometimes takes 150 to 200 lifts to move all the parts of one rig from one spot to another. Most of the work on the ground must be done in ankle-deep mud because it rains in excess of 300 inches a year there.

Considering the extremely difficult conditions for drilling and the heavy expenses, the Trend people felt they were lucky indeed when they struck oil in the first well that they sank, in October, 1972. This well was only a modest success, producing about 1,680 barrels of crude daily, but the find was extremely encouraging to all parties concerned. "Had not this come early," Tom Jordan says, "our group might not have had the financial staying power to remain with the project until success was won. After all, most of our backers were relatively small companies." The second well proved to be a dry hole, but a few weeks later, early in 1973, new life was breathed into the Trend endeavor when the third well, known as KASIM 3, started out by producing 23,600 barrels daily. This transformed the enterprise into a commercial success.

The only "metropolis" in the area is the little town of Sōrong, originally built by Shell, which had a native population of between 3,000 and 4,000 at the time oil was discovered, but which now numbers 75,000 persons. The town has an airstrip and a small hospital with a doctor who works three days a week. The forests surrounding the swamps contain mahogany, teak and ironwood trees, some 200 feet tall. There are also many sago palms with a starchy center which the natives cut in big hunks and eat.

No dangerous animals inhabit the surrounding jungles, and, although large pythons occasionally are sighted, these great snakes don't seem to bother anybody. The most dangerous reptiles are crocodiles in the rivers and deadly poisonous sea snakes in the ocean. But these latter do not seem to discourage the oil crews from swimming and surfing in the waves. At this writing, no one had been fatally bitten. The approximately 400 expatriates who do the more complicated jobs—Europeans, Australians, Canadians and Americans—also entertain themselves by playing darts and cards and various ball games. For a while, the company showed movies for entertainment, but Indonesians put a stop to that since they didn't think much of the quality of American films. The expatriate workers live in little metal boxlike houses, some on an offshore island called Lugo, the remainder in a cleared area, where in 1975 the company was building a permanent camp. These oil crews work for two weeks, then get a week off, when the company flies them to Jakarta or Singapore for a holiday.

The skilled and semiskilled Indonesians who work on the job are rotated on the same basis. Most of them take their week off at Jakarta or at home. The main body of the approximately 4,000 workers on the job are unskilled nationals clearing for drilling sites, helicopter pads and trails through the jungle. They use chain saws for felling the larger trees and have their own method whereby they pick the largest tree in an area to cut down first. It is so intertwined by vines with other trees that when the big tree falls it carries perhaps ten or fifteen others down with it.

"We have quite a number of nationals doing skilled and semiskilled jobs," Jim Wilson says. "A number of them have attended trade schools. The native workers drive caterpillar tractors and other heavy equipment. Some are mechanics and some of the Indonesians have taken over the more difficult jobs on the rigs. We are attempting—and this is in the best interest of the project—to Indonesianize the work force as rapidly as possible."

It required a year after that first well hit before the project was able to ship out any oil, pending the clearing of land and installation of four 300,000-barrel storage tanks. Two more tanks of the same size were completed in 1975. The company had also moored two large barges side by side for additional storage. Oil is now piped from these storage barges through a submarine pipeline to export tankers that anchor in the Sele Strait, the nearest navigable water for large ships. The channel, in 1975, could float a tanker of 50,000 deadweight tons and was being dredged to accommodate even larger vessels.

The Indonesian oil discoveries by Trend Exploration, Ltd. are the more remarkable because the Shell Oil Company explored and drilled in this general area for about twenty years and never made a successful commercial oil discovery, after spending almost $160,000,000 and drilling more than forty wells. By contrast, Trend spent only about $4,000,000 before making its first commercial discovery. In short, Trend did in a couple of years what Shell had not been able to accomplish in ten times that time. This does not mean that Shell was incompetent. The main reason why Trend succeeded where Shell failed, according to Jordan and Wilson, is that oil-finding technology generally and the seismic sciences in particular have improved vastly since 1958, when Shell quit the Irian Jaya area.

"The Shell explorationists built a road from the Sele Cape inland to the area where they drilled several unsuccessful wells," Jim Wilson points out. "This road goes within a few hundred yards of every important discovery we have made. Shell built its road right past where its people should have been drilling. This was unfortunate for them but fortunate for us. The techniques for finding oil available then were simply nowhere near as advanced as they are now."

And therein lies a main hope for discoveries in the future of new oil sources in these energy-scarce times. Some experts estimate that there is still more recoverable oil in the ground than has yet been brought up. Perhaps even more advanced techniques in the seismic sciences will help in the discovery of vast new oil supplies and thus replenish the world's fuel for a long time to come.

In exploring for oil on its own, MAPCO's Production Division uses techniques similar to those employed by Trend in its studies of oil potentials in Indonesia. The Irian Jaya discoveries, plus some of MAPCO's own oil-finding successes in Oklahoma, Texas, Kansas and Utah, have helped to keep that company's oil operations in the black and thriving—despite the misgivings of some years past by the New York Society of Security Analysts.

Finding Oil Ain't Easy!　25

The ability to grasp the great oil potentials in Irian Jaya more quickly than the other participating companies and its enthusiasm for joining in the project typifies two notable qualities of MAPCO's Production Division: It is relatively small and made up of knowledgeable, imaginative geologists who believe in working practically around the clock in analyzing a prospect when a good-looking one arrives. Once convinced that an area is sufficiently promising, it moves quickly and aggressively to lease land and explore for oil, or, if others are involved, get a piece of the action.

Tom Jordan, who organized Trend Exploration, Ltd., was much impressed by these qualities when he approached MAPCO with his Indonesian oil proposition. "MAPCO's Production Department is relatively small," he points out, "without a debilitating chain of command, and when they had the opportunity to study our data, they acted swiftly, secured the approval of MAPCO's top management and were in on the deal. When MAPCO came in, it rounded out the financing we needed and we were able to proceed.

"In many of the major oil companies, the level of their geological attitude was such that they could not appreciate the potentials resulting from our studies in Indonesia. A great big oil company is like a big bureaucracy, like the Government in a way. When companies get extremely large, they can become stodgy, very bureaucratic and set in their ways, reluctant to listen to new ideas, new approaches. Everyone is scared to take a chance."

MAPCO began its program of oil exploration in July, 1969, after the company had acquired the oil- and gas-producing properties in Oklahoma and north Texas of the Bradley Producing Corporation, of Wellsville, New York, along with Bradley's western personnel of some thirty people. Prior to this, MAPCO had done only a very modest amount of development drilling in the Westpan and Hugoton properties it had acquired some time earlier, but had done no exploration in new areas. The Bradley Producing lands consisted of 20 properties in 14 locations and contained 378 wells that produced 1,250 barrels of oil a day and about 1,000,000 cubic feet of natural gas. These acquisitions doubled MAPCO's oil production.

J. Lee Wright, Senior Vice President in charge of its Production Division, came to MAPCO in the Bradley deal, as did Edwin J. Milt, Vice President in Charge of Operations, Guy Irvin, Exploration Manager, and other key people in the company's oil and gas exploration and development effort. Mr. Wright is a likeable, quiet-spoken man, but extremely aggressive when it comes to oil exploration. It has been principally his policies that, since 1969, have taken MAPCO's oil and gas explorations far afield—principally into Canada, the Rockies, the Gulf Coast and to Indonesia, half way around the world.

The Bradley enterprise is one of the oldest in the oil industry in America. The original Bradley brothers drilled an oil well in Ontario even before Colonel Edwin Laurentine Drake brought in the first petroleum well in the United States, at Titusville, Pennsylvania, on August 27, 1859, and put this country into the oil business. In 1881, the Bradley brothers formed the Empire Gas and Fuel Company and developed gas- and oil-producing properties in the area of southwestern New York State and in Pennsylvania.

Lee Wright, who joined the Bradley organization in 1949, says: "I felt we certainly ought to get into the oil business out here in the West, so I moved to Oklahoma and started a Bradley office in Tulsa in 1952. I moved my family out in 1953. This was the first time Bradley had gone into the oil business in these parts. We'd had royalties out in this part of the country for some time, but no operating company. We worked very hard, acquired some oil-producing properties and were quite successful in Oklahoma and Texas, and then we expanded operations into Illinois, with Ed Milt in charge of the Illinois office.

"In 1969," Mr. Wright went on, "the Bradley family decided to de-emphasize further investments in the oil business and increase their equity in other companies by entering the stock market. I was Vice President in charge of Bradley's oil operations in Illinois, Oklahoma and Texas, and wanted to continue in the oil business. Bob Thomas and I got together, and he decided to buy Bradley's mid-continent holdings—mostly waterflood, or secondary recovery properties. This means that you stimulate an apparently exhausted oil field to give up more oil by pumping water into the ground. It forces out oil that would not have come without such stimulation. Sometimes you can recover as much—even more—oil by these rejuvenation methods than a well produced during its primary recovery period.

"But my staff and I had long entertained more ambitious ideas than working the old oil fields. After moving over from Bradley to MAPCO, we got the opportunity to put some of these ideas into effect. I've always been interested in the Rockies, feeling that they presented one of the last domestic frontiers that have not really been properly explored for oil.

"Knowing that southern Louisiana has been, and will be for many years, a marvelously well-established source for gas, especially gas from the deeper zones, I felt that we should be represented there and also along the Gulf Coast of Texas. We are there now as part of the Florida Gas exploration group," Mr. Wright says. "Here in Oklahoma, our geologists are working on our own prospects and we know that in one part of the state we have good potentials, particularly in the deep zones. Years ago, a 5,000-foot well was considered very deep in Oklahoma. Now it is a shallow well."

Admittedly, the business of oil exploration and recovery is chancy and tough. As they say, "A wildcatter puts his money on the line and hopes he is right, while knowing that the deck is stacked against him most of the time." Wildcatting, incidentally, is drilling for oil in areas removed from any known production. This can mean drilling a mile or more from production or at a new depth. The location of the well, its depth and the difficulties and expenses in drilling and operating it dictate how much oil the well must produce to break even. A shallow well in Oklahoma can be profitable while producing no more than 30 to 50 barrels a day. A 200-barrel-a-day well is practically a gold mine. In Utah, where the wells generally run three or four times as deep in more difficult territory, one must produce at least 300 barrels a day to break even. In the North Sea—where MAPCO does not operate—a well would probably have to produce 10,000 barrels a day to be profitable.

To date, MAPCO has been extremely fortunate in its wildcatting, with a 30 percent average of success, compared with a national average of slightly less than 10 percent. In other words, three out of ten of MAPCO's wells have paid off, whereas less than one out of ten have paid off as a national average. "Back before they were plagued with tax problems and regulations," Ed Milt says, "the major oil companies developed much new oil on a profitable basis. They have continued to be successful despite many mistakes; they are so big they're hard to untrack. Smaller companies try harder but often haven't the finances to withstand dry holes or really compete on an international basis. Up to now, I think MAPCO has been at the right place at the right time, most of the time. Part of this is good fortune; a lot is in knowing the probabilities. We feel that MAPCO undertakes only high-grade prospects, skimming off the cream. Our Production Division has a distinct advantage because we are given lots of leeway. When a prospect comes in that we can really strongly recommend, management will usually see to it that we get the capital to go ahead.

"Many oil operations are hamstrung by 'The Budget,'" Mr.

Milt went on. "Top management will say to Production, 'You have $20,000,000 for exploration—and that is it.' Then sometimes even if Production seems on the verge of making an important discovery and the money runs out, the entire project may be abandoned. On the other hand, if Production does not have an especially promising project and the money is available, it will probably be spent. Thus a strict budget can be a severe limitation, or it can cause foolish expenditures because the money is available. Mr. Thomas does not operate our Division on that kind of a fixed budget on new ventures. He believes in us and if we can come up with a strong recommendation, he generally comes up with the money. MAPCO won't spend money just because it is there."

Exploration Manager Guy Irvin, who also came with MAPCO with the Bradley organization, has these observations: "Mr. Wright and Mr. Thomas don't *tell* us to work hard—they show us how. We have more than twenty-five people in the Production Department now in Tulsa, and not a bad apple in the bunch. Everybody has the same attitude toward work and getting things done. It's hard to understand how a group as small as ours accomplishes as much as we do. We have no playboys—no clock watchers; everybody is interested in what he is doing."

To better appreciate the problems and accomplishments of explorationists, the reader should have a rudimentary idea of how oil and gas were formed and how they are discovered. In the first place, there are no "pools" of oil in subterranean lakes. Oil lies underground in tiny particles occupying the pores of rock, mainly sandstone and limestone. A section of oil-producing rock looks something like a hunk of concrete that might have been removed from the driveway of an automobile service station, then washed, leaving only the oil that had permeated into the concrete's pores. Nobody knows for sure how oil and gas were created, but it is generally believed that they were formed by immense quantities of organic matter—some animal remains, but mainly plant life such as tremendous accumulations of seaweed and kelp that were deposited in ages past in the quiet, lagoonal areas of the ocean. It is believed that oil and gas were usually formed in marine areas because the seawater helped protect the deposits from oxidation after they had died and before they were finally surrounded by sedimentary rock, such as shale, which was gradually formed from the silt washed down into the seas by streams. Shale is perhaps the best of all source rock that generated oil and gas because it is so fine-grained that it held the decaying materials within its structure during the process of maturization. This required probably millions of years and enormous pressures from the overburden of thousands of feet of rock and immensely high temperatures which finally transformed the onetime seaweed, kelp and other organic matter into liquid oil and gas. The pressures are so great that finally the hydrocarbons are forced out of the source rock into "reservoir rocks," which are porous and allow the oil and gas to migrate slowly through them seeking a way to escape.

Water is nearly always found with oil and gas. It is salty because much of this water was once a part of a sea, buried below ground during the earth's upheavals of bygone times. Other salt dissolves into the water from surrounding mineral deposits. Water, which is heavier, is always on the bottom. The lighter oil is on top of the water and the still lighter gas is above the oil. All of these liquids are trying to travel upward to escape the great pressures—especially the lighter oil and gas.

They follow the grain of rock, which lies in wavy strata, like the waves on the sea or the track of a roller coaster. Finally the oil and gas reach the highest possible point available to them, where they either escape through the earth's surface or are trapped by some formation they cannot penetrate. These structural traps are a sort of underground dome, called an anticline, and that is what the oil seekers look for. (There is another type of oil trap called a stratigraphic trap, that we will discuss in the following chapter.)

The earliest oil discoveries were made by people who happened to see trickles of it escaping from the earth. During the late 1800's and the early 1900's oil was often found in so-called sheepherder anticlines—rock formations that may be seen outcropping from the earth's surface that indicate proper conditions below ground level for an oil trap. A sheepherder, for instance, might stumble across an oil-bearing formation by noticing that the grain of the rock dipped in his direction when he was walking up one side of the hill and then after he had crossed over the top and started down the other side he could see it dipping in the other direction. This meant that the grain of the rock had reached some kind of peak or dome between these two inclines.

Anybody can see what the rock formation is probably like underneath by looking at the grain of rock in a highway cut. But even if the rock looks promising, there is probably no oil down there these days. The rock has likely already been observed and the subsurface explored. Thus, most of the shallow-well prospects have long since been fully exploited in this country. Starting in the late 1930's, oil seekers began employing geophysicists, using seismic methods in searching for oil anticlines so far below the surface of the ground that no indication of them could be observed aboveground. MAPCO's consulting geophysicist is John Botkin, an energetic and loquacious man with "Farmer Brown" chin whiskers, who is regarded as one of the most accurate oil finders in the business.

Basically, a geophysicist "shakes the earth" and listens to the echoes he causes in locating rock structures far below the surface that could hold oil. This is done most effectively by setting off a heavy charge of explosives hundreds of feet below the earth's surface. The detonation shakes the earth several miles below, and the various rock formations down there reflect the shock back like an echo. Sensors record the time required for each "echo" to arrive. This data is then fed into computers, and the results studied by the geophysicist and his staff. The data are usually exact, but the analysis and conclusions are strictly up to the geophysicist and his people and subject, naturally, to human error. It is something like forecasting the weather. The data are correct—provided the seismic blast has been properly set and recorded. The trick is in knowing how to interpret it.

In searching for oil, the explorationists want to find formations that could generate oil, also formations that allow oil to migrate and a trap that could hold a vast accumulation of hydrocarbons. It is also extremely helpful to know that oil has been produced in the immediate area. That is why wildcatting is so chancy. A geophysicist might make a perfect analysis showing that conditions are exactly right, say, 15,000 feet down—but the only way to be sure oil is there is to drill. Sometimes it is; sometimes it is not. The oil may have escaped and dissipated into the atmosphere a million years ago, or there may never have been enough organic material in that particular area to have formed oil in the first place. Thus, as anyone can see, finding oil ain't easy.

In 1975, the MAPCO Production Department's biggest income producer was its interest in the Indonesian oil fields. MAPCO's take from this enterprise amounted to 3,000 to 4,000 barrels a day, and that promised to double in 1976. The second-largest producer was natural gas liquids from the West Panhandle Gas Fields in Texas. "The field is declining now but we can probably take natural gas liquids out of it at our present rate for another ten years," Mr. Wright says. "We should be able to produce some liquids from that field until the year 2,000. I think we will have liquids from other domestic sources by that time, however. I'm optimistic about this. The idea that oil and gas reserves are pretty well shot in this country is overstated, in my opinion."

MAPCO's Production Division's greatest investment by 1975 was in its Utah wells. Next came Indonesia, and third the Province of Alberta in Canada. "We are still getting production and drilling new wells here in Oklahoma and Texas," Mr. Wright says, "but these areas are not nearly as important as our explorations in Canada, Utah, Indonesia and elsewhere, particularly in the Rockies. Yet we *do* have two new discoveries in Oklahoma—one very small. I believe the other can be important, however, if it continues to develop the way we hope. We are drilling several wells there now. We have a settled production in Oklahoma and Texas that has been giving us oil for years. We brought most of these properties to MAPCO from Bradley, although some are new. The Oklahoma and Texas operations, however, are the base or foundation on which we have built our other oil explorations."

One pleasant, sunny day in the spring of 1975, I visited some of MAPCO's old and new Oklahoma oil fields about 150 miles southwest of Tulsa, accompanied by two members of the company's Production Department, Frank McQueeney, District Superintendent for Oil and Gas Exploration in the Shawnee area of Oklahoma, and Mark Marken, a reservoir engineer. My main impression from the experience was surprise that the giant oil industry, which supplies so much of our national energy, depends to the degree it does upon the little wells that give out oil in driblets. Of course, there are immense producers here and there throughout the world, but more of our oil than one would think comes from these little wells that produce in humble amounts, showing how hard the industry has to work and scrape for us to have the domestic oil production that we do.

Southwest of Tulsa is rolling, cattle-raising country, characterized by clay formations and growths of white oak. The infrequent farmhouses are plainly built, often with a trailer as a nucleus. After 30 or 40 miles, in the pastures and fields alongside the highway, you begin to see the oil-pumping units, which are called "horses heads," because they vaguely resemble a grazing mechanical horse. The entire assembly is probably 16 to 18 feet long and from 8 to 15 feet high, with an electrically powered unit that moves a walking beam with counterweights at the rear, a "bridle," and the part that most resembles an actual horse's head at the front end. That is a big iron connection with a polished steel rod that plunges up and down into the ground, pumping away stolidly and bringing out the oil. Some of the pumping units make up little mechanical "villages" covering several acres, each pump 660 feet from its nearest neighbor. Other pumps stand by themselves out in the boondocks with none of their kind nearby. Somehow they look lonely and forgotten as they slowly nod up and down, like one of those toy birds that perches on the rim of a glass and dips away tirelessly.

Some of the units are still. The Oklahoma Corporation Commission regulates the amount of oil any well in the state is allowed to sell over a given time, and various units are shut off now and then to keep from getting ahead of their allotment. Others probably just haven't got enough oil left down there to keep them busy all the time. You see a good many old, abandoned pumping units, some still with their ancient, rusting gasoline engines that supplied the power in earlier times. And now and then a rotting old wooden oil derrick stands as another reminder of early oil-field days. In these times, the drilling rigs have portable steel derricks that are removed from the field along with the rest of the equipment when the well is completed. But years ago the derricks were built permanently of wood at drilling site and a few of them are still standing as monuments to those days when Oklahoma's land was bursting with oil and the oil fields were rowdy and exciting, like the gold rush in California in 1849.

By the time we had reached Sulphur, Oklahoma—so-named because of the sulfur water springs in the area and the Platt National Park that surrounds them—we were in rich limestone country. Limestone is significant to oil production because its porous texture allows the oil to migrate. And just west of Sulphur is one of the most prosperous-looking oil fields along the route—the East Davis property, where all of the pumping units look new and efficient and most of them are working away industriously. From the East Davis field you can see the Arbuckle Mountain range rising in the west, although these mountains do not reach impressive heights. Geologists believe there may be great untapped quantities of hydrocarbons down among those deep subterranean folds of rock at the base of the Arbuckles, possibly at depths of 25,000 to 30,000 feet.

The deepest drilling equipment yet developed will go down at most 35,000 feet—but, then, that is nearly seven miles. And it is terribly expensive to go deep. It costs about $2,000 a day to drill a 7,500-foot-deep oil well, but the price jumps up to about $10,000 or more a day when you go down to 30,000 feet or even 20,000 feet. At those depths, more horsepower, heavier equipment and more men are needed. Beyond that, the deeper you go, the greater the chance for some sort of subterranean foul-up. Oilmen call the Arbuckles "crooked hole country," because those subterranean mountains are so shoved and tangled together that the rock formations go off in all sorts of crazy angles. These tend to confuse the drilling bit and sent it off course. Elsewhere in Oklahoma you can drill a 7,500-foot-deep oil well in about 25 days. In the Arbuckles, it may take 80.

Typical of the small producers in the area is Pickens #1, drilled by MAPCO in the Summer of 1974 on the farm of the Pickens family on the edge of the Arbuckles. You reach Pickens #1 after opening, driving through, and closing several wide farm gates, fastened with chains hooked onto a nail. Then you follow along a narrow dirt road through some brushy, wooded pasture lots, where an occasional cow stares at you through the buck bushes. The pumping unit sits out there alone in the woods, its big metal "horses head" nodding and pumping away, bringing up about 30 barrels of crude a day from some 5,000 feet down. The crude goes into a separator tank that looks like a large version of one of those old-time hot-water tanks that used to stand beside the kitchen range. Gas separates from oil inside the tank. Some of the natural gas goes as fuel into the gas engine that powers the pumping unit; the rest is vented into the air. Not enough gas is produced here to make it commercially practical to lay a line and transport gas for use. When a float in the separator tank reaches a certain height, the oil is vented into a 400-barrel metal stock tank about 100 feet away. Every few days a truck from a refinery in the area arrives and loads up from the stock tank.

Mr. Pickens, a rugged Oklahoma rustic, is employed by MAPCO to keep an eye on the pumping operation and check it once or twice a day to be sure everything is working right. One of his duties is to see that a chemical compound is fed regularly down the annulus to keep the paraffin in the crude in suspension. This oil is so thick that without the chemical it will clog the pump. (The annulus is the space between the steel tubing and the steel casing of the well. The tubing is the smallest pipe in the string— 1¼ to 3½ inches in diameter in these fields—at the center, through which the oil comes up. The casing is a larger pipe—4½ to 7 inches in diameter—that surrounds the tubing.)

You drive four or five miles along a meandering country road, shaded by cottonwoods and willows, which border a little stream that flows nearby. Then, on a lower level of one of the small mountains, you come to Howell #1, which is part of the "important" discovery that Lee Wright mentioned earlier. It is a free-flowing well, with enough gas in the oil to give it sufficient pressure to rise to the earth's surface without need of a pump. Instead of a "horses head," Howell #1 is equipped with a "Christmas Tree," a collection of pipes and valves on the surface above the well that is said to resemble faintly the holiday fixture from which its nickname derives. The flow of oil is regulated by adjusting a choke in the well head. The choke is set at $^{10}\!/_{64}$ ths of an inch to allow 180 barrels of oil a day to go into a stock tank, somewhat larger than the one at Pickens.

A quarter of a mile or so away, up near the top of the same mountain, a rig and crew were busy drilling Howell #2—a development well. From the drilling site, you could look out across the skyline at a stimulating view of little, rounded-topped mountains that somehow resembles a rolling sea, adorned with scrub cedars. The drilling was progressing one foot every 12 minutes. The hole was now down to 1,939 feet after 23 days of drilling, and the crew—made up of three four-man shifts—would probably be on the job another couple of months before getting to the oil.

This was a medium-size rig with a 125-foot-tall jackknife derrick and the usual equipment on the drilling floor—each with its colorful nickname: the Kelly, the rathole, the mousehole, and halfway up the mast the monkey board, with its Geronimo line. When the drill pipe is being hoisted up to change the drill, one man is stationed on the monkey board to help manipulate the joints as they are stacked vertically in a tall holder. The Geronimo line, named after the traditional cry of paratroopers when bailing out, is there to allow the monkey board occupant to escape quickly in case of emergency, such as a "blowout." The Geronimo line is fastened to the derrick beside the monkey board, and descends in a fairly steep slant to where it is anchored to a post driven in the ground several hundred feet away. In case of a blowout, the man on the monkey board can leap into a bosun's chair and quickly scoot away to safety along the declining rope.

A blowout, incidentally, is the oilman's name for what the public calls a "gusher." And—contrary to what most laymen think —a blowout is the last thing an oilman wants, except a dry hole. A blowout is difficult to bring under control. It is likely to hurt somebody; it fouls up the equipment; it may waste days and cause untold effort, and it definitely wastes a great deal of oil. Every rig has an elaborate set of equipment intended to prevent blowouts, which seldom occur nowadays.

Some 50 miles southwest of the Howell wells is MAPCO's Westbrock Penn unit—700 acres containing 88 old wells that the company had purchased back in 1972, one of the waterflood or secondary recovery projects, in which vast amounts of water are pumped into the ground in an effort to create enough pressure to force the oil out of the old wells that had almost quit giving. In the summer of 1974, the company started pumping water into the ground from one unit with a capacity of 4,500 barrels a day. After a year of this, some of the old wells in that pump's vicinity had increased their production from four or five barrels a day to 40 and 50 barrels a day and, in a few cases, as high as 100 and 200 barrels a day. The MAPCO engineers, in 1975, were installing three more 4,500-barrel-per-day pumps to pick up production throughout the entire 700 acres. The wells in the waterflood area pump out water and oil together. Both go into a "free water knockout tank" that holds about 400 barrels. Here the water separates from the oil. The oil goes into a pipeline to a refinery. The residue water is pumped back into the earth to encourage more oil to come out and make itself useful.

The impression a layman gets from visiting these southern Oklahoma oil areas is that these fields are mostly old and tired and during the next few years the last of their oil will be squeezed from them. But in this same part of the country under the "buried" Arbuckle Mountains—25,000 feet or more down—some geologists think there may be fresh, untapped treasures of black gold, perhaps even in greater amounts than the oil that has already been taken out of Oklahoma. Some exploration companies have already begun to do some deep digging in western and south-western Oklahoma. MAPCO, however, has reserved its heavy expenditures for deep drilling for areas farther west and north into the Rocky Mountains—in Utah, Alberta in Canada, and Wyoming.

But it is still occasionally possible to find highly profitable oil deposits by sinking shallow wells even in Southern Oklahoma, as proved to be the case with MAPCO's wells on the Howell property. Howell #2, which was completed during the summer of

1975, struck two producing zones. This means that MAPCO is allowed to recover from it twice as much oil as the 180 barrels permitted daily from a single well. Since completing Howell #2, the company has drilled four more wells in that area. All are producing the allowable limit. One of these four also has two *producing* zones. Thus, in the fall of 1975, four of the six wells in the Howell area were producing 180 barrels a day, and two were bringing up 360 barrels a day each.

The Positive Thinkers 26

Oil explorationists may well be humanity's most adamant Positive Thinkers. As they say: "In this business, you've got to be aggressively optimistic, or you're dead."

The other main impression a visitor is apt to bring away from a sojourn in the oil fields is one of amazement that gasoline, heating oil and such do not retail at, say, about $5 a gallon. Most people just don't realize the effort and expense involved in finding petroleum and bringing it out of the earth and to market. And this is to say nothing of the mental anguish that explorationists and their financial backers probably endure, although most of them claim to be able to block out of their minds worries about dry holes, drilling difficulties and unforeseen problems involved in harvesting the oil once it is found.

Although MAPCO has been three times as effective in finding new oil as the national average of exploration companies, an outsider cannot help but admire the ability of its Production Department to maintain great confidence in the face of the many difficulties and disappointments in the early stages of some of its projects. "In this business you have to put your neck out every time you go into one of these ventures," Vice President Ed Milt observes. "A person in oil exploitation cannot get the feeling, 'Well, I've made it—why take a chance this time?' When you take that approach, nobody has to tell you what is going to happen. You quit growing. And in the oil business, you are working with a depleting asset, so you have got to keep drilling to survive. For every barrel of oil you produce today, you need to replace it with two, just to take care of additional costs, taxes, dry holes and the unforeseen. And this means that you have got to keep laying it on the line."

Seismology, as applied to oil exploration, has been so perfected and refined in recent years that it has probably saved the oil industry billions of dollars in finding new oil without the necessity of drilling an unacceptable number of dry holes. And yet, wildcatting remains such a chancy thing that it continues to retain much of its old-time mystique. There are still characters around who claim to be able to find oil in the ground by using various inscrutable means, including witchcraft, partnership with God and the Heavenly Hosts, and the time-worn "Black Box," a device which has often been employed by charlatans to bamboozle gullible investors since the days of the oxcart and the whale-oil lamp.

" 'Black Box' is the term used throughout the industry to describe all sorts of exotic bogus oil-finding devices," according to John Botkin, MAPCO's Geophysical Consultant, who has had many encounters over the years with "Black Box Operators." " 'Black Box' has become a generic term in the oil industry because these great 'oil finders' generally have some kind of a box and it is usually black. They are very secretive about what is inside and how it works. When you do get a look into a 'Black Box,' it generally contains radio tubes and dials and stuff—electronic things to make the operator appear to be more sophisticated than the old wick and stick type."

Some bucolic "scientists" rely on a plumb-bob arrangement to indicate where oil deposits lie. Others use various versions of the old water-witching wand. Some employ crystal balls, or have oil-revealing dreams, which they will impart to oil companies if they are paid to reveal this information. And there are others who write extravagant claims to oil-producers, including MAPCO, such as one Alan Hammer, whose letterhead proclaims: "A God And Hammer Enterprise. (We can do anything.) Alan Hammer and God Almighty, Oklahoma City, Oklahoma 73102. Crude Petroleum and Natural Gas Exploration . . . Development . . . Production . . . Our references include all the Hosts of Heaven . . . (Signed) Alan Hammer and God Almighty."

MAPCO has managed to make out better than any of the other—except one—of the hundreds of U.S. oil exploration efforts over the past four years, according to Ed Milt, without depending upon black boxes, the Occult or any direct assistance—as far as the department is aware—from the Heavenly Hosts. MAPCO's Production Department relies heavily on the analyses and judgments of John Botkin, whom Laddie McDade, Senior Geologist for MAPCO's Northern Production, calls "one of the world's finest explorationists—a great oil finder. How he accomplishes as much work as he does in 24 hours is beyond my comprehension." MAPCO's own staff geologists work pretty hard themselves—sometimes most of the night. They study data, make maps, examine the logs of wells drilled by others, both dry holes and good producers. They evaluate electrical recordings of the goings-on deep down in the oil wells, study aerial photographs and try every known way to conceive as accurately as possible where oil may be concealed down there in those porous rocks.

"The staff of our Production Department has about average ability," Exploration Manager Guy Irvin says. "We have no exceptionally brilliant people. What makes the difference is hard work—and enthusiasm. Our staff works like hell and we are positive in our approach and enthusiastic about it; these are the main reasons for our success. This attitude on our part is maintained by management's willingness to do the things we think should be done. You can have the greatest people in the world, but if no action is taken by management on their recommendations, you kill their enthusiasm."

Shortly after joining MAPCO Lee Wright sent his Number one man, Ed Milt, to Billings, Montana, to open a MAPCO office in 1969 and prepare for oil exploitation throughout the northwestern U.S. and southwestern Canada. Mr. Milt worked alone at first out of a tiny office, but operations and personnel increased rapidly until by 1975 MAPCO's Northern Division of Production had forty-two people, including four resident geologists. They had moved into more elaborate quarters, and Don Holliman had become the Manager of Operations. Ed Milt had been made a MAPCO Divisional Vice President and moved to Tulsa. By this time, Northern Production was heavily involved in oil exploration and production on three fronts—Alberta, northeastern Utah and north central Wyoming.

MAPCO's first big oil-finding project in the Northwest was —and is—in Canada, principally the Hamilton Lake field in central Alberta, about 125 miles northeast of Calgary, where the temperature dips to 60 below in winter. It is barren, lonely country, with only an occasional isolated farmhouse in sight. Wildlife is sparse—no jackrabbits, no coyotes—only a large population of little gophers called "picket pins." They got that name during the latter 1800's when Army cavalrymen on duty in the Northwest picketed their horses at night to metal pins driven into the ground. When the gophers indulge in their habit of sitting on their hind legs to look curiously at people, they so closely resemble the picket pins that a cavalryman would sometimes bend over to tie his horse to one and the picket pin ran away. Road signs along the highway warn northern-bound motorists, "No gasoline—no service—no nothing." Other signs tell motorists the way to "nearby" towns, such as Ghost-Pine, 120 miles along a dirt road. It is a wild, wide-open and bleak country. But 2,900 feet below the surface lies a 5-foot-thick band of sandstone that tests—made before MAPCO became interested—indicate might contain more than 1,000,000 barrels of commercially recoverable oil under each section of 640 acres. The Hamilton Lake field covers several hundred square miles, of which MAPCO has acquired about 55 sections, and drilled more than 100 wells during 1972 and 1973.

The company also built and put into operation four large injection plants capable of pumping 55,000 barrels of water into the ground every day to start the reluctant oil flowing at a profitable rate. This had been expected to begin in the Fall of 1973, but by the Fall of 1975, the injection plants had pumped more than 20,000,000 barrels of water into the ground—and MAPCO had sunk upward of $13,000,000 into the project—and the wells were still not producing enough oil to pay the electric bill. The producing wells were giving only one to ten barrels of crude a day. "We are looking for 100 to 200 to 250 barrels a day per well," Don Holliman says. "And we are confident that we *will* get that production eventually. It is just taking longer than we had expected to saturate this area with enough water to force out the oil. This is something like pouring water into a bucket of sand. You can fill a bucket with tightly packed sand and still you can pour a lot of water into it before the bucket runs over. Loosely grained sand will absorb a lot more water than the finer sand that packs more tightly together. The subterranean sand in the Hamilton Lake field is more loosely grained and will absorb more water than we had anticipated."

MAPCO's largest outlay of money for oil exploration—around $30,000,000 by late 1975—and its most frustrating experiences up to that time have been in the Uinta Basin in the northeastern corner of Utah. A number of problems exist that delay drilling time and make it difficult to bring out the oil and gas once the wells are down. For one thing, the oil lies 15,000 to 17,000 feet down, which is quite deep, and that makes drilling expensive in the first place—around $1,500,000 or more per well. The natural gas associated with oil is under extremely high pressure, which necessitates cautious drilling and the use of especially heavy drilling mud to prevent blowouts. The area is isolated, the terrain is rough, and the winters are brutal, wind-whipped with temperatures of 30 below and colder. Because the oil is unusually waxy, it will not flow at temperatures lower than 120°F. In fact, at ordinary temperatures it is like heavy grease. All of the oil companies drilling in the area, including MAPCO, are experiencing these problems.

Oil production in the Uinta Basin dates back to 1949 with the discovery of the Roosevelt Field by the Carter Oil Company, now the Humble Oil and Refining Company. Eight wells were drilled, and three were still producing in 1975. Other fields in the area, including Flat Mesa, Blue Bell and Starr Flat, were discovered in 1950. But with oil selling at $3 a barrel, these wells, considering the many problems in getting out the oil, were not profitable. In the early 1970's, however, the price of new oil rose to $10 a barrel and that made it desirable to exploit the Uinta Basin. Whereupon, northeastern Utah became the center of the biggest oil boom this country had seen for a number of years. The population of the little town of Roosevelt, in the oil area, jumped from 2,000 to 5,000 in a few months; motels in the area were overflowing, lines waited at restaurants, and no houses were left to rent. The Uinta Basin, which once held an ancient lake, is about 50 miles long and a dozen miles wide and contains more than a dozen oil fields. The most active, since it was discovered by Shell in 1972, has been the Altamont Field, where more than a score of heavy rigs have operated at one time, representing a number of oil companies, both majors and independents.

MAPCO got 50 percent of the drilling rights to six sections of the Altamont Field on a "farm-out" from Chevron Oil Company, which was having trouble finding more drilling rigs and its short-term leases were about to run out. (The 1,650 drilling rigs in the U.S. were in great demand at the time because high prices had revived oil-boom fever.) A "farm-out" means that the original lessor, Chevron in this case, shares none of the work and expense of developing the field and gets a minor part of the production. MAPCO's two partners—Basin Petroleum Corporation and Apache Exploration Company—got 25 percent each. Since then MAPCO has acquired other leases and drilling rights, so that by 1975 it owned about 53 percent of the oil production under 14,925 acres in northeastern Utah.

MAPCO and its partners brought in their first Utah well on April 19, 1973—Number 1 Fisher, drilled to 17,244 feet—a free-flowing well that tested as high as 2,825 barrels of oil a day. It has continued to produce about 1,000 barrels a day ever since and has long since paid out.

According to Don Holliman, the Fisher well was drilled on a farm owned by George Fisher, "a grizzly old milk-cow farmer, who had been broke all his life and was trying to eke out a living on that poor property of his. Now, as a result of this well, he has built himself a $60,000 home and furnished it on the royalties he gets from his oil. He's probably worth half a million dollars now. Mr. Fisher is a nice type of guy—the sort you like to see do well. We dug another well on the farm of a fellow named Art Timothy, called Timothy Number 1. His family never had much either, but they are becoming wealthy now. That well is putting out 500 to 600 barrels of oil a day and is going to produce more."

At this writing, MAPCO had drilled 23 wells, some with partners, others on its own, in northeastern Utah. Five of the wells were considered highly successful; 16 good; two "not so good" and needing stimulation for profitable production; and two "very bad." The five best wells and one dry hole are on the first sections where MAPCO acquired drilling rights. The 18 wells drilled on the other acreage to the west will require an artificial type of lift, either by introducing gas into the well to lighten the oil, or with a hydraulic pump, or an electrically powered pump lowered into the well to the oil-producing zone. The stimulating equipment will probably cost between $150,000 and $200,000 for each well.

"We are reasonably sure there is a lot of oil in that rock in Utah, and that it will come up when we use these methods," Lee Wright said in the fall of 1975. "I'm a little disappointed so far because I had expected our wells to be better than they are. But the Utah enterprise is a profitable operation and, therefore, I'm happy about it. We will probably be producing the Utah wells for 15 or 20 years."

In 1975, MAPCO production was seriously involved with oil and gas exploration in the Big Horn Basin of Wyoming, which Laddie McDade describes as "a good oily state." Wyoming has been the best oil-producing state in the Rocky Mountains for many years, and the Big Horn Basin has had the most fertile oil fields in Wyoming. "It has produced over one billion barrels of oil already, and some geologists believe there are at least five billion more barrels there to be recovered," according to Mr. McDade, who says the Big Horn Basin has produced oil since the late 1800's, but it is still in more or less a virgin state of exploration insofar as stratigraphic traps are concerned. And finding oil in stratigraphic traps is going to be the next big phase of exploration.

Unlike structural oil traps, stratigraphic traps cannot be effectively detected by seismic or any other scientific methods as yet. A stratigraphic trap occurs when the porous rock through which the oil has been migrating changes into a nonporous rock that stops the migrating oil and causes it to accumulate in large quantities. There are no underground domes or anticlines of rock from which seismic shocks can bounce back to be measured on the surface. Geologists believe that effective methods eventually will be perfected to find stratigraphic traps, but at present the best way to discover them is by drilling a number of wells—mostly dry holes— sampling the nature of the rock deep down and gradually zeroing in on the place where, say, porous sandstone changes to nonporous shale. But that sort of procedure is extremely expensive.

During the summer and early autumn of 1975, MAPCO Production's Northern Division was most interested in a well being drilled in the Big Horn Basin near Buffalo, Wyoming. This site is above a deep structural trap that was discovered, according to geologist McDade, as a result of "an excellent piece of seismic work by John Botkin. In the past, four other companies did seismic exploration in this area and failed to find it. We don't know yet whether the trap is full of oil, but we are drilling to find out. Right now," Mr. McDade said in early August, 1975, "our target where we expect to strike oil is 15,500 feet, but literally we do not know how deep we will have to go. We would like to drill down to 20,500 feet if we don't find oil at 5,000 feet above that. But whether we go that far depends on the decision of Mr. Thomas. And there are some ramifications that might eventually change our mind about drilling deeper in this particular sector. There is still another prospect in that general area that we are pretty excited about. That one we share with another company. To strike oil there, we feel we will have to go down to a depth of 22,500 feet, and that is awfully deep by anybody's standards."

On a fine Saturday in early August, 1975, Loffland Brothers Company of Houston, Texas, which was drilling the Buffalo, Wyoming well, were hosts at a barbecue at the drilling site for people concerned in the project. Guests included MAPCO Production's Northern Headquarters staff from Billings, Montana, as well as representatives of service companies that supply mud, drills and other equipment, and families of landowners in the area whose property has been leased for drilling. About 130 people dined on barbecued ribs and sausages prepared on a portable cooking outfit that Loffland Brothers often use on such occasions. After the meal, guests were taken on tours of the drilling site to inspect the rig and associated equipment. The drilling was being done by a National 110 Rig, which is considered medium-large. MAPCO pays a rental of about $8,000 a day, which covers use of the equipment, salaries of the drilling supervisor and three shifts of five men each who work around the clock, as well as costs of the drilling bits, the steel casing that lines the hole and the drilling fluids. The entire rig is "winterized," meaning it is completely housed to help withstand temperatures that get 30 degrees below zero and colder. Otherwise everything would freeze up. In fact, everything often does, which causes the drilling in the middle of winter to shut down for two or three days while the pipes are being thawed out. A boiler keeps warm the abundance of water needed for the drilling, which runs around the rig in numerous pipes and hoses. But if the boiler breaks down, the water immediately freezes and things come to a standstill. The drilling of the Buffalo well, however, had begun in June and benefited from warm, pleasant summer and early autumn weather.

On the day of the barbecue the hole was down to 11,210 feet and the drill was progressing through shale at an average of six feet an hour. If the formation should change to soft sandstone, the drill would probably make 20 feet an hour. There had been no indications of any oil from the well drillings, but there were still 4,000 feet—another 60 days—of drilling to go before reaching the target of 15,500 feet, and so optimism was high. It had taken 47 days to get this far, but the deeper a well goes, the slower. One reason is that as the well deepens, more joints of drill pipe must be added to reach the bottom. And the longer the "string" of drill pipe, the longer it takes to change a bit after it becomes dull from constantly chewing away at the underground rock formations. A drill looks something like the iron housing that encloses a big pulley, perhaps a yard long and a foot and a half in diameter. This contains several bits that resemble cog wheels, each about six inches in diameter and set at various angles. The teeth of the bits being used on this job were of tungsten steel, and each drill costs $2,400. One lasts only five or six days. Then it must be brought to the surface and replaced with a new one. The old drill is discarded;

it can't be resharpened. A regular rock drill costs only about $480, but it doesn't have the cutting or lasting power for use at great depths.

The procedure involved in taking a drill out of a deep hole and putting down a fresh one involves a formidable amount of time and hard effort. At 11,210 feet down at the Buffalo well, it required ten hours of hard work to make a drill change. This, briefly, is what is involved: The drill in the Buffalo well was attached to the bottom end of the bottom unit of 21 "collars." The collars are heavy pipes, each 30 feet long, about 6 inches in diameter and weighing 3,000 pounds each. They are attached to the power unit of the drilling rig at the surface of the ground by a "string"—in this case, of 375 joints of drill pipe. Each joint is 30 feet long, about 3 or 4 inches in diameter and weighs 600 pounds. All of that combined weight is so great it actually stretches the steel in the drill string. (When Loffland Brothers reached the bottom of the 31,441-foot-deep well they drilled in western Oklahoma —the deepest anywhere today—the weight of the string actually stretched the steel 60 feet.)

The rig's power unit, two big diesels, generates 1,800 horsepower that turns the string, which turns the drill. When it is time to change the drill, the power unit lifts the string up—three lengths of drill pipe, 90 feet, at a time. The top of the next section of drill pipe below the unit out of the ground is anchored with a heavy iron collar to keep the rest of the string from falling down into the well. The 90-foot section out of the ground is being held temporarily at the top of the derrick, which in this rig rises 136 feet above the drilling floor, itself 20 feet above ground level. The 90-foot section is unscrewed from the string still in the ground and stored temporarily in a perpendicular position to wait there while the laborious process proceeds of bringing up the string 90 feet at a time, until the worn-out drill finally emerges. It is changed and the whole process is repeated in reverse to put the drill back down to the bottom of the hole. Drilling resumes and continues five or six days until time to repeat the whole complicated process.

Each of the three crews consists of five men: a driller, a derrick hand, an engine man, and two floor men. The driller, top man of the crew, is in charge of some gauges, wheels and indicators making up a central board situated on the drilling floor. The gauges and indicators tell him what the bit is doing at the bottom of the well, the weight of the string, the pump pressure, and the rate of circulation of the mud. It also indicates whether there is danger of a blowout, so that precautions can be taken, such as adding more weight to the drilling mud to hold down the pressure in the well. Drilling mud, which comes as dry powder in sacks, is made basically of natural clay with various chemicals. The drilling rig at the Buffalo well was using about 1,000 pounds of dry mud a day, which, when mixed with water, amounts to about 200 barrels. This is circulated by pumps down along the drill string to the bottom of the hole, where it serves as lubrication for the bits. As it comes up through the annulus, the mud brings cuttings from the bottom of the hole to the surface.

The emerging mud is watched carefully to see if it shows any signs of oil. A small stream of the drilling mud is piped into the "mud logging trailer"—a motor trailer containing scientific equipment that, in effect, sniffs through the mud stream and draws from it any gases that might be contained. The instruments inform the operator as to the amount of gas being encountered and the relative percentages of each type of gas—methane, ethane, propane, butane. This can indicate whether the drill is approaching an oil deposit.

The Loffland Brothers barbeque was held on a magnificently clear, cool summer day in a spectacularly scenic area of the Rocky Mountains. The drilling site sat in the middle of a great basin, and for perhaps ten miles on all sides the green-coated basin floor seemed to roll off toward the distant mountains in gently rounded hillocks that gradually lifted their elevation as they approached the base of the range. In the distance, this storybook setting was framed by the stately grandeur of the Big Horn Mountains, rising in two tiers, like the lower and upper decks of a great stadium built for the gods. The ring of nearer mountains rose about 7,000 to 8,000 feet and seemingly immediately behind them was the larger, higher ring of mountains going up to 13,000 feet, which, in the late summer, was still capped with snow.

It was a happy day for all those present, and everybody seemed to assume that just 4,000 more feet down the drilling bit would encounter a great abundance of black gold that would make the project as profitable as it had been colorful on this day. During the long ride back to Billings in the Holliman station wagon, I asked Don if he did not worry sometimes that all this effort might result in nothing more than a dry hole. After all, he and his geologists, working with John Botkin's seismic data, had strongly recommended this project, and MAPCO's top management had backed their judgment to the tune of probably $2,000,000 or more. But so far there was no sign of oil whatever and there was not another producing well anywhere in that vicinity to give an indication that there was any oil down there.

"Well, I used to get uptight about things like that," Don Holliman said. "But after you've been in this business as long as I have, you learn to put anxieties and worries out of your mind. After all, the oil is there or it isn't."

Nearly three months after the day of the barbecue, on October 28, 1975, the drilling bit reached a depth of 15,766 feet in the Buffalo, Wyoming well—and still no sign of oil. The well was "plugged" that day, and the whole expensive enterprise that had generated so much hope and enthusiasm back in August, was declared a "dry hole." But Vice President Lee Wright of MAPCO Production and his people were still convinced there was oil in the area and intended to keep on trying.

As we say: you have to be an aggressive optimist—a Positive Thinker—to stay in the business of exploring for oil.

Silhouetted against a clear winter sky is the big rig during the drilling of Fisher #1—MAPCO's first oil well in the Altamont Field of the Uinta Basin in northwestern Utah. Fisher has turned out to be one of MAPCO's most productive wells in Utah. It is free-flowing, 17,244 feet deep and its production of crude has been tested as high as 2,825 barrels per day. The well is on the property of George Fisher, "a grizzled old cow farmer who had been broke all his life" until the well hit. Now he has built a $60,000 home from his oil royalties, and MAPCO production people estimate his worth at probably half a million dollars.

J. Lee Wright (right), Senior Vice President in charge of MAPCO's Production Division, stands with Edwin J. Milt, Divisional Vice President in charge of Operations, behind a "Christmas Tree" at a recently-drilled MAPCO oil well in Murray County, Oklahoma. "Christmas Tree" is oil man's slang for the above-ground installation that carries crude oil from a free-flowing well into storage tanks or a pipeline.

A battery of storage tanks that serves MAPCO's six new (in 1975) and highly productive oil wells is outlined against one of the little, rounded, cedar-studded mountains of the ancient Arbuckle Range in south central Oklahoma. The Murray County wells constituted MAPCO Production's most pleasant discovery of 1975. They are relatively shallow, about 4,500 feet, and therefore relatively inexpensive to drill.

The Man Behind MAPCO

27

Robert E. Thomas is anything but a garrulous man, especially in matters concerning his personal life. His family's derivations, his early strivings, personal likes and dislikes, his hopes, dreams and the inspiration back of the energy that impels him are little known, even to some of those closest to him in business, including officials of the company he heads. It was, therefore, surprising to the people at MAPCO when, during a speech to the Tulsa Chapter of the National Association of Accountants, Mr. Thomas told in public about a boyhood ambition that helped to inspire and guide him into his career as a big-business executive.

"Few of you know that at one time I was an accountant of sorts, and my father was an accountant—and a good one, too," the MAPCO Chairman and President said. "Back in the early 'thirties, after graduating from high school, I worked for a year at the Firestone Tire and Rubber Company in Akron, Ohio, for two reasons: First, I needed to save some money for college and, second, I needed time to figure out what I wanted to do with my life. The latter proved to be much easier than saving the money to go to college.

"My duties at Firestone occasionally took me into a portion of an office floor known as 'Mahogany Row.' This was an area of mahogany-paneled offices, each containing two mahogany desks—a tremendous rolltop desk against the wall and a flat-top desk facing the visitors' chairs. The executives who occupied these offices had many privileges. One I remember was that their big limousines were brought around to the front door each evening and waited there until each executive was ready to go. All of this was extremely impressive to me at the tender age of seventeen.

"After a few weeks at Firestone, I told my father one evening that I had made up my mind on what I wanted to be in life. It was simple. I just wanted to sit in one of those offices in 'Mahogany Row,' preferably one of the two offices at the far end—either the President's or the Chairman's. 'Mahogany Row' at Firestone was merely a general, rather than a specific, boyish goal for me. Because of certain family reasons, I did not want to try to make it to the top at Firestone. But I had learned by now that every company had something comparable to Firestone's 'Mahogany Row,' and I sure thought that one of these areas would be a worthwhile place to spend my working life."

Robert E. Thomas, who is both Chairman and President, has no "Mahogany Row" as such at MAPCO. Until the company moved into its own ten-story office building in 1976, Mr. Thomas' office for fifteen years had occupied a sizable portion of the northwest eighth-floor corner of the Skelly Oil Center Building in Tulsa. His domain contains no noticeable outlay of mahogany. The decor these days might be described as "Latter 20th-Century Executive Standard," with the usual thick carpet and hangings, a long littered desk, batteries of telephones, and groups of easy chairs, sofas, coffee tables and lamps, arranged tastefully here and there about the carpeted expanse. Adornments and decorations consist mainly of photographs showing the Chairman and President together with other captains of industry or MAPCO employees, gathered at various notable occasions, along with a number of trophies signifying sundry industrial triumphs. No limousines await without the MAPCO offices in Tulsa. The Chairman and President and all of his executives drive their own cars when they are in town.

But when he is traveling, which takes about half of his time these days, to speaking engagements, board and business meetings and to investigate new sources of energy for possible acquisition by MAPCO, Mr. Thomas goes in the streamlined manner of the modern day business executive. Chairman and President Thomas generally flies in the company's French-built Falcon fan jet, a sleek-looking, white airplane trimmed in MAPCO blue with a small U.S. flag painted on its tail. The Falcon seats eight people, flies at 525 miles an hour, and its graceful lines almost always inspire envious comment wherever it lands.

In flight, Mr. Thomas may entertain his guests with food or liquid refreshment, providing a social respite from the business talk that occupies most of the hours aloft. But more often he flies alone in the cabin. Bob Thomas boards these flights with a fat mail bag full of correspondence and two bulging brief cases. He spends most of his time sitting at his desk in the cabin doing paper work. If meal time arrives on one of these flights, he subsists on sandwiches. If he is tired or the flight is late at night, the divan at the plane's rear is made into a bed, where Bob may sleep until the Falcon lands. A typical Thomas day of hop-scotching across the country to business meetings began with a breakfast session in New York City, followed by a late luncheon board meeting in Chicago and then an early evening session in Los Angeles. His plane left California around 9:30 that night. After doing some paper work in flight, Bob kicked off his shoes, lay down and slept until the flight landed at Tulsa. He was at home in his own bed by 2:30 A.M.

"Even though Mr. Thomas is a demanding man, he never

tries to influence us when we have to make technical decisions about our flights," reports Don Elgin, who had been flying the boss for about seven years in 1975. "Occasionally we have to cancel a flight or delay one because of weather. If that is our decision, he never objects—no matter how important it might be for him to get where we're going. Mr. Thomas never enters into these decisions. And he is always considerate of the crew. If he goes some place to stay three or four days or longer, he sends us home to be with our families. Then we go back for him when he is ready.

"The whole time I have flown him, we have had only one tight situation. That was in November, 1969, when we were flying a converted World War II bomber, a B-26. We lost an engine and blew an oil line in the other while flying over Colorado. Mr. Thomas had been with us up in the cockpit, but when the first engine lost power he left and went back and sat in the cabin so as not to be in the way. The only thing we heard from him was a call on the intercom. He told us that oil was escaping from the other engine. That is the only time that I ever recall him giving us any sort of suggestion or advice about flying. We landed in Denver with only about three or four minutes flying time left. This didn't seem to upset him much, but shortly after that, we got another airplane."

Don Elgin and Fred Cassel, the pilot and copilot respectively, talked about the Falcon and their boss while we were drinking coffee at the restaurant of the Orange County Airport in California, waiting for Mr. Thomas to return from a business meeting in progress at a hotel several miles away. At four o'clock, Don looked at his watch and said, "We'd better get back to the airplane. The boss said he will be back at 4:30 and he is never late. He's got a clock in his head. He is very organized. I bet he knows right now exactly what he'll be doing this time next week. I don't mean just what he will be doing *that day*—I mean at *this hour* on that day. He makes use of every minute, but he never seems to rush. It's all at a steady pace." Sure enough, we had been waiting beside the Falcon for only 20 minutes when Bob Thomas appeared walking through the iron gates. He was perspiring under the hot California sun and carried his jacket over his shoulder. It was exactly 4:30 P.M.

Mrs. Barbara Thomas, his wife of 26 years in 1975, agrees that Bob does seem to carry some sort of mental timekeeper. She has observed this especially when they are cruising on his yacht, the *Seabird*. "He can predict within a few minutes the time we are going to arrive at our destination—even on longish trips such as those we make from Florida to the Bahamas," she reports. "He is usually right on the nose, practically to the minute. He just figures out these times in his head. Once we were caught in fog off the Jersey coast, and we didn't have radar on that boat. It was patchy fog—very dense in places where we could not see at all and then we would run out into a spot of good visibility. This meant slowing down and speeding up the boat constantly. Barbee, our daughter, was on the bridge with him and I was up forward trying to see or hear any other boats in the area. Bob was changing speeds all the time and calculating and keeping track of our position. Finally he said to Barbee, 'At this moment we should sight Barnegat Light.' A few seconds later, the boat emerged from heavy fog into a patch of clear air, and Barbee shouted, 'Daddy, there *is* Barnegat Light.' "

After yearning for a yacht ever since his college days, Bob got his first one in 1966. "She was pretty much a stock boat," he says. "Then I got a second, *Seabird,* which is custom-built, fifty-five feet long. Now I'm having this third built, sixty-five feet. The old one has only two state rooms, the large one for the owner, and a guest room. To cruise farther out than we have been doing, we need a sailor aboard and that means another room on the boat. My wife doesn't like the idea of us going out as far to sea as I have in mind with only the two of us aboard."

Mrs. Thomas reports that as the *Seabird's* master her husband does not suddenly become a domineering, overbearing "Captain Bligh-type"—a personality change that often occurs in land-based businessmen when they put to sea in their own boat. "Bob is very good at navigating and he gets extremely involved with it; it is sort of second nature with him," Mrs. Thomas says. "But he remains quite calm the whole time. He has always been excellent with anything to do with figures of any kind. But," she goes on, "Bob is no fisherman. The *Seabird* is strictly a cruiser; we're not set up for fishing. I would sort of like to fish, but Bob isn't interested in it. He says when they used to go fishing when he was a boy, he was always the one who never caught any fish."

As for the motivation that drives her husband in business, Mrs. Thomas says, "It is just something built inside him. I think a person has to be born with it. He's got an awful lot of drive—it is there; that's all. A lot of people who know him—especially business people—see only that side of him, though. We, in the family, and his closest friends, see another side. Actually, Bob is quite mild in many ways. I don't think many people realize that.

"The company's success has been absolutely fantastic, of course, and many people credit Bob with making instant and almost-always-correct decisions. I don't think he makes quick decisions. I think he labors over them. And when he has to fire some people, that bothers him tremendously. He has got a lot of heart, and I would call him anything but 'cold-blooded.' He has very high standards and I can't imagine him any other way. I wouldn't want him any other way. But he is very outspoken. If he believes in something, he is going to say it.

"Besides boating, Bob likes to read for relaxation," Mrs. Thomas reports. "In years gone by, he enjoyed mystery books

—one at a sitting, since he is a natural speed reader. But nowadays he doesn't have much time for fiction. He reads all the boating magazines and everything he can find to do with business. He doesn't care for movies for the most part, but once in a while he enjoys an old movie, if it has quite a bit of humor in it, when one comes on TV. He thinks violence on TV is awful, but he does like to watch old Perry Mason reruns late at night. There is some violence in those, but it is restrained violence.

"If he goes to a play, he wants to laugh—to be entertained. He wants it to be funny. Bob doesn't like heavy dramas. When he goes to a show he doesn't want to have to worry about somebody else's problems—even a fictional somebody else." His favorite play of all time, according to Mrs. Thomas, was *No Time for Sergeants,* the misadventures in the Army of a hillbilly from Georgia, starring Andy Griffith. "Bob laughed so hard at that one," she says, "that he almost fell out of his seat, and he bumped his knees against the back of the seat in front of him so hard and often, I thought the person sitting there was going to turn around and hit him."

Mrs. Thomas, who at that time lived in Belmont, Massachusetts, reports that she met her husband one November day in 1948 when they happened to be riding horseback through some woodland near Boston. It was an Election Day, she recalls, and both of them were away from work. "We got to talking," she says, "and learned that we both worked for investment funds. He was with Keystone and I was secretary to one of the trustees of the George Putnam Fund. We were married about a year after we met."

Their one child, Barbara Ann—the family calls her "Barbee"—is married to Brian Kennedy, a native of New Jersey. In 1976 they were living in their recently purchased house in Atlanta, Georgia, where Brian was a salesman for a heating and air-conditioning company and Barbara Ann worked as a computer programmer for the Trust Company of Georgia. Barbee first became interested in computers as a little girl, she says, when she used to accompany her father when he went down on Saturdays to work at the office. She would play tick-tack-toe with a Mid-America week-end-working employee on a primitive type of computer the company then owned.

Barbara Ann, a tall, firm-featured, outspoken young woman of twenty-five in 1976, met her husband when they were students at Duke University. "I started in college majoring in Math," she says. "Math runs in our family. My dad can go down a row of figures, adding them up in his head like mad, and I thought that's what I wanted to be into. But they put me in theoretical Math at college, and I was really interested in practical Math. Then I started getting disillusioned about school. I was really up a creek. This was bad because my father is big on college—*very* big on college. He thinks everybody should have a college degree—at least, *his daughter should.* So he took time out from his business trips, shuttling between New York and Washington, and flew down to Duke and sat down and talked it over with me and calmed me down and got me thinking in other directions. And so I changed over and majored in French." As things turned out, like her father, Barbara Ann finished her four-year college course in just over three years.

"My father has always been a perfectionist, I'm sure," his daughter says. "Not long ago, my grandmother—his mother— was telling us about the time they had a tennis court in their backyard at home. But there was a definite slope to it. So one summer when my father was home from college, he spent almost the entire summer hauling wheelbarrows full of dirt to one end of that court to level it off. They couldn't afford to hire somebody to do this, so he was going to get a flat tennis court—a perfect one—if it killed him.

"And he still strives for perfection in everything he does. His boat is an example of it. It is probably not only the best-built boat in the world, but also the best-equipped. When he goes into something, he tries to find out everything there is to know about it. Or else he tries to get people who know everything there is to know about it. He knows how to pick people really well. That is one of the qualities, I guess, that makes him the President of a company. My father has a lot of ideas that might be called old-fashioned nowadays, about dignity and formality, and he doesn't believe in bringing business problems home to worry the women folks. He sees business as a man's world. Some people might consider these attitudes Victorian but, as far as I am concerned, he's just a gentleman—and these days you don't find too many of them.

"Sometimes my father can be an awesome person," Barbee says. "But I can handle him pretty well, although he is practically always in control of every situation." She enjoys relating instances when her father was not entirely in control, such as a couple of times when he fell off his boat into the Chesapeake Bay. This may be because Barbara Ann likes to think of Robert E. Thomas first as her father, as opposed to the great business executive—as a man with weaknesses as well as strengths, human emotions and love for his family, rather than an always-correctly-calculating business machine wearing a gray flannel suit. She likes best to remember occasions such as the time she was returning from a trip around the world and her father came down in a limousine to meet her at the pier in New York City. "I was all involved in customs with about nine pieces of luggage," she says, "and it took me a long time to get through. And here he was on the other side of the barrier, and we were waving madly at each other. Finally, when we got all that luggage out, he put it in the limousine and we started away and I suddenly remembered I had left somewhere back in customs my stuffed elephant, embroidered with sequins, which I had gotten in India. I told my father I needed that elephant and we had to go back and get it. So he had the car turned around and we went back and after a lot of crowds and confusion and all sorts of trouble, he retrieved the elephant. It is still at home in my room in Tulsa.

"Then there was the time when several girl companions and I came home from Europe and landed in Philadelphia. My father was there to meet us in a big car with its soft seats that felt so good to us after riding third-class on those hard wooden seats all over Europe, that we just bounced up and down all the way to my father's hotel. We were having a fine, jolly time when my mother telephoned from Tulsa. I noticed that my father was talking to her in a serious tone and looked quite sad. Then he told me that our family dog, a golden retriever named Rocky, had died that day. This made me sad, too. But somehow I felt good that my father was so touched by this. I could see that beyond all his interest in business, he had in him a real sentimental, tender streak.

"And then there was my wedding day. We had a big church wedding at four o'clock in the afternoon, and I was busy and excited all that day before the wedding, running around in all directions not getting much of anything done. At lunchtime, my father came home from work and decided I must be hungry. So he went into the kitchen and fixed me a sandwich. It was a lamb sandwich, I remember, and it wasn't very good. My father is definitely no cook. In fact, this may have been the only domestic moment of his life—but I have always been happy that he was thinking about me when he had that moment.

"After lunch, my father came into my room, which was a complete mess, and asked if there was anything else he could do. I said I needed some toothpaste and a tube of makeup. He had never bought anything like makeup before. I told him what kind I wanted and the shade and he went to the drugstore and had long discussions with the people there about just what shade was needed, and they didn't have it. So he spent a good part of that afternoon going from one drugstore to another and having these long, involved conversations with the sales people trying to match up the right kind of makeup. Finally, he found a drugstore that did have the right kind, and he bought out the entire stock. When he got home with it, I said, 'My goodness, Dad, you've got a five-year supply for me.' My husband, Brian, says this is typical. My father figured that if all those stores didn't have this type of makeup, it must be in short supply, so it was good business to buy it in quantity. It was sort of like building that first propane pipeline because there wasn't any other such thing at the time. My interpretation of my father spending all that time looking for my makeup and buying out the store, though, is somewhat different from Brian's.

"My brother's wedding was quite different—to put it mildly—from mine, which was traditional, formal and solemn in the

Episcopal Church," Barbee says. "My brother and his bride sent out no formal invitations to their wedding, in the winter of 1975. It was held in the yard of his little house, which my brother built himself from an old avocado shed. It is not far from the beach at Oceanside, California. The guests were asked to bring finger foods for the refreshments after. The bride, who is a wonderful girl named Fritzie (Huber), wore a simple shift-type dress with Indian embroidery down the front. My brother wore a similar sort of shirt she had made for him, slacks and no jacket. The minister, also a part-time bartender, wore a shirt and jeans. He was a very nice guy and interesting to talk to. Bob and Fritzie said their vows to each other, and so they were married.

"The night before the wedding we had a dinner, and Fritzie, who comes from a family of trapeze artists, told me she intended to perform out in the yard before the wedding. But there were so many people milling around, and time got so short she didn't do it. I was kind of disappointed. During the pre-wedding dinner, my brother made a good comment about my parents. He said, 'There are going to be so many different kinds of people present, I just hope they (Mr. and Mrs. Thomas) can last for the hour or so it is going to take.' Well, they lasted all right, and seemed to have a fine time—especially our father. He was smiling at everybody and rushing around the place snapping photographs in all directions."

The informal nature of the Huber-Thomas nuptials reflects the personality and life style of Robert E. Thomas, Jr., who is ten years older than his half-sister—tall, lean and sinewy, with a rather serious and severe cast to his facial features. He has strong convictions and attitudes, as does his father, but Bob Jr.'s are as unorthodox as his father's are "good, right-wing conservative." Like his father, young Bob loves the sea, but instead of a luxurious yacht, he sails a frail catamaran—a primitive sort of craft that floats on two pontoons, under a sail—a modern, sporting version of the traditional outrigger canoe in which natives of the South Pacific have defied the sea for centuries. He has sailed one of these cockleshells as far out to sea as Santa Catalina Island and back to California, despite the concern of his father, who regards such a long trip in such a fragile craft as just plain dangerous. Young Bob finds it exhilarating.

After finishing college, Bob, Jr., worked for a while as a loan officer in a bank, but found that so stultifying that he resigned and traveled in Australia and Hawaii. Returning to the continental United States, he worked for a bank again, then opened a sales agency at Oceanside, for catamaran boats and seagoing clothing and gear. He was operating this establishment in 1976 with the help of his new wife.

"I am a fatalist," he says. "I believe whatever is going to happen happens, no matter what you do. My father does not believe that way at all. He maintains his airplane in top condition.

271

If you are well prepared, you are not going to have problems. My father believes in doing everything safe and sound. I remember an argument we had in Florida, when I was twenty-six, because he wanted me to wear a safety belt while water skiing. I didn't want to wear a safety belt, and left Florida. Getting ever-bigger yachts with twin-engine diesels and air conditioning and freezers and washers and dryers aboard is all part of my father's picture of security. Ever since he was a kid and worked for Firestone and saw those mahogany doors in the executive office suite and the limos picking up the dudes at night, those sorts of things have represented security to him. My father went through the Depression of the 1930's. He has fought for everything he's got. He wanted this security status and that is one of the things he has been working for. That is probably one reason I am leading the life I am. I suppose I am rebelling against those things. Maybe I see them as meaning too much to my father and removing him from me. When a person travels as much as he does, I see him as a lonely man. But that is his job. He is a totally dedicated man, and I understand that completely. I cannot do anything without being totally dedicated, although the goals toward which our dedications are directed are quite different.

"I don't get to see my father very often," Bob, Jr., was saying one night when I was having dinner, of charcoal-broiled shark, with him and Fritzie in their tiny house, which Bob had neatly carpentered with many cabinets, closets and cupboards, like the cabins of a small boat. "I see my father only when he comes out here to visit or when I go back home for Christmas or something," young Thomas went on. "He has been to my house only once for dinner. My father insists on taking *me* out to dinner, but I had much rather have him here. Now that I am married, maybe he will figure that my wife can cook better than I can, and come more often. My father and I have had a hard time communicating, because when I visit him he hauls me to all those fancy places where you have to change your suit three times a day. I am happy working in shorts, sandals and a T-shirt. I just can't enjoy eating all that rich food all the time. I don't feel good when I do. I can't enjoy that life.

"My favorite time that we had together was once when he came out here to see me and we went hiking to a place called Black Mountain. It is quite a long hike up there, and he took off his tie and put on his soft shoes, and we went for this hike and walked to the top of the mountain, and looked over to where you could see the Tijuana border, all the way to the ocean. We had a nice conversation. It was like we were friends. There wasn't any of this stuff about what he expects of me.

"I have been interested in hearing that my father has started making speeches around the country about energy," Bob, Jr., said. "I could not travel as he does and think of it as fun, but I realize he does it because he has a strong sense of duty. I know he believes strongly in everything he says. I'm sure he enjoys it, too, because we all have a bit of actor in us, and when you make a speech, you are acting. I have never been invited to go on one of his speech-making trips. I don't know if I would enjoy it. I had enough trouble when I was working for the bank and had to go to luncheon meetings or business dinners. The food they served and the whole atmosphere was just too pretentious for me.

"I am steering away from the Executive Life. I have no desire for those lonely nights on the road. I am not interested in having the peer group that my father admires and that pats him on the back. I would have trouble relating to them. I think what life is about is totally different from that.

"But, don't get me wrong: I greatly admire my father and respect him. I admire any man who is doing what he truly believes in and what he truly believes is right. And my father certainly believes in what he does and in what he says. But each person has to find what he feels is his niche or role. We have to produce for others in such a way that we feel is right for us. Fritzie and I were talking about that the other night. We had sold a couple of catamarans to two policemen. One is a detective and one has been driving a squad car for nineteen years. We feel that when they go sailing in the boats they got from us, we will have helped to make their lives happier and easier, and maybe because of the feelings they get from this sport, they will make it easier for somebody else. So we have served.

"My father, in his way, is doing the same thing. He is providing heat and energy for people. He is helping to make their lives easier and better for a great many people. Really, isn't that what we are here to do? You do what you feel is your thing in society."

Energy's Energetic Evangelist

28

Robert E. Thomas, Sr., says he "loves" making speeches and "enjoys" being interviewed about energy on television and radio, although "years ago the thought of making a speech terrified me. Back in 1948, before making my first important speech—to a group of railroad finance people—I rehearsed for weeks with my wife as coach. She came to listen when I made my speech, and before it was over she got so nervous she could hardly sit there. Barbara did not get up enough nerve to hear me speak again until January, 1975. She says my speaking ability has vastly improved. It should have; I've made enough of them."

Mr. Thomas began regular public speech-making early in the 1960's, not long after Mid-America commenced operations, discussing pipelining, natural resources and finance before organizations of accountants, securities analysts, politicians, oil and other trade groups. In 1972, he also launched a career as a vigorous speaker on the energy crisis, presenting the side of the energy producer—straightforward, hard-hitting talks, "telling it like it is," as he sees it. Orator Thomas often bears down on the fact that only a few States—most of them relatively sparsely populated—produce energy, while the great majority of the States and the preponderance of the U.S. population consumes energy. Thus, he says, the media and politicians, in their utterances and actions, favor the great consuming public with sentiments and legislation that are killing the energy industry's ability to produce.

"I started speaking out on energy," he says, "because I became convinced that Chief Executives of energy companies had to begin speaking out—to 'hang together,' as they say, or 'we would all hang separately.' Now, I am getting more invitations than I can fulfill. I write my own speeches, and, basically, it is the same speech over and over again. But it has to be modified and changed almost daily, because of the antics of our politicians in Washington. Any energy speech over twenty-four hours old is subject to revision. Most of my talks are abrasive. They are intended to be, because I don't think you can stimulate people into action with a lot of high-sounding, carefully analytical phrases designed to appeal to college professors. After all, I am talking to plain people. Basically, I am trying to change attitudes in this country about energy, because I am sincerely convinced that if many things are not changed in the energy picture, we are going to have a lower standard of living, more unemployment, all the problems of having too little energy, because a high standard of living is supported mainly by a relatively high energy consumption."

He is especially emphatic in his contention that the Federal Power Commission is stifling exploration for natural gas in this country because of the price ceilings it imposes at the producer's level. Mr. Thomas is also annoyed that many States, especially along the Eastern Seaboard, are content for the energy-producing Gulf Coast States to mar their coastlines with offshore oil equipment—but the Atlantic States want nothing like that debasing their own shorelines.

An example of the Thomas "abrasive" approach was a newspaper interview in Boston when he was quoted as saying, "If I were a Texas or Louisiana legislator, I would introduce legislation that would prohibit the transportation of petroleum products into Massachusetts until that State agreed to off-shore drilling. . . ." The Boston *Globe* headlined this interview: "He'd Shut Off Our Oil Until We Let Them Drill."

The general theme of most of the Thomas energy speeches is contained in this excerpt from a talk in May, 1975, to the Land Use Conference in Denver, Colorado. Mr. Thomas quoted a *Wall Street Journal* article saying that "the corporation today is largely defenseless—a nice, big, fat, juicy target for every ambitious politician and a most convenient scapegoat for every variety of discontent . . ."

The speaker went on: "Collectively, we are on a collision course with economic disaster. Unless some drastic changes occur, unless Congressmen from the heavy oil-consuming States in particular stop playing games, our country is headed for lower business activity, lower standards of living, lower employment and other unpleasant consequences.

"It is so sad and so completely unnecessary. We do have vast quantities of energy, we have the manpower, talent, expertise and money—in short, we have the foundation for energy independence in our time, provided—and this proviso is a *must*—clear-cut guidelines are established by the Congress, and Congress ceases its political vendetta directed at destroying our energy companies. Only if you and other concerned citizens become aroused, only if you and other concerned citizens across this great land of ours maintain steady pressure on your Congressmen and Senators, can we hope to accomplish such a result. Many connected with energy are belatedly doing their best. But we badly need the help of every concerned American."

On his trips in behalf of reducing energy consumption,

Robert E. Thomas consumes a great deal of his own personal energy. A typical such expedition was his journey from Tulsa to Salt Lake City, March 12–13, 1975. The MAPCO Chairman and President, accompanied by his assistant, Robert J. Swain, left Tulsa aboard the Falcon late in the afternoon, ate dinner aboard the jet and landed at Salt Lake City in the early evening. They were met at the flying field by Roger Shelley, the MAPCO Account Executive with the public relations firm of Ruder & Finn, of New York City. Mr. Shelley had been in Salt Lake City all day, checking on the Thomas schedule and arrangements. He was accompanied by a local public relations associate of Ruder & Finn. The party was driven to the Hotel Utah, where all the rooms had been registered in advance.

Thirty minutes later they were en route to KCTY, the local ABC television outlet, situated on the outskirts of the city. It required about two hours to set up and conduct a taped interview with Thomas by two of the station's local news commentators.

Mr. Thomas and his group were back in the hotel and in bed by midnight, but they were up before daylight and away to KUTV, the NBC television outlet, which is situated downtown. They stumbled around in a dark alley for several minutes trying to locate the rear door to the station's building, the only one open at that hour. After they got inside, Mr. Thomas was interviewed on tape for thirty minutes by one of the early morning newsmen.

After breakfast at the hotel, Mr. Thomas held a business conference in his suite for an hour or so. Then he and his group walked half a dozen blocks to the offices of the local daily newspapers, where he was again interviewed, this time by the business columnists of *The Salt Lake Tribune* and *The Deseret News.*

When that was over, the party hurried back to the hotel, where the Salt Lake City Kiwanis Club membership was assembling for its weekly luncheon, with Robert E. Thomas as speaker. Following the usual civic club good-fellowship high jinks, several hundred Salt Lake City Kiwanians listened to the Thomas discourse on energy troubles, while digesting their roast beef, applauding frequently, and, at the meeting's end, vowing to contact their Congressmen about energy—immediately, if not sooner. En route back to Tulsa, the Falcon landed at a small city not far from Salt Lake, where Messrs. Thomas and Swain spent several hours inspecting the work of a laboratory that is experimenting with hydrogen as fuel for automobiles, heating and other purposes.

Besides his energy talks, Bob Thomas continues to address groups of securities analysts, financial organizations and other trade bodies. He also attends, as a member, Director's meetings of the Perkin-Elmer Corporation, the Founders Financial Corporation, the Transportation Association of America, the American Petroleum Institute, Midwest Research Institute, and the Bank of Oklahoma, and Trustees' meetings of the University of Tulsa. In all, according to MAPCO's chief pilot, Robert E. Thomas flies more than 200,000 miles a year.

One of the men who knows Bob Thomas best is Charles Lipton, Chairman of the Board of Ruder & Finn., Inc., a leading public relations firm in New York City that, at this writing, has represented MAPCO for nearly a decade. Mr. Lipton, a friend of Robert E. Thomas for nearly twenty years, summarizes the MAPCO Chairman and President's business and personal qualities this way: "Bob is one of the most interesting executives I've ever met. He has great strength—a pronounced ability to get from Point A to Point B without standing for any nonsense. When he wants to accomplish something, Bob is going to do it if it is humanly possible.

"A great many executives have strong opinions about various subjects, as he does, but many times many executives are incorrect. I won't say that Bob is always right, but he usually is. An example is his disagreement, back in 1968, with the Accounting Principles Board, a national body that helps regulate accounting practices. When the Board objected to MAPCO's method of calculating earnings per share, Bob responded that the APB's basis of accounting was 'more misleading than enlightening,' and took the body to task. Later, the APB reconsidered its stand and changed its method of computing earnings per share more in line with Bob's ideas.

"The fact that he runs a fine company is a matter of record," Mr. Lipton went on. "I think Bob is excellent at delegating responsibility. He knows how to get people to do the things they are capable of doing and has the ability to make them think along with him. Bob hasn't always selected the right person for a specific job, but he has gotten rid of those who haven't been able to 'cut the mustard,' and stayed with those who can do the type of work he wants. The company has grown mainly, I think, because Bob has not had to burden himself with too many details. By delegating authority, he has been able to think about matters beyond the routine, to point the company in new, progressive directions.

"In some ways, Bob is such a conservative that he is more to the right than Barry Goldwater. In other ways, his conservative bent is more like that of the late Senator Bob Taft, of Ohio. But he is an interesting mixture. For a man who is basically conservative in his thinking, he will move into new areas of business more readily than most executives. An especially good example is his decision to take MAPCO into coal production when coal was not an especially profitable commodity.

"Very often, people who meet Bob for the first time find him cold and austere. Actually, I feel he is just the opposite of such first impressions. I believe Bob would go down to the wire for anybody for whom he has high regard. I find him warm, sympathetic, easy to talk to. That early austere impression is part of his conservative image. Bob can get more out of people than most executives do. I know that he has gotten greater effort out of *our* company in the striving that our people put forth for him. And because he *does* cause our people to try harder and develop themselves, he is a good man, from our selfish point of view, for us to work for. People both inside and outside his company who have done work for him seem most anxious to please him. And he secures all this loyalty and hard work through no display of force and bluster. I have seen him get angry, but never heard him raise his voice. He is under control at all times. And, of course, that is most important for a top-rank business executive."

Nowadays, Bob Thomas spends much more time away from Tulsa than during the early years of Mid-America. "This is made possible," one associate outside the company observes, "because Bob has built an organization that can function very well when he is not there. He has instituted sensible policies and procedures, and has surrounded himself with competent people, operating in a very conducive environment, so that he can now spend a great deal of time away from the company doing other things, and the company doesn't suffer. This is the measure of his organization. He has trained his people so well that he can say, 'Here, go do it.' If MAPCO were a so-called one-man company, the President would be the type who says, 'I don't trust you to do this. *I'll* do it myself.' The measure of a good President is one who has created an organization that can operate without him, so that he does not have to get involved in things that can be done by other people just as well, or better.

"When Bob Thomas travels, he goes first-class. But that is the way he is thinking—he is thinking first-class. There is nothing second-class about Thomas or his company. He will not spend money foolishly, and he doesn't want others in his company to do it, either—but he is not afraid to spend money—and a great deal of it—when that is indicated. He sets an example of high achievement and establishes respect. Some people may think at times he is harsh. He is merely setting himself apart. He has to. He can't ever become too close to his management, because then he would lose some of the contribution he has given, and that is leadership. Leadership always has to be above and apart. You have to look up to leadership."

Robert E. Thomas says he plans to retire at age sixty-five, but there are people who doubt this, among them his daughter, Barbara Ann. "My father used to say his ambition was to retire when he was fifty years old," she says, "but that has already gone by the boards. He has got it written into the rules, or into his contract, or somewhere, that the President of MAPCO cannot serve longer than age sixty-five. But he wrote the rules, and I guess he can change them. I think, even if he retires as President, he will keep pretty much running the company as Chairman until he is seventy—at least."

"I am definitely looking forward to his retirement when he is sixty-five," Mrs. Thomas says. "But I am sure he is going to continue to be active, although not to the degree he is now. He just couldn't be inactive. He is too dedicated to his business."

Mrs. Thomas demonstrated several years ago just how dedicated to business she believes her husband to be, when they were flying east to have Thanksgiving dinner with their daughter, who was in school at the time in Connecticut. On this trip, Mr. Thomas encountered the only flying accident of his much-traveled career. The converted bomber, a B-26, which MAPCO had leased, suffered a brake failure while landing at Meigs Airport, on the edge of Lake Michigan, near downtown Chicago. The airplane ran off the end of the runway and a good distance out into the lake.

"I didn't realize at first we were having a brake failure," Mrs. Thomas recalls. "But Bob did. While we were still tearing along the runway, he pulled down the cabin's decorative ceiling and opened an emergency door up top. He was very collected. After we hit the water, Bob told me exactly what to do, and he helped me out onto the wing of the plane. Then he rescued his briefcase." (Some observers have commented upon Bob Thomas' chivalrous action at this time, because he saw his wife to safety before rescuing his briefcase, filled with his working papers. Many business types, they point out, would have rescued the briefcase *first*.)

"We were not very far offshore," Mrs. Thomas recalls, "but the water was very deep, and there were those big, dangerous-looking rocks. The owner of the plane, who had come along for the ride, kept yelling, 'Don't worry. This plane can float forever.' One of our two MAPCO pilots, who was swimming to save himself, yelled back, 'For a plane that can float forever, this one seems to be sinking mighty fast.'

"By the time the plane *did* sink, a rescue helicopter had sat down in the water beside us. I was helped out onto one of its pontoons. Bob was out there in the water swimming. About that time, I saw his 'Little Black Book' float by. It was the book containing all of his appointments and the names, addresses, private telephone numbers and other information about all of his important business friends and associates—the sort of information most vital to a business executive.

"When I saw the book there in the water," Mrs. Thomas recounts, "I started to tell him. But then I got afraid that Bob might drown himself in trying to save this vital business repository. So I just sat there and watched it drift away and sink out of sight into Lake Michigan."

DATE DUE